'An up-to-date and comprehensive survey of Kashmir's rich tradition of Islamic architecture, connecting the region's built environment with its political and cultural history. This book intelligently explores the dialogue – and the tensions – between esthetic elements rooted in the valley's medieval and pre-Muslim past, and Persianate elements subsequently brought in from outside.'

Richard M. Eaton,
Professor, Department of History,
University of Arizona, USA

'Hakim Sameer Hamdani's volume is the best available survey of the Islamic architecture of Kashmir, spanning the entirety of Muslim rule in the Valley, from its inception in the fourteenth century to the eighteenth century. It brings together a corpus of buildings, many of them little known and so far unrecorded, which are documented with exact measured drawings as well as textual references that anchor the buildings chronologically and contextually in their time. The book highlights the syncretistic distinctiveness of Kashmiri architecture expressed in its mosques, shrines and tombs, and will be an indispensable reference work for any reader interested in Islamic or Indian architecture.'

Ebba Koch,
Professor, Department of Art History,
University of Vienna, Austria

'Dr Hakim Sameer Hamdani's volume fills important gaps in the history of Kashmir's Islamic architectural heritage, broadly defined to encompass Sufi khanaqahs, Rishi shrines and garden complexes, as well as detailed analyses of mosque architecture. The book considers multiple historiographical perspectives on Islamic architecture in Kashmir, and it addresses the dynamic historical geographic context of architectural development of five major periods from the fourteenth century onwards. This combination of historical, cultural and formal approaches supports the book's argument for, and reflections upon, syncretic traditions of Kashmiri architecture.'

James L. Wescoat Jr.,
Aga Khan Professor Emeritus of Landscape Architecture and Geography,
Department of Architecture, Massachusetts Institute of Technology, USA

The Syncretic Traditions of Islamic Religious Architecture of Kashmir (Early 14th–18th Century)

This book traces the historical identity of Kashmir within the context of Islamic religious architecture between early fourteenth and eighteenth century. It presents a framework of syncretism within which the understanding of this architectural tradition acquires new dimensions and possibilities in the region. In a first, the volume provides a detailed overview of the origin and development of Islamic sacred architecture while contextualizing it within the history of Islam in Kashmir. Covering the entirety of Muslim rule in the region, the book throws light on Islamic religious architecture introduced with the establishment of the Muslim Sultanate in the early fourteenth century, and focuses on both monumental and vernacular architecture. It examines the establishment of new styles in architecture, including ideas, materials and crafts introduced by non-Kashmiri missionaries in the late-fourteenth to fifteenth century. Further, it discusses how the Mughals viewed Kashmir and embellished the land with their architectural undertakings, coupled with encounters between Kashmir's native culture, with its identity and influences introduced by Sufis arriving from the medieval Persianate world. The book also highlights the transition of the traditional architecture to a pan-Islamic image in the post-Independence period.

With its rich illustrations, photographs and drawings, this book will interest students, researchers and professionals in architecture studies, cultural and heritage studies, visual and art history, religion, Islamic studies and South Asian studies. It will also be useful to professional architecture institutes, public libraries, museums, cultural and heritage bodies as well as the general reader interested in the architectural and cultural history of South Asia.

Hakim Sameer Hamdani is Design Director, Indian National Trust for Art and Cultural Heritage (INTACH), Kashmir Chapter, Srinagar, Kashmir, India. With his primary research focused on Islamic architecture, he has published his work in various journals and book chapters. Among his major conservation projects are the Reconstruction of 18th-century Wooden Shrine of Pīr Dastgīr Ṣāhab (2020–12) and Conservation of ʿAālī Masjid at *ʿĪdgāh*, Srinagar (2007) – both of which were longlisted for the Aga Khan Award for Architecture. Others include the Conservation of the *Khānaqāh-i Mʿaulā*, Srinagar (2018); Restoration of Mughal Monument of Thag Bābā at Srinagar (2011); and Conservation of Historic Mughal Gardens of Kashmir (2007–10).

The Syncretic Traditions of Islamic Religious Architecture of Kashmir (Early 14th–18th Century)

Hakim Sameer Hamdani

Routledge
Taylor & Francis Group
LONDON AND NEW YORK

First published 2021
by Routledge
2 Park Square, Milton Park, Abingdon, Oxon OX14 4RN

and by Routledge
52 Vanderbilt Avenue, New York, NY 10017

Routledge is an imprint of the Taylor & Francis Group, an informa business

Disclaimer: The views and opinions expressed in this book are solely those of the author and do not necessarily reflect those of the publisher. The analyses based on historical research material are intended here to serve general educational and informational purposes and not obligatory upon any party. The author has made every effort to ensure that the information presented in the book was correct at the time of press, but the author and the publisher do not assume and hereby disclaim any liability with respect to the accuracy, completeness, reliability, suitability, selection and inclusion of the contents of this book and any implied warranties or guarantees. The author and publisher make no representations or warranties of any kind to any person, product or entity for any loss, including, but not limited to special, incidental or consequential damage, or disruption alleged to have been caused, directly or indirectly, by omissions or any other related cause.

British Library Cataloguing-in-Publication Data
A catalogue record for this book is available from the British Library

Library of Congress Cataloging-in-Publication Data
A catalog record has been requested for this book

ISBN: 978-0-367-55009-7 (hbk)
ISBN: 978-1-003-09652-8 (ebk)

Typeset in Sabon LT Std
by KnowledgeWorks Global Ltd.

TO MY FAMILY, ... AND THE LAND
THAT IS HOME

'[...] for everyone has a tension towards his origin, a yearning to attach himself to his mine and source. All things are drawn by their own gravity'

Shahāb al-Dīn *Suharwardī Maqtul*
(*An Introduction to the History of Sufism*, A. J. Arberry, 75)

CONTENTS

List of figures and plates x
Acknowledgements xiv
Note on transliteration xvi

1 Introduction 1

2 The formative period: 1320–1389 CE 21

3 Establishment of a style: 1389–1586 CE 54

4 The mughal interlude: 1586–1752CE 127

5 Resurgence of the local idiom: 1752–1847 CE 166

6 Conclusion: Transition to a pan-islamic image in post-independence period 187

Appendix: The origin of Major Sufi orders in Kashmir 200
Glossary 202
Bibliography 204
Index 214

FIGURES AND PLATES

FIGURES

1.1 Quwat-al Islam mosque: symbolizing the advent of Muslim rule in Northern India, Delhi, 2018, © Vipendra Singh. 16

2.1 Kashmir at the time of establishment of *Shahmīrī* sultanate, © Hakim Sameer Hamdani. 23

2.2 Martand sun temple with the peristyle showing Greek influences, Martand: 2013, © Hakim Sameer Hamdani. 31

2.3 Loduv temple: the circular sanctum of the temple indicates its pre-Hindu origin. The mosque in the vicinity reflects the continuing 'narrative of sacredness' associated with place, Loduv, 2012, © Hakim Sameer Hamdani. 32

2.4 Mosque of Rīnchanā: plan with the entrance door on the northern side, © Hakim Sameer Hamdani. 36

2.5 Shāh Hamdan mosque, main eastern elevation: image of the mosque from early 20th century, Pampore, early 20th century, © ASI. 40

2.6 Temple at Alchi: the woodwork at Alchi represents the oldest surviving example of Kashmiri wooden architecture, Alchi: 2011, © Hakim Sameer Hamdani. 41

2.7 Shāh Hamdan mosque: details of wooden eaves resembling similar detailing at Alchi, Pampore: 2007, © Randolph Langenbach. 42

2.8 Sarnath: square motifs arranged in a diagonal pattern provided the inspiration for similar motif in wooden architecture of Kashmir, Sarnath: 2018, © Hakim Sameer Hamdani. 43

2.9 Mīr Hamdan mosque, plan of the mosque, © Hakim Sameer Hamdani. 44

2.10 Shrine of Shāhmīr at Anderkote, plan of the shrine, © Hakim Sameer Hamdani. 47

3.1 *Mazar* of Sultan Quṭub-al Dīn, trefoil arched opening in the eastern façade, Srinagar: 2015, © Hakim Sameer Hamdani. 63

3.2 Centralized octagonal plan: both at the *Mazar* of Quṭub-al Dīn and Dumath, the octagonal plan is achieved through rotation of a square, with rectangular projections along the main cardinal directions, © Hakim Sameer Hamdani. 64
3.3 Plan of *Khānaqāh-i Naū*, © Hakim Sameer Hamdani. 72
3.4 Plan of the temple, showing mosque extension, © Hakim Sameer Hamdani. 74
3.5 Extension to the temple on the northern side. Note how the builders have tried to match the original texture of the structure in their reconstruction, Srinagar: 2018, © Hakim Sameer Hamdani. 75
3.6 Malik Ṣāhab mosque, plan, © Hakim Sameer Hamdani. 77
3.7 Malik Ṣāhab mosque, entrance door to the building framed by a semi-circular pediment, Srinagar: 2017, © Hakim Sameer Hamdani. 78
3.8 Mosque of Madnī, plan of the precinct, © Hakim Sameer Hamdani. 79
3.9 Mosque of Madnī: entrance doorway to the tomb. The wooden door of both the tomb and the mosque comprises a series of panels with arabesque (*islim*) motifs, Srinagar, © INTACH, Kashmir. 82
3.10 Jamia Masjid: Ground floor plan of the mosque with the centrally located *hauz* (pool) in the courtyard, © INTACH, Kashmir. 84
3.11 Zaina Lank, western façade: the mosque and its immediate setting. The approach ghāt can be seen in the foreground, Zaina Lank: 2017, © Hakim Sameer Hamdani. 86
3.12 Zaina Lank, mosque plan, © Hakim Sameer Hamdani. 89
3.13 Makhdūm Ṣāhab shrine precinct, Srinagar: 2019, © Mukhtar Ahmad. 93
3.14 Zakir Masjid:plan, Srinagar: 2018, © Hakim Sameer Hamdani. 94
3.15 Zakir Masjid: shallow domed *muqarna* ceiling, Srinagar: 2018, © Hakim Sameer Hamdani. 95
3.16 Aālī Masjid, south eastern façade: the wooden *dalān* is an eighteenth-century CE addition, yet the building retains its original spatial layout, Srinagar: 2018, © Hakim Sameer Hamdani. 96
3.17 Aālī Masjid: Ground floor plan © INTACH, Kashmir. 98
3.18 Aālī Masjid: longitudinal section, © INTACH, Kashmir. 98
3.19 Entrance gateways: (t to b) i. Malik Jalal, ii. *Mazar-i Salātīn*, iii mosque of Madnī, and iv. Mīr Masjid (ASI). 102
3.20 Rahim Sāhab, plan, © INTACH, Kashmir. 106
3.21 *Ghār-i Sharīf* at Tapil: plan, © Hakim Sameer Hamdani. 110
3.22 *Ghār-i Sharīf* at Shree Gupwara; plan, © INTACH, Kashmir. 113

3.23 Courtyard plan in Kashmir, Jamia Masjid Srinagar (L) formed the inspiration for designing of *Mʿārak* (R), © Hakim Sameer Hamdani. 115

4.1 Sangin Darwaza: Akbar's symbolic entrance gateway to the nāgar Nagar, Srinagar: 2018, © Hakim Sameer Hamdani. 130

4.2 Masjid-i Naū, eastern façade: notice the cusped arches set within the rectangular recessed panels, Srinagar: 2018, © Hakim Sameer Hamdani. 133

4.3 Masjid-i Naū, plan and longitudinal section, © INTACH, Kashmir. 134

4.4 Stylistic resemblance: the setting of a cusped arch within a recessed rectangular frame, a surrounding star motif and carved plinth stone at Masjid-i Naū (L) and Mullā Shāh mosque (R), Srinagar: 2018, © Hakim Sameer Hamdani. 135

4.5 Mullā Shāh complex: Mullā Shāh mosque (1), terraces (2), terrace with cells below (2a), cells (3), pavilion (4), pool (5), Dārā Shukoh hammam mosque(6), open well (7), © Hakim Sameer Hamdani. 136

4.6 Mullā Shāh Bāgh masjid, plan, © INTACH, Kashmir. 142

4.7 Tomb of Madnī, eastern elevation: comparison between the mughal entrance gateway to the tomb (top) and sultanate period entrance gateway to the tomb (bottom), © Hakim Sameer Hamdani. 146

4.8 Thag Bābā shrine: view of the marble cenotaphs over the grave, Srinagar: 2010, © Hakim Sameer Hamdani. 148

4.9 *Khānaqāh-i Mʿaulā*, ground floor and upper floor plan, © INTACH, Kashmir. 157

4.10 Mughal mosque at Hasanabad, ruins of the mosque. Note the heavy brick masonry of the walls, Srinagar: early 20th century, © ASI. 160

5.1 *Khānaqāh-i Ghusīyah*, ground floor plan, © INTACH, Kashmir. 175

5.2 *Khānaqāh-i Nazkī*, ground floor plan, © INTACH, Kashmir. 177

5.3 *Khānaqāh-i Khawājā Masʿud*, north-eastern façade of the building, Pampore, 2007, © Hakim Sameer Hamdani. 180

5.4 Shrine of Sayyid Qasim, Budgam: 2010, © Mukhtar Ahmad. 182

6.1 Kheer Bhawani, the main miniature marble temple at Kheer Bhawani, constructed in 1912, Ganderbal: 2018, © Hakim Sameer Hamdani. 193

PLATES

1 Kashmir: The image of a Himalayan Paradise, Kishansar-Vishansar lake, Kashmir: 2019, © Niraj Kumar.

2 Jhelum river front: The riverfront as a maker of the city's cultural ethos, the mosque of Rīnchanā is in the foreground, Srinagar: 2018, © Hakim Sameer Hamdani.

3 *Dumath*: Mausoleum of Zain-al Ābidīn's mother, based on a centralized octagonal plan, showing deep influences of Timurid architecture, Srinagar: 2019, © Niraj Kumar.

4 Mosque of Madnī, main eastern façade, the Mughal gateway to the tomb of Madnī is located on the right of the main mosque, Srinagar, 2019, © Zubair Ahmed.

5 Jamia Masjid: Northern *iwan* from across the central courtyard, Srinagar: 2007, © Hakim Sameer Hamdani.

6 ʿAālī Masjid: Hypostyle hall with Deodar wooden columns, Srinagar: 2010, © Ram Rehman.

7 Achabal bāgh: The *bāgh* owes its development to two women: the Empress Nūr Jahān and Princess Jahān Ārā, a reminder of Kashmir's fascination for the imperial household, Achbal: 2011, © Hakim Sameer Hamdani.

8 Zafar Khān Aḥsan (blue dress) holding a majlis at his *ḥavelī* at Srinagar. The rich Mughal decorations of *ṣubedars ḥavelī* contrast with the rustic appearance of a Kashmiri shrine which can be seen in the background (from the window), manuscript: c. 1073 AH/ 1662 CE, © Royal Asiatic Society.

9 *Khānaqāh* of Bābā Nasib: The *Khānaqāh* from the south-east with the modern masonry pillars replacing wooden columns in the entrance porch, Bijbehara: 2017, © Hakim Sameer Hamdani.

10 *Khānaqāh-i Mʿaulā*, Main eastern façade with painted naqāshī work on the walls and door frame. Most of the colours have undergone through a gradual change during successive repair works in the post-1945 period, Srinagar: 2018, © Niraj Kumar.

11 Interiors of the *Khānaqāh-i Ghusīyah*, Srinagar, 2019, © Niraj Kumar.

12 *Asār-i Sharīf*, Hazratbal, the new building at Hazratbal was inspired by Mughal architecture, especially Taj Mahal, Srinagar: 2018, © Mukhtar Ahmad.

ACKNOWLEDGEMENTS

It was after finishing my graduation, somewhere in the years in between 2000-2001 that I first started going around the narrow lanes and by lanes of Srinagar, simply registering the imagery of wood and brick that formed this old city. And walking down the streets amongst the decay, chaos and exuberance of life hidden in between, I discovered not only the architecture of this resilient city but also bonded with my own roots. This work is part of that journey and rediscovery, ongoing and unending.

This work has benefitted from invaluable advice and suggestions from Ebba Koch, James Wescoat and Manu Subti. I would specially like to thank Ebba Koch for sharing her thoughts on many of the issues relating to Kashmir in general and Mughal Architecture in particular. Over the years her scholarship has increased my understanding on a myriad of issues relating to Mughal architecture. This work has benefitted from the help of many people, colleagues as well as friends. I would like to express my gratitude to Nasser Rabat, Shehzad Bashir, Chitrelekha Zutshi, Susan Stronge, Avinoam Shalem and Abid Gulzar for their help during the days of my initial doctoral research. Priyaleen Singh at School of Planning and Architecture, Delhi, my thesis advisor, deserves my thanks and gratitude, both for her patience as well as her valuable insights and criticism which helped in shaping my research. I would also like to thank my thesis examination committee, especially R C Aggarwal who first suggested publishing my thesis in the form of a book.

I would like to express particular gratitude to Saleem Beg, who initiated me on the path of researching Kashmir's Islamic religious architecture. Over the years since joining INTACH in 2004, I have listened to numerous anecdotes that he has recollected that revolve around the changing dynamics of Kashmir's society. I would also like to thank INTACH Kashmir for supporting my doctoral research which has resulted in this work. A special thank is owed to my colleagues at INTACH: Sumaira Hakak, Imran Butt, Umer Farooq, Taha Mughal, Tawakul, Zubair and also Vipendra Singh who interned with us; Mehran Qureshi, who was a constant colleague in my journey with his queries, conversation and insights; Niraj Kumar for his friendship and support in sourcing material at Delhi. Particular gratitude also goes to the staff of Research Library, Srinagar. I thank the original sources and copyright owners of the illustrative material for their permission to reproduce them here. At Routledge I would like to thank Lubna Irfan and Rimina Mohapatra for their patience and support.

My family owes special thanks, especially my wonderful nieces, Fiza and Zuha as well as Zulfikar Ashraf; my uncle Munshi Ghulam Hassan, who passed away before this work took the shape of a book. His memory of places, events and individuals is something that I will always cherish. This work has mostly been written in the silence of nights, and I cannot thank my wife Rakhshanda and daughter Parirou, enough for their sacrifice and support. Also, I would be amiss not to thank Rakshanda for those unlimited cups of tea, which helped me through some of Kashmir's cold nights. To my parents I owe my love of books and reading, which has not only helped me in this work but also enriched my life. And to my sisters, those unending gift of books during my teenage years, which I hope to finally return with this work. Thanks!

Srinagar
August 2020

NOTE ON TRANSLITERATION

Arabic and Persian transliteration follow a modified system based on the standard of the *International Journal of Middle East Studies* (IJMES). Kashmiri transliterations are largely based on the same convention. The use of diacritical mark for non-English words has been kept to a minimum and reserved for cases when no common transliteration in English language text is available. The use of diacritical marks for name of places has been avoided.

1

INTRODUCTION

Kashmir: Imagining a place and its historical memory

Within the wide swathe of land that has been associated with Islam, Kashmir assumes a marginal and remote association. Located in the northernmost part of South Asia, the region has traditionally been seen as a provincial part of the wider Indian empire, with its claim to fame based mostly on its geographical location: the abundance of bountiful water, snow-clad mountains and a pleasant climate. Within the Indian context, Kashmir is also renowned for its crafts, some of which, like *pashminā* shawls, have been famed in the court of emperors and kings – Asian as well as European. Nestled in the lofty and virtually impenetrable folds of the Himalayas, the valley has carved a distinct identity for itself, politically as well as culturally, of which its architecture is visually the most dominant expression.

Historically, Kashmir for its inhabitants has been the epitome of a heavenly paradise on earth – a tradition that has carried itself well into our own times too. Writing earlier, in the eighteenth-century CE, Khawjā Azam Dedhmāri weaves the narrative of this heavenly imagery in his introduction to his general history of Kashmir, *Tārīkh-iʿ Uẓmā in*, these word:

> This book has been written about that wonder of the Creator's creation which is commonly referred to as the unrivalled paradise – the land of Kashmir [...][1].

Similarly, for Pīr Hasan Shāh Khuihāmī, a nineteenth-century CE historian, Kashmir because of its natural beauty has always been perceived as a paradise – not to be seen anywhere else, by learned men, divines and nature lovers from time immemorial[2]. Whereas for most the imagery of paradise can be seen as a lyrical expression of the surrounding physical environment, some have even attempted to quantify it. Khuihāmī elaborates on fifteen distinct traits that for him are to be found in Kashmir alone, characteristics which for him assume a quality uniquely Kashmiri, quintessentially heavenly[3]. To a large extent, Khuihāmī's list reads like an echo of the Hindu scripture, *Nīlamata Purāṇa* (ca. sixth-eighth century CE), in which the blessings of Kashmir are recounted as:

> [...] Filled with rows of rice-fields [...], inhabited by the people who perform sacrifices and are engaged in self-study and contemplation – virtuous ascetics [...] it is bedecked with the temples of the gods and all the holy places, and is auspicious [...] all the sacred places, which are on the earth, are there. Thronged with the hermitages of the sages (it is) pleasant in heat and cold [...] Unconquerable by the enemy [...] it is devoid of the fear of famines [...] enjoyable, holy, beneficial for living beings, endowed with the qualities (of producing) all grains [...] Full of gardens and pleasure-grove [...] Laden with various types of flowers, fruits, trees [...] possessed of all the sacred places[4].

This image of an earthly heaven is not, however, confined to native Kashmiri writers alone [Plate 1]. For over the centuries, visitors to this isolated mountainous valley ranging from emperors, wandering poets, dervishes to European visitors, have echoed the words of the inhabitants and celebrated the land for its beauty[5].Yet, for Kashmiris, the land is not only the recipient of nature's graces but was also seen in the distant past as the abode of gods[6]. It is a land which 'since early times has been pre-eminently a country of holy sites and places of pilgrimage of all kinds'. As the oldest surviving text on Kashmir, *Nīlamata Purāṇa* brings to fore the sacredness of the land, through legends celebrating the very evolution of life in this area as a divine favor – intervention leaving a mark of holiness all over the land[7]. It is to *Nīlamata Purāṇa* that we owe the legend not only of origin of life in Kashmir but the vary name 'Kashmir' itself.

Along with the image of a paradise and sacredness is the associated impression of a homeland; Kashmir as a defined physical entity enclosed within its mountainous surroundings which sets it apart from the rest: the others[8]. The mountains not only contained the land but, more importantly, formed a visual boundary; easily recognizable for what Kashmiris down through the history saw as their homeland. For Kashmir, the mountains not only 'isolated its population from the rest of India' but also bestowed on the land 'a historical existence of marked individuality'[9]. This sense of what made Kashmir unique was captured both in textual writings and in the architectural manifestation of the region in pre-Muslim medieval Kashmir. Representing a shared awareness of the land, it, to borrow the words of Diana Eck[10], can also be said to symbolize a whole for the inhabitants of the land. An all-encompassing whole in its formation of linkages between myths, legends, sacredness and the place – a wholeness that assumes a character far more distinct and concrete then that of a regional variation of larger idea that may be constructed as the greater Indic civilization. An important element in establishing this sense of Kashmiri-ness was that of the frontiers: of those insurmountable natural barriers that acted as safeguards and harbingers of the land and its culture. Frontiers, which have acted not only as physical barriers but also as enablers of Kashmiri identity.

And, when fate would separate the people of Kashmir from this homeland, they would still reminisce about the land, as the eleventh century CE poet Bīlhanā does in these verses:

> Where the beauty of the women's breasts
> Warmed through a gentle application of saffron,
> Raṅku deer blankets, releasing the fragrance of musk,
> And boat-bourne bath houses at the Vitastā's shore
> Each in their abundance during the winter months
> Point to the pleasure of heaven[11].

Historically, Kashmir would remain the valley of the river Jhelum (Vitastā) and its tributaries. The Pīr Panjal mountain range forms its cultural as well as geographical extent along the south and the central Himalayan range separating the Jhelum and Indus drainage system its northerly extent. Even though the destiny of the surrounding hill states of Poonch, Rajouri, Badarwah, Kishtwar, Padar and Jammu would keep on being intertwined with that of Kashmir, fostering close cultural linkages, yet these areas were never seen as being distinctly Kashmiri. Similarly, in spite of intermittent cry for aid or even occasional adventures of conquest launched by the kings of Kashmir into the Indian plains or the high mountains of Ladakh and Tibet, these lands remained always the 'outside' for the inhabitants of the land[12].

Yet, the land located as it was on one of the branches of the Silk route[13] leading into the Indian sub-continent was never totally devoid of external influences. Kashmir was not only a recipient of traditions from the east, of China and Tibet, but at various points of its history also formed a part of wider empires originating from mainland India, like that of the Mauryas under Ashoka, the Kushans under Kanīshkā, the White Huns[14] or the Mughal in the medieval period. This resulted not only in the introduction of foreign elements (and races) in the overall cultural and social life of the inhabitants of the region but also a certain cross fertilization of ideas[15]. Nevertheless, such a fusion, synthesis always reflected a sense of continuity with the past, culturally as well as politically, reinforcing the Kashmiri self-image of being unique and distinct.

Justifiably, in this self-image that the inhabitants of the land created for themselves, one does not find the distinctiveness as associated with a modern concept of a nation, yet a sense of exclusiveness, a sense of a shared identity, an understanding of us and them is always present as is the notion of a homeland. This can also be seen the work of the twelfth century CE poet Maṅkha, who conveys a sense of Kashmiri distinctness by contrasting it with the other: the lands that are different from Kashmir. This difference is again articulated in terms of the physical landscape, the climate as well as social customs of the people of Kashmir, all contributing to a sense of

Kashmiri identity[16]. To a large extent, it is the geography much more than descent or language that defines the image of Kashmir during the medieval period. In this image, different political epochs, change of dynasties, kings, all form a collective narrative of the land; a shared memory of the past. That this identity is not articulated in specific political terms, that there may be other multiple identities based on communal, sectarian and social level present throughout the course of history does not negate its very existence.

Islam and (its) architecture: Narrative and interpretations

Islam is a religion; it is also a cultural force and is seen as a distinct civilization too. Historically, since its birth in the year 610 CE, Islam, after an initial stage of persecution and hostility, would within years after the passing of its founder advance into territory away from the deserts of Arabia, areas culturally rich and part of older civilizations and empires. And, over the centuries, Islam in turn gave rise to new empires and kingdoms as it travelled to geographical territories as vast and diverse as Spain in the west and Indonesia in the east.

The revelation, or what can be seen as the propagation of faith of Islam, had resulted during the Prophet's own lifetime in the creation of a distinct Muslim society, forming an Islamic state based on certain principles[17]; principles that were introduced socially and politically in all areas that came under the sway of the religion. For the Muslims themselves, Islam identifies not only with an act of faith but also in being a part of a community of believers (*umma*), ruled and governed by a series of universal values, the articles of faith, the economy of worship and a law of governance[18].

Combined with a shared value system, there has also been a predisposition to see within the vast geographical expanse that has been a part of the Islamic world, the region of Middle East as 'both the homeland and the heartland of *Dār-al Islam* (Abode of Islam)'[19]. Historically, this notion holds true for the Arabian Peninsula – the land of the Prophet of Islam, of the revelations (Quran) and the house of God (Kaaba). In so far as the land contains the historic memory of not only the Prophet of Islam, but all major events marking his life and acts: *sunnah* (the Prophetic practices)[20], this relationship is deeply entrenched in the collective Muslim consciousness, reinforced by the mandatory annual pilgrimage: *hajj*. In its early formative post-prophetic years, this notion of sacredness also came to include various locations in the east, mostly in Iraq connected with the Shiʿa thought, and in the west with Jerusalem, which came to be referred to, in traditional Muslim accounts, as *Bait-ul-Muqaddas* (The Holy House).

In so far as the 'principle of purpose' – *niʿyah* – forms one of the key theological themes of Islam in regards to human acts and their reckoning[21], one can use the argument that it also forms a key component of any collective community expression in a specific geographical setting. This would hold true not only for areas where a functional Muslim polity existed at a point of time in their past or even today, but also in settings which were culturally predominantly Muslim. Such an argument would imply specific cultural meanings which have translated into motifs of expressions in the field of arts, languages and architecture. As the inherent meaning behind such an expression was to be derived, deliberated and accepted by a collective community; therefore, it lends to the entire process of arriving at an expression a certain dynamism linked to the geographical and temporal frame of reference within which that decision was made. In so far as this study is concerned with the examination of religious architectural expression, it would also involve our understanding of Islam as a cultural force with an architectural image and its manifestation in a geographical area which was derived from the local experience of the community, thus making each experience unique to its setting and period of occurrence. This does negate a more traditional view of Islamic architecture, as an expression realized at a specific point of time, immutable in its essence which is derived not from the community but based on doctrines of faith, as an eternal and enduring truth. This is an argument that will be the focus of this study in understanding the experience of Islam as religion in a specific geographical setting – Kashmir.

Our understanding of Islamic art and architecture is governed by three different and distinct set of narratives. The European discourse that emerged in the colonial times, though with a conceived understanding of the oriental, was still seminal in nature in the way they undertook a study and overview of the subject[22]. As Robert Hillenbrand puts it, 'Islamic architectural history is a field invented by Westerners and cast in Western terms'[23]. The post-colonial approach to the subject involves two contrary expressions both approached by their exponents with a wide range of analytic subtlety. Of these, we have the traditionalist looking for a deeper meaning, symbolism and unity of purpose behind the visual image and a view that emerged in the 1970s, re-examining the whole idea of what actually constitutes Islamic art-architecture. Since the publication of Edward Said's seminal work, *Orientalism*, the very notion of Islamic architecture has been critically examined and re-examined as a part of post-modern, post-colonial discourse[24]. Overall, in this post-colonial discourse, in terms of the expressions and understanding, we find a broad range of intellectual nuance, of views highly divergent in what has also been termed as an 'unwieldy field of Islamic art and architecture'[25].

For the traditionalists, or as they have also at times been termed the symbolists, there exists a universal field of Islamic architecture, an architecture which is seen as a physical manifestation of a deeper, symbolic meaning, many a times highly esoteric version of the religion itself. In a view wherein 'everything in creation is a symbol'[26], any and virtually all artistic expressions are a reflection and manifestation of such symbols, their understanding and their meanings. For architecture in Islam, such symbols and their association, all originate from the divine revelation, the word of God: Quran[27]. It is from symbols that the notions of form, space, color, geometry, calligraphy as used in creation of a building derive their meaning. Thus, in Titus Burckhardt's view, Islamic art represents a synthesis of wisdom '*hīkmāh*' and craftsmanship '*fann* or *sināh*'[28]. *Hīkmāh* which for Sayyid H Nasr, one of the leading exponents of this viewpoint translates into 'theosophy or traditional philosophy'[29], may also be interpreted as workmanship[30]. Interestingly, it is to this highly symbolic field of traditional philosophy that writers like Nader Ardlan, Laleh Bakhtiar, Nasr and others look for explaining their understanding of Islamic architecture and its symbols.

That Islamic architecture did not exist in an artistic vacuum but had precedents in earlier traditions is not contested in such a world view. Yet, when Muslims started building, they not only incorporated these earlier architectural elements in their buildings, but gave birth to a new artistic form in their creations, wherein older architectural and structural elements are synthesized with the yearning of new spiritual order in creation of a uniquely new art form – the Islamic architecture[31]. As Marcus Hattiens explains it:

> [...] The bond of common religion, many distinctive local, cultural and ethnic features developed quite early, since Islam absorbed elements of cultures it had conquered or converted[32].

Such a universal overview of Islamic architecture as a visual expression of Islam does not for its advocates assume isolation between the sacred and the secular, much like the religion itself wherein no such delineation exists.

But this notion of unity, which some have taken for granted as a fact, has also been critiqued as a 'myth'[33]. As has been variously argued, in traditional Muslim societies, architectural writing never emerged on a scale and depth as seen in the western world or even in various Asian cultures, like the *shilpā shāstras* in South Asia, and the few that were written, never acquired a canonical status[34]. This lack of a written discourse on architecture contrasts with the actual event of Islam, which in the words of Marshall Hodgson actually, 'intensified historical awareness'[35].

The idea of an art-architectural tradition rooted in Quran has also been critiqued based on an understanding of early muslin history, best illustrated by Oleg Grabar's argument that:

> [...] The infant Islam of Medina had no feelings on the matter of art, because it did not penetrate into its consciousness[36].

Unfortunately, Grabar's view, though purely academic, would also find resonance in certain sections of Muslim society today, who arguing for the same would tend to condemn any artistic expression as a sacrilegious innovation of later-day Muslims-a *bid'a*. The recent unfortunate events in Syria, Iraq, Mali and earlier in Bamiyan (Afghanistan) resulting in desecration and destruction of cultural sites, both Islamic and pre-Muslim, is a sad reflection on how ingrained such a discourse has become in small but vocal sections of the Muslim society today. Hodgson's view that 'Muslim puritans, like others, would no doubt prefer to avoid all art of any sort'[37] can be seen as sad but insightful realization of the argument.

The narratives questioning the notion of a single Islamic artistic expression mark the shift from traditional universalism of Islamic art and architecture to a diversification of how and what it is, without actually redefining it. Primarily, this approach reflects a deeper understanding of regional idiosyncrasies; dynastic epochs, of varied building typologies and art mediums. The shift from Islamic to Islamicate, as first argued by Marshall Hogdson in 1974, continues to define the narratives related to material culture of Muslim societies. In this definition, Islamic would pertain to that limited matrix of artistic outpouring which are primarily of religious use as opposed to the wider cultural traditions not directly linked to Muslim faith but produced in Muslim cultural settings: the Islamicate. A modification of Hogdson's view can be seen in some contemporary arguments such as Nasser Rabbat's, in whose view:

> Islamic architecture is of course the architecture of those cultures, regions or societies that have directly or via some intermediary processes accepted Islam as an integral component of their epistemological and socio-cultural makeup[38].

We also have arguments such as Ernst Grube's who look for an understanding of Islamic architecture as a genre of contemplative inward-looking spaces[39], while Edward Madden suggests for a quality which is 'non-directional [...] timelessness, eternity and infinity which excludes all thing temporal and historical'[40] as the essence of what may be understood as Islamic Architecture.

Amongst contemporary writers, Yasir Tabbaa[41] tends to see a transforming nature of Islamic arts, representing social, cultural and political tensions resulting in new forms and expressions – a society very much like any other society with an element of continuity as well as chaos and change inherent to its functioning and development. In such a society, it is not a perennial, un-mutated essence which is at the roots of all artistic expressions but rather societal pressures which find and lead us to newer expressions which have been bestowed with new meanings. This is a viewpoint that is reflected in this study also, as I will explain how the experience of Islam in Kashmir in the fourteenth century CE is quite dissimilar to that of the same religion in the rest of the South Asia, especially in the adjoining plains of Punjab and Delhi. In the end, though the faith retained its essence wherever it went, the culture that was associated with it differed from region to region, era to era. In certain cases, the differences were negligible while in others they were more profound. Though the needs of articles of faith remained same, the understanding of the faith remained same, the doctrine of faith remained same, yet its cultural expression did not.

This study does recognize the fact that during the medieval period, which saw the development of Islamic artistic expressions, religion formed the basis of identity of the individual as well as the community. Yet, unlike in jurisprudence wherein a certain consensus had been evolved by the ninth century CE regarding major issues of law, architectural developments and innovations were neither curtailed nor consecrated into a written or even unwritten dogma at any fixed point of time. Certain tradition of esthetics that had been established were circulating in different parts of the Islamic world in a manner that made it a part of the entire Muslim civilization irrespective of time or place, a similarity which at times make it difficult even today to decide upon the provenance of certain artifact conclusively, yet there were differences too; differences linked to the regional setting and regional identity, the strength of such a regional identity and the way such an identity was assimilated, erased or transmitted into Islam.

To rephrase Grunebaum, the identity of an individual as a part of his society in the medieval ages was primarily governed by religion, then locale and finally a larger racio-geographic entity[42]. In such an environment, it is hard to argue that religion did not weigh on the artistic-architectural traditions that were evolving or assuming a certain degree of permanence within the society. While we can say that 'but' for Islam, monuments linked to Muslim societies and its traditions could not have evolved, yet to accept such a building tradition as a formal expression of the religion would not only negate the vary evolution of this building style but the principles of religion itself.

This study sees in the civilization of Islam a transnational culture with certain fixed religious values interacting with different cultures and regions in evolving a flexible identity for itself, shaped by the particular circumstances and environments in which such an interaction was undertaken.

Islam in Kashmir: The prelude

In so much as Islam represents a universal religious value, Kashmir as the land represents a regional context with a self-definition of local distinctiveness, local uniqueness. Though the actual advent of Muslims in the region may have happened as early as latter part of the eleventh century CE, yet the establishment of a nascent Muslim community in the region dates to a much later period – of early fourteenth century CE. Thus, by the time Islam marked its presence felt in Kashmir, those great dynasties marking the golden age of the medieval Islamic world bestowed with the politico-religious authority of a Caliphate, that of the Umayyad (634–749 CE), the Abbasids (749–1258 CE) and the Fatimids (910–1171 CE) had already waned away.

Many of the legal arguments regarding various societal mores and values, issues of faith and doctrine, jurisprudence, permissibility of various acts and expressions within the Muslim community had been resolved with the formation and consolidation of various legal schools amongst both Shi'a Shia and Sunnis. The Hadith of the Prophet Muhammad (d. 632 CE) as transmitted down the ages orally had been consolidated and recorded as written works. Historically, this collective body of Hadith would form the theocratic background against which the *ummah* (community) was supposed to adjust, affirm or reaffirm the religious validity of various forms of social expressions, and at times also formed the theological background for any transformation or reformation agenda in the society[43]. In so far as the compilation of these books was coeval with cultural and artistic development taking place in the Islamic empire during the medieval ages, they also assume a certain degree of vindication of contemporary social practices (*'urf*) while also convening disapproval of some. Similarly, philosophical, mystical, sectarian and political discourses had assumed a well-defined outline and recognizable identity for their various adherents as well as opponents.

Socially as well as architecturally, institutions like mosque, *khānaqāh*, madrasa, tombs and mausoleums had continued to be built and an acceptable and recognizable visual imagery was bestowed on them. The hypostyle mosque and what would be referred to as the Iranian mosque had both already been perfected. Even the prototype for a future Ottoman mosque had already been constructed by the Seljuks, though the actual creation of an Ottoman state (1299 CE) would be almost coeval with the establishment of Muslim rule in Kashmir. Monuments of Islamic architecture such as the Dome of Rock (c. 691 CE), the Great Umayyad Mosque (c. 634 CE, rb. 706–15 CE), various Caliphical mosques of the Abbasids in Iraq, Great Mosque of Samara, Iraq (c. 848 CE), the Fatamid madrasa of Al Azhar (c. 970–72 CE), the Seljuk Masjid-i Jamia (1086–88 CE) at Isfahan, had all been constructed.

In South Asia, Muslim dynasties had been continuously ruling from Delhi since 1210 CE, while Muslim rule had been established much earlier in the eleventh and twelfth century CE in Punjab and adjoining areas[44]. The invading Muslim armies of the Ghurids (r. 1150–1210 CE) arriving in the North India had also resulted in introducing cultural, especially artistic predilection of Indian artisans to a Persianate world as represented by the Ghurid court. Subsequently, with the establishment of Delhi Sultanate, we see a gradual transformation in building traditions: from initial attempts at salvaging temple material into workable structures[45] as seen in the Quwat-al Islam mosque (1193 CE) at Delhi [Figure 1.1] and the Arhai-din-ka Jhonpra mosque (1200-06 CE) at Ajmer to a well-defined style of the Khiljis (1290–1320 CE) and the Tughlaqs (1320–1413 CE) which also involved structural innovations[46]. Thus, by the time Islam reached Kashmir in the early fourteenth century CE, it had already established a cultural milieu for itself as well as establishing a visual medium for representing itself.

Narratives behind Kashmirs's Islamic built traditions: Overview of sources

Our basic and rather limited understanding of the development of Kashmir's built traditions related to Islamic religious architecture is based primarily on political histories (*tārīkh*), a select few of which are coeval with the actual development of this architectural style.

Unfortunately, none of these historic writings are actually devoted to architecture or offer any direct report about the architectural concerns of a nascent Muslim society in the region. The importance of these accounts primarily lies in way they help us in analyzing the political and social forces in vogue at the time of introduction of Islam in the region and the development of a Muslim society over the years. They also provide us with a chronology of certain major monuments linked with Muslim faith. Aside from the political history, we have numerous *taẕkira* (hagiographic accounts) of various Sufi masters and orders which provide us with additional information about the people and the institutions for whom many of the buildings and structures where built. Of these that of *Tuḥfatūl Aḥbāb* dealing with the *Nūrbakhshī* Sufi order, an order that had adherents in the last sovereign Muslim dynasty of Kashmir – the Chaks – is rich in details about the architecture of the *khānaqāh* associated with this order. Additionally, the work is filled with references, wherein esoteric meaning has been lent to the actual architecture of a building.

In terms of architecture, especially history of the architecture of the region dating to Muslim rule, virtually our entire knowledge on the subject is limited to what has been written by early twentieth century CE colonial writers like James Fergusson, Percy Brown and W H Nicholls. Others like Alexander Cunningham, Aurel Stein and Henry Cole have also briefly remarked on the subject, though most of their work is devoted to study of the pre-Muslim past of the area. An earlier generation of European travelers to the region including Baron Hugel, François Bernier, G T Vigne, and Rev. Lowenthal, stuck by the quaintness of the Muslim religious architecture, have also included brief passages in their travelogues on the subject. George Forster, who visited the valley during the Afghan rule, is dismissive of local Kashmiri architecture, reserving his praise for surviving Mughal monuments in the region.

Similarly, William Moorcroft who arrived in Kashmir in the mid-nineteenth century CE seems to have been singularly unimpressed by the Muslim architecture of Kashmir. His visit coincided with a turbulent political period in the land and consequently one comes across frequent description of decay and ruin in his travelogue[47].

On the other hand, Baron Hugel proved to be a more discerning observer. Writing about one of the most celebrated monuments of Kashmir, the *khānaqāh* of Shāh Hamdan at Srinagar, he observes:

> [...] Shah Hamedan Musjid is a modern looking building, the prototype of every mosque in Kashmir, and if not exactly resembling

> a Chinese temple, is certainly unlike Indian architecture in general [...] This form is common throughout the valley of Kashmir, from the simplest village temple, to the richly ornamented mosque of the capital [...][48].

Amongst the writers of twentieth century CE, R C Kak, a native archaeologist, in a pioneering work describes the architectural styles of Kashmir. Kak was well-versed with the physical landscape of his native land and the architectural traditions associated with it. His work is of immense value while appreciating the pre-Islamic traditions of Kashmiri architecture, but with regards to the Islamic religious architecture of the land itself, his description is rather perfunctory. While his writings on this architectural genre are almost entirely based on Nicholls description, Kak's own understanding can be gleaned from his statement:

> [...] Muslims in Kashmir were in the beginning far too few to initiate an architecture of their own. All they did was utilize the materials of disused Hindu temples for construction of their mosques. The result was peculiar [...][49].

For Kak, this peculiar architecture is exemplified by two mosques, that of Madnī and Zaina Lank. Yet, both these buildings date from the reign of Sultan Zain-al Ābidīn (r. 1420–70 CE), a ruler who came to the throne almost a century after the establishment of Muslim rule in the valley.

A basic premise of Kak is the contention that all major Muslim religious buildings of Kashmir have been constructed on ruins of ancient Hindu temple[50] – a premise that ignores the evolution of localized architectural response in the society to the introduction of Islam. Interestingly, the prejudices of Kak are also reflected in Hermann Goetz. In his seminal work on the medieval arts of Kashmir, he observes:

> In Srinagar, there is hardly a house in the foundation of which fragments of old Hindu temples have not been built in[51].

Goetz work was finished in 1969, when the population of Srinagar city was more than four hundred thousand!

Given the fact that Kak's book was published at a time when the issue of religious identity was increasingly defining the tone of the political debate, not only in Kashmir but across South Asia, the question remains whether the book was also a response to some of these troublesome issues[52]. An important question that arises from a reading of Kak's work is that if the Muslim society, or at least the Muslim polity, was actively involved in destroying symbols associated with non-Muslim communities as his study implies, then why was the physical form of Muslim places of worship so similar to them? If the formative stage of Muslim rule is seen as a period of conflict between communities essentially identified by their religious belief, then would not the interests of the Muslim community best be served in carving a distinct and separate image for itself? Especially when we see that such a phenomenon did take place under the sultans of Delhi, the nearest Muslim neighbors of Kashmiri sultans.

Where Kak adds to our information is in the actual description of some of these monuments, providing us with a textual vision on some of the main Muslim monuments of the valley as they existed in the early part of the twentieth century CE before later-day additions and alterations. Unfortunately, sometimes even here Kak's descriptions end up as being factually incorrect, as is the case of Khānaqāh-i Shāh Hamdān, a hospice dedicated to the memory of Sayyid ʿAli Hamdanī, which he describes as 'the tomb of the saint'[53]. Similarly, he confuses the ruins of Sultan Quṭub al-Dīn's mausoleum with that of a saint, Pīr Haji Muhammad, an altogether different structure though both exist within the same precinct[54].

While Kak in his description of Muslim architecture of Kashmir draws heavily on Nicholls, the writings of Nicholls are an echo of an earlier European writer, Sir Alexander Cunningham, whose work relates to a narrative that is best characterized as:

> [...] A part of a purportedly dispassionate historical exercise of providing the genealogies of Kashmiri Muslim shrines but which also traced their origins in the destruction of temples[55].

Nicholls description of individual buildings is primarily based on visual observation, coupled with a textual reading as could be derived from European sources. In undertaking his limited study, he completely ignores vernacular and court historians, as well as the various hagiographical accounts related to these buildings. Nicholls' unfamiliarity with the vernacular historical accounts as well as unfamiliarity with building epigraphy leads him to assuming the entrance gateway to the shrine of Madnī to be coeval with the construction of the actual mosque, though the gateway is from a later date and belongs to a different architectural tradition.

Unfortunately, even in the post-Independence period, the unique architectural tradition of Kashmir as seen in the design of its Islamic religious architecture has remained ignored. A basic survey of various buildings and typologies associated with this building tradition does not exist even today. Neither have major monuments linked with it been studied in detail. Most of the works written in this period are devoid of any original contribution on the subject. G M D Sufi's work is both a celebration of the Islamic culture of Kashmir as well as an apology for Muslim rule in the valley. Regarding the architecture associated with Muslim buildings in Kashmir, the book merely reiterates what had already been written on the subject by earlier European writers. By associating wooden architecture in the valley with Muslim rule asserting that the 'wooden style owed its origin to Muslims'[56], he conveniently ignores both historical and archaeological references that prove the existence of a distinct wooden architectural style way before the commencement of Muslim rule in the region.

Mohibbul Hasan, like Sufi, attempts at reconstructing the history of Kashmir during the Muslim rule. Regarding the Muslim architecture of the region, Hasan uses the same sources as Sufi, though slightly digressing from him by acknowledging the fact that building in the wooden style was not all together unknown in pre-Islamic period[57].

Recent architectural studies including those of Catherine Asher, Ebba Koch, J W Bulmahn and James Wescoat, Sylvia Crowe are entirely devoted to the Mughal Architecture of Kashmir and offer little insight on the development of local architectural traditions or the impact of Imperial Mughal architectural style on them. Simultaneously, due to political upheaval affecting the region and natural disasters, many of the important monuments linked with this tradition have been lost which make understanding the evolution of this architectural tradition difficult with each passing day.

Research need

In an interesting assessment of the diversity of forms prevalent in mosque architecture, Ismail Serageldin[58] argues for a syncretic relationship between a common liturgical practice that pervades in all geographical settings where Islam made its foray – the basic functionality of the building and a form which tends to be rooted in the culture of the native community. It is an architectural experience wherein it is local geographical, climatic and morphological features and social practices that give a 'sense of place' to particular location and 'character' to an environment[59]. As an argument, it would explain the regional currents that have always been prevalent in the wide body of what has been termed as Islamic architecture. Such an approach would tend to see Islam being engaged in an interactive dialogue with the local cultures helping in evolving a synthesis of form, between the needs of a new faith and existing artistic and cultural tradition. This relation, or rather partnership, of ideas resembles a participatory exercise in which Islam plays an accommodating if somewhat patronizing role with prevailing local traditions so as to create a new image for itself from what was available in the host community.

In so far as the dominant visual image of designing mosques and shrine in South Asia, especially in North India, at the time when Islam made its presence in Kashmir was and even remains the dome and minaret, any attempt at a contra-image certainly needs to be seen beyond the immediate possibility of material and technology specific necessities. Thus, almost a century before the establishment of Muslim rule in Kashmir, as the Sultanate of Delhi (1206–1526 CE) was being established, Islam, or rather the polity that was Islam, made conscious attempts to obscure or replace established images within the native community. And, the state through its acts as well as patronage did tend to popularize the landscape with this new architectural language derived from the Turko-Persian traditions of the Persianate world: traditions on which, over a period of time, local customs, practices and esthetic sensibility would get grafted on[60].

The religious architecture of Islam evolved in Kashmir in an age and milieu when the immigrant missionaries who introduced the religion in the region were deeply conscious about the Islamic-ness of their native social and cultural mores. Individual mystics some of them leading a solitary life of a religious recluse, were as much a part of this journey as were communities of wandering missionaries well equipped with zealous preachers and attendants. These group of people undertook what would in those times best be described as a hazardous journey along narrow mountain passes into *mūlk-i Kashmir* (land of Kashmir). Most of these missionaries, who were part of this endeavor to proselyte in Kashmir, belonged to Iran or rather the wider Persianate world of Iran proper as well as parts of Central Asia, especially Khurasan – areas rich with Persian influences. They acted as conveyors of Islamic values, both ideological and cultural – acting as agents of cultural ethno-centrism. Self-identifying with the image of acting as Islam's standard bearer in a new territory, they represented not only the religion but the entire cultural outpourings of their native lands, whether it be language, dress or architecture. Yet, the architectural style that emerged and came to be associated with Islam in Kashmir remained rooted in local building traditions and rejecting any outside image manipulation. The purpose of this study is to enhance understanding of this phenomenon, to study the social and political forces behind it. This study aims to fill the large and substantial gaps in our understanding of the Islamic religious architecture of Kashmir gaps which '[...] nobody has hitherto been able to explain satisfactorily [...]'[61].

Taking its point of departure from the prevailing understanding of the subject, this study sees in the religious architecture of Islam in Kashmir a recasting of a primordial identity that was rooted not in Islam the religion but in the memory Kashmir the land. The study investigates the historicity of a transcendent Kashmiri identity within the framework of Islamic religious architecture in the region, arguing that this genre of architecture *transcends the established non-native building traditions linked with Muslim faith, traditions that were adopted in designing of Muslim religious buildings outside Kashmir in the wider geographical swathe of the South Asia, in a time period contemporaneous to the establishment of Muslim rule in Kashmir.*

This study seeks to explore and understand the specificities of this architectural genre that define its regional character and uniqueness, a study so far unexplored and undocumented. This research involves a study on a subject wherein the primary source of study exists in the form of buildings or their archaeological remnants. These extant buildings serve as the primary source of study, evaluated and tested against available historical records. Iconographic analysis is used to establish the meaning of a building studied to establish dates, provenance and stylistic classification. The findings so generated are then critically analyzed to arrive at an iconological understanding of the phenomenon that defines the study.

By cross-checking these sources, the study demonstrates that the Islamic religious architecture of Kashmir represents a process by which the cultural manifestation of Islamic principles – functions were realized in a syncretic idiom of the existing Kashmiri identity.

Structure rationalization

Chapter 1 focuses on how historically, Kashmiri's have seen their land and described its uniqueness, drawing from ancient texts to writings in the medieval period. It is in this uniqueness, reinforced by the geography of the land and its frontiers that has helped in framing the tradition of inter-determinacy between the land and its people, giving rise to a shared feeling of sameness. In discussing the land and religion, which is the subject of this study, the chapter looks into the ways this definite regional identity had been established for Kashmir well before the introduction of Islam into the region. It also, examines the essentials of Islam the religion and its relation with the architectural traditions which are associated with it.

Chapter 2 focuses on the establishment of Muslim rule in Kashmir which in its formative period laid the ground for a cultural syncretism. It examines the archaeological traces from this period and illustrates how, rather than standing apart from the prevailing society by creating victorious monuments to faith, the Muslim Sultans of Kashmir tried to blend in with local customs and architectural practices. From the initial decades of the formative period, the study expands in Chapter 3, to the late fourteenth-fifteenth century when the Sultanate of Kashmir expanded from its natural boundaries, drawing contact with surrounding lands and attracting attention of missionaries from the wider Persianate world. In analyzing the period, the focus is on how, even though new ideas, materials and crafts were introduced in the region, yet local building traditions continued to be promoted by both the court and patrons outside the court. The chapter focuses on the role of native Kashmir Sufis linked with the *Reshī* order who effectively promoted preservation of pre-Islamic cultural symbols, in face of an orthodox view emanating from non-native Persian-speaking Sufis. It also examines the iconoclastic campaign that was launched by these non-Kashmiri missionaries in their efforts to remake Kashmir in a more orthodox image and the role of the *Reshīs* in helping to assimilate past traditions within the boundaries of expanding Muslim community of Kashmir. How this process of assimilation was advanced within the boundaries of architecture is exhibited through a case study of cave shrines of Kashmir linked with the *Reshīs*.

The fall of Kashmir to the Mughal Empire in the sixteenth century resulted in two centuries of Mughal rule in Kashmir. Chapter 4 examines how Mughals viewed Kashmir as a terrestrial paradise to enjoy; and embellished the land with their architectural undertakings. Built in stone, the architectural outpourings of the Mughals in Kashmir marked the projection of an image of permanence of Mughal power and hold over Kashmir as well as their munificence in creating new spaces of worship for the locals. Focusing on the various mosques and a shrine that the Mughal constructed in Kashmir, the work examines how these buildings were used to portray the durability of Mughal rule in Kashmir, yet were mostly abandoned by the Muslim community of Kashmir. The study argues that the architectural tonality of Mughal architecture in Kashmir and its rejection of local established building traditions was the reason why this architectural phenomenon lacked public acceptability. The unenthusiastic reception of Mughal religious buildings amongst the Muslim community of Kashmir is contrasted with the reconstruction of the *Khānaqāh-i Mʿaulā* during the closing years of Mughal rule in Kashmir. An analysis of how the reconstruction was undertaken in native Kashmiri idiom at a time when central Mughal authority had collapsed in Kashmir helps in establishing the actual architecture of the building within the socio-cultural realities of its construction. The work expands on the narrative of image, official patronage and local community involvement and the resultant shape that the reconstruction took. Continuing with the theme of decline of central authority located outside Kashmir, Chapter 5 analyzes how the local image

Figure 1.1 Quwat-al Islam mosque: symbolizing the advent of Muslim rule in Northern India, Delhi, 2018, © Vipendra Singh.

linked with designing of mosques, *khānaqāhs*, shrines and *imāmbādas* was re-established in the region, drawing on from community patronage, following the collapse of Mughal rule in Kashmir. The chapter focuses on how under adverse socio-political condition linked to Afghan and Sikh rule in Kashmir, the Kashmiri Muslim community remained the source of patronage for both preservation and construction activities of Muslim places of worship. Expanding on the theme of a resurgent native architecture, the research posits that the community-based patronage of native architectural enterprise is both a testament to the existence of a real 'community identity' that the research associates with Kashmiri-ness as well a celebration of its syncretic culture. A culture that encompasses not only the architecture but also the entirety of the shrine traditions linked with the Muslim community of Kashmir.

In conclusion, in order to show the contemporary relevance of this architectural tradition as well as the cultural meaning behind it, Chapter 6 offers an overview of the Islamic religious architecture of Kashmir in the twentieth-century Kashmir, drawing on issues of traditions, change, identity, image, conservation and changing perceptions about past.

Notes

1 Khawjā'Azam Dedhmārī, transl. (Urdu), Z S Azhar, *Waqāt-i Kashmir* (Srinagar: Gulshan Publishers, 2003), 22. For an earlier depiction of the same, see Kalhānā, transl. M A Stein, *Rajatarangini,* 2 vols. (Srinagar: Gulshan Books, 2007), 10. For a brief review of how pre-Muslim Sanskrit texts imagined Kashmir and its place within the Indic civilizational ethos of the time, see Luther Obrock, 'Landscape in its place: the imagination of Kashmir in Sanskrit and beyond', *History and Theory*, 59, no. 1, March 2020.

2 Pīr Hasan Shāh Khuihāmī, transl. (Kashmiri), Shams-ud Din Ahmad, *Tārīkh-i Hasan*, Vol. I (Srinagar: J&K Academy of Arts, Culture & Languages, 1999), 110. In the twentieth century, the idea of Kashmir as a physical paradise was again revisited in major works such as G M D Sufi, *Kashīr, Being a History of Kashmir from the Earliest Times to Our Own*, 2 vols (Srinagar: Gulshan books, 2008), R K Parimu, *A History of Sikh Rule in Kashmir, 1819–1846* (Srinagar: Jammu and Kashmir Government: Department of Education, 1977) etc. On the other hand, Chitralekha Zutshi would argue that the 'axiom of Kashmir as paradise' was coined by the Mughal Emperor Jahangir, which is historically incorrect; see Chitralekha Zutshi, *Languages of Belonging.* (Delhi: Permanent Black, 2003), 29.

3 See Khuihāmī, *Tārīkh-i Hasan*, 110–117.

4 *Nīlamata Purāṇa*, Vol. II, transl. Dr Ved Kumari, (Srinagar: J & K Academy of Art, Culture and Languages, 1994), 4–7.

5 See Khuiāmī, *Tārīkh-i Hasan.*

6 M A Stein, *Ancient Geography of Kashmir*, (Srinagar: Gulshan books, 2005), 46. 'In that country [...] there is not a space as large as a grain of *sesamum* without a Tīrāthā', Kalhānā, *Rajatarangini,* 9.

7 For a brief description of Nīlamata Purāṇa as well other ancient texts, refer to Stein, *Ancient Geography of Kashmir*.

8 'That country may be conquered by the forces of spiritual merits, but not by forces of soldiers', Kalhānā, *Rajatarangini,* 9.

9 Ibid, 30.
10 Eck argues for a narrative of Indian-ess that was conceived in the imaginations of the inhabitants of the land, linked by a sacred geography of place-myth, pilgrimage and legend, see Diana Leck, *India: A Sacred Geography,* (New York: Three Rivers Press, 2012).
11 *Vikramāṅkadevacarita*, 18.31, transl. Luther Obrock, also see Anthony Kennedy Warder, *Indian Kāvya literature: The Art of Storytelling*, Vol. 6 (Delhi: Motilal Banarsidass Publishers, 1992), 653.
12 Of the various kings of Kashmir, two stand out in this regard, the seventh century CE monarch, Lalitāditya Muktāpīda (d. 757 CE) and the fourteenth century CE sultan, Shahāb al-Dīn (d. 1373 CE), see H Goetz, *Studies in the History and Art of Kashmir and the Indian Himalayas*, (Wiesbradan: Otto Harrasswitz, 1969), 13–22, 25, and Mohibbul Hasan, *Kashmir under the Sultans* (Srinagar: Ali Mohammad and Sons, 1974), 49–51.
13 An early reference to the route links it with the salt trade by referring it to as the salt route; see Kalhānā, *Rajatarangini*, 395.
14 See Goetz, *Studies in the History,* 1.
15 This cultural melting pot, resulted in the evolution of a Kashmiri style that was 'highly eclectic, and constantly gathered new influences throughout its early development [...]', John Siudmak, *The Hindu-Buddhist Sculpture of Ancient Kashmir and Its Influences* (Lieden: Brill), 22.
16 See Kashi Gomez, *Beyond Sacred Landscapes: Poetic Illuminations of Local Experience in Maṅkha's Śrīkaṇhacarita* (MA Thesis: University of California, Berkeley, 2016).
17 'Religion had spawned a society and its government. This is the situation in the Prophet's Medina, Patricia Crone, *Slaves on Horses: The Evolution of the Islamic Polity* (Cambridge: Cambridge University Press, 2008), 296.
18 As Hattstein views it, in Islam, 'the individuals need for salvation was set within the framework of a well regulated community, and Islam became "God's law" on earth', M Hattstein and P Delius, ed. *Islamic Art and Architecture.* (Königswinter: Konemann, 2004), 24.
19 See L C Brown, *Religion and State: The Muslim Approach to Politics* (New York: Columbia University Press, 2000).
20 See A Guillaume, *Islam* (England: Penguin Books Ltd., 1982), 92.
21 A J Arberry, *An Introduction to the History of Sufism* (UK: Orient Longman Ltd., 1992), 56.
22 See Nasser Rabbat, *What Is Islamic Architecture Anyway?*, *Journal of Art Historiography*, no. 6, 2012, 1.
23 Robert Hillenbrand, *Islamic Art and Architecture* (London: Thames & Hudson Ltd., 2004), 5.
24 Avinoam Shalem, 'What do we mean when we say 'Islamic art?' A plea for a critical rewriting of the history of the arts of Islam', *Journal of Art Historiography*, no. 6, 2012, 1.
25 See Sheila S Blair and Jonathan M Bloom, *The Mirage of Islamic Art: Reflections on the Study of an Unwieldy Field*, *The Art Bulletin*, vol. 85, no. 1 (Mar., 2003), 152–184.
26 Laleh Bakhtiar, *Sufi: Expressions of the Mystic Quest* (London: Thames and Hudson, 1976), 25.
27 Ibid, 27.
28 See Titus Burckhardt, *The Art of Islam: Language and Meaning* (London: World of Islam Festival Publ. Co., 1976).
29 Seyyed Hossein Nasr, *The Garden of Truth* (New York: Harper Collins, 2008), 82.

30 'Wisdom' (*Al-Hikmah)* is defined as 'knowledge which puts everything in its place', and therefore implies application and 'workmanship', S M H Tabatabai, transl. William C Chittick, *A Shi'ite Anthology* (Tehran Ansariyan Publications, 1980), 65.
31 The view of Ernst Grube also broadly follows the contours of such a discourse, wherein the architecture in its physical manifestation displays features which are 'inherent in Islam as a cultural phenomenon', Rabbat, *What is Islamic architecture anyway?*, 3.
32 Hattstein and Delius, *Islamic Art and Architecture*, 9
33 See Shalem, *What do we mean when we say 'Islamic Art'*.
34 Thus we have the words of the Andalusian judge, Ibn Abdun who stated 'as an architecture is concerned, it is the haven where man's spirit, soul and body find refuge and shelter', A Ahmad, W Mujani and R Othman, *Architecture according to the Perspective of the Quran: An Evaluation*, International Journal of Academic Research in Business and Social Sciences, Vol. 7(8), August, 2017, 2.
35 Marshall G S Hodgson, *Islam and Image*: *History of Religions*, 3(1), 1964, 238.
36 Note by Grabar in Hodgson, *Islam and Image*, 259.
37 Ibid, 240.
38 Rabbat, *What is Islamic architecture anyway?*, 15.
39 Ernst J Grube, in *Architecture of the Islamic World: Its History and Social meaning*, ed. George Michell, (London, Thames & Hudson, 1978), 10–15.
40 Edward H Madden, *Some Characteristics of Islamic Art*: *Journal of Esthetics and Art Criticism*, 33 (4), 1975, 428.
41 Yasser Tabbaa, *The Transformation of Islamic Art during the Sunni Revival* (London: University of Washington Press, 2001).
42 See Gustave E Von Grunebaum, *Medieval Islam: A Study in Cultural Orientation* (Chicago: University of Chicago Press, 1969), 85.
43 In the Muslim community of medieval times as Crone argues, 'Government now formed an almost completely detached circle of its own, devoted to Islam but not generated by it. But as far as society (or at least urban society) was concerned, the overlap remained total. Insofar as one can tell, society continued to be largely based on the Shari'a […]', Patricia Crone, *From Arabian Tribes to Islamic Empire: Army, State and Society in the Near East c. 600–850*. (New York: Routledge, 2008), 396.
44 Muslim presence in India both in Sindh and in peninsular India, especially Kerala dates back to Ummayad period, see Finbarr Barry Flood, *Before the Mughals: Material Culture of Sultanate of North India, Muqarnas* (Leiden: Brill, 2019), 1.
45 A Lambah and A Patel, (2006), *The Architecture of Indian Sultanates* (Mumbai: Marg Publications, 2006), 136.
46 Like Balban's tomb where we see the use of first true arch and dome or ʿAla'-i Darwāzā which saw the use of radiating voussoirs in the construction of the dome, see Flood, *Before the Mughals*.
47 W Moorcroft and G Trebeck, *Travels in the Himalayan Provinces of Hindustan and the Punjab; in Ladakh and Kashmir, in Peshawar, Kabul, Kunduz and Bokhara*, 2 vols. (Srinagar: Gulshan books, 2000), 118–123.
48 Baron C Hugel, *Kashmir and the Punjab* (Jammu: Light & Life Publishers, 1972), 117.
49 R C Kak, *Ancient Monuments of Kashmir* (Delhi: Sagar Publications, 1971), 70.
50 Ibid, 81, 83, 91, 92, 136, 164.
51 Goetz, *Studies in the history and Art of Kashmir*, 63.

52 Kak's work had to be expunged of certain passages before its publication by the India Society, London precisely for the same reason, see Mridu Rai, *Hindu Rulers, Muslim Subjects.* (Ranikhet: Permanent Black, 2004), 205.
53 Kak, *Ancient Monuments of Kashmir,* 79.
54 Ibid.
55 Rai, *Hindu Rulers, Muslim Subjects*, 206.
56 Sufi, *Kāshir,* 509. Yet in his introduction to the section on architecture, he is far more measured in his opinion, '[...] the wooden architecture of Kashmir [...] originated, in its present form, with, or rather was popularized by, the Muslims, as Buddhists, too, had a wooden style of their own', Sufi, *Kāshir,* 505–06.
57 Hasan, *Kashmir Under the Sultans*, 268.
58 Ismail Serageldin, *Introduction: The Regionalism* in *The Mosque: History, Architectural Development & Regional Diversity*, ed. Martin Frishman and Hasan-ud Din Khan (London: Thames & Hudson, 1994).
59 Ibid, 72.
60 Flood, *Before the Mughals*, 1. In recent studies the extent of Persianate influences on Sultanate architecture has also been questioned in favor of a more native Indian origin for some of the main architectural features employed, see Yves Porter and Richard Castinel, *Jahanpanah's Jamiʿ Masjid (circa 1343): A Reassessment*, *Muqarnas*, vol. 35 (Leiden: Brill), 2018. Significantly even at a later date, we have Ibn Battuta's testimony on how during the reign of Sultan Muhammad bin Tughlaq (r. 1325–1351 CE) foreigners were patronized as 'courtiers, palace officials, ministers of state, judges', Ibn Battuta, transl. H A R Gibb, *Travels in Asia and Africa*, 1325–1354 (Delhi: Low Priced Edition,1999), 184. Nevertheless, both Ibn Battuta and the historian Zia-al Dīn Baranī write about a society, reflecting a level of pluralism and tolerance between the Muslim ruling elite and the majority Hindu population. For Baranī, see Irfan Habib, 'Baranī's Theory of the History of the Delhi Sultanate', *The Indian Historical Review*, vol. VII, no: 1–2 (Delhi: Motilal Banarsidass)1980: 99–115.
61 Goetz, *Studies in the history and Art of Kashmir*, 52.

2

THE FORMATIVE PERIOD: 1320–1389 CE

> Kashmir lies on a plateau surrounded by high inaccessible mountains [...]. They are particularly anxious about the natural strength of their country, and therefore take always much care to keep a strong hold upon the entrances and roads leading into it. In consequence, it is very difficult to have any commerce with them. In former times, they used to allow one or two foreigners to enter their country, particularly Jews, but at present they do not allow any Hindu whom they do not know personally to enter, much less other people.
>
> Abu Rayhan Muhammad ibn Ahmad al-Biruni, ***Kitab-al Hind***, Vol II, 206.

This chapter takes a look at the Islamic religious architecture that was introduced in Kashmir, with the establishment of the Muslim Sultanate in the region, in the early part of the fourteenth century CE. While looking into the chronology of the Muslim rule in Kashmir, it also examines the cultural and architectural traditions that were inherited by Muslim rulers and formed the immediate reference for the builders, from which to borrow and select.

Given limited archaeological material evidence from the period, the chapter explores available textual references related to this time to address the new building typologies that came up catering to the need of Muslim faith. It investigates how these early Muslim religious buildings are reflective of a conscious attempt by the nascent Muslim community of Kashmir to merge both socially and culturally with past inherited traditions. The absence of a hegemonic rhetoric in the new architecture, or a portrayal of power through monumentalizing of new religious building typologies, ensured the power or cultural force linked with Muslim rule remained rooted in the local land.

The chapter through a study of archaeological evidences from the period establishes the narrative of syncretism that forms the roots of Islamic religious architecture in Kashmir. This narrative of cultural syncretism and co-existence, that can be seen in three of the buildings studied. These case studies include the mosque of Rīnchanā at Srinagar, the *ziyārat* of Shāh Mīr at Anderkote and the Mīr Masjid at Pampore. These building were used to articulate an image of continuity with past building traditions, bringing to fore the assimilative nature of this early Muslim culture of Kashmir.

The chapter also includes an understanding of how Sufi *khānaqāhs* became a part of the new language of Muslim rule in Kashmir, emerging as institutions of religious propagation as well as of modes of cultural transformation, a phenomenon that became more apparent at a later stage and will be studied in the next chapter.

Kashmir at the beginning of the Muslim rule

In describing the political trials and tribulation of his time, Kalhānā speaks of *Turuskā* (Muslim) soldiers who were in the service of King Harsadeva (r. 1089–1101 CE), a king who was also responsible for extensive iconoclastic activities in the country[1]. Yet, only less than a century before Harsa's reign, under King Samgramarāja (r.1003–28 CE) a contingent of Kashmiri soldiers had gone to assist the last king of Hindu Shahiya[2] dynasty in their fight against the *Turuskās* – the invading army of Mahmud of Ghazni[3]. Given the turbulence on its western borders, Kashmir had at this period also closed its frontiers to all foreigners. The presence of foreign Muslim soldiers of fortune in the service of Kashmiri kings a century later is indicative of the fact that not only were these restrictions relaxed but a nascent community of Muslims had also been established in the land before the actual commencement of Muslim rule[4]. A community that had adapted to local conditions and customs, and whose members were gradually becoming involved in the affairs of the land. The mural painting at Sumstek temple (c. twelfth century CE) in Alchi (Ladakh) undertaken by artisan from Kashmir, in their depiction of the costumes worn by various depicted figures are a material witness to the influence of this Muslim community on contemporary Kashmiri society[5].

Historically, before the commencement of Muslim rule in Kashmir, the region was ruled by a series of local dynasties as well as being part of empires with their base in the wider Indian subcontinent.

In his narrative, Kalhānā traces the history of the land to a mythological past, but it is only with the Kushans that one can establish the history of the region with some certainty[6]. Though, in the accounts of Kalhānā, the first historical ruler we come across is Emperor Ashoka, yet no physical evidence of the Mauryan rule in Kashmir has been discovered, this is in spite of Kalhānā ascribing the foundation of Srinagar to Ashoka[7]. After the Mauryas, the land passed into the hands of Kushans at the beginning of the Christian era, when Kanīshkā (78 CE) conquered Kashmir. It is believed that the Fourth Buddhist Council was held during Kanīshkā's reign at Harwan [Figure 2.4]. Traces of a stupa and *vihāra* were excavated at the site during the early part of the twentieth century CE. The Kushans were succeeded by the Gonada dynasty, which historians see as a line of native kings that helped in re-establishing the Hindu faith in the region. The Gonadas were succeeded by the kings from the Hūṇas (White Ephthalites). The most famous king of this dynasty, Parvarsana II (580 CE), founded the city of Parvarapora in the heart of the present-day Srinagar city, on the foothills of the Hari Parbat hillock. The Huns were followed by the Kārkoṭa (627–950 CE), the First Lohara (950–1101 CE) and the Second Lohara dynasty (1101–1320 CE). Of the various kings who ruled during this period, the reign of Lalitāditya (725–753 CE), Jayapīda (751–82 CE), Avantivarman (855–83 CE stands out for the promotion of arts and crafts in the region as well as their architectural proclivity.

Mūlk-i Kashmir: The making Muslim rule in Kashmir

Coeval with existence of a Muslim community in Kashmir, in the wider Indian subcontinent, the Delhi Sultanate had stabilized under the Tughlaqs, with Sultan Ghiyās-al Dīn (r. 1320–25 CE) ruling in Delhi [Figure 2.1]. Historically, Muslim rule in Kashmir is said to begin with the conversion of Rīnchanā (r. 1320–23 CE)[8] to Islam at the hands of an obscure Muslim shaykh, Būlbūl Shāh (d. 1327 CE/727 AH), sometime after this native Ladakhi chieftain ascended to the throne of Kashmir[9]. While the story relating to the conversion seems anecdotal, which came into vogue when Muslim rule was well-established in the region[10], it does help in understanding the way Kashmiri Muslims during the medieval period looked at their

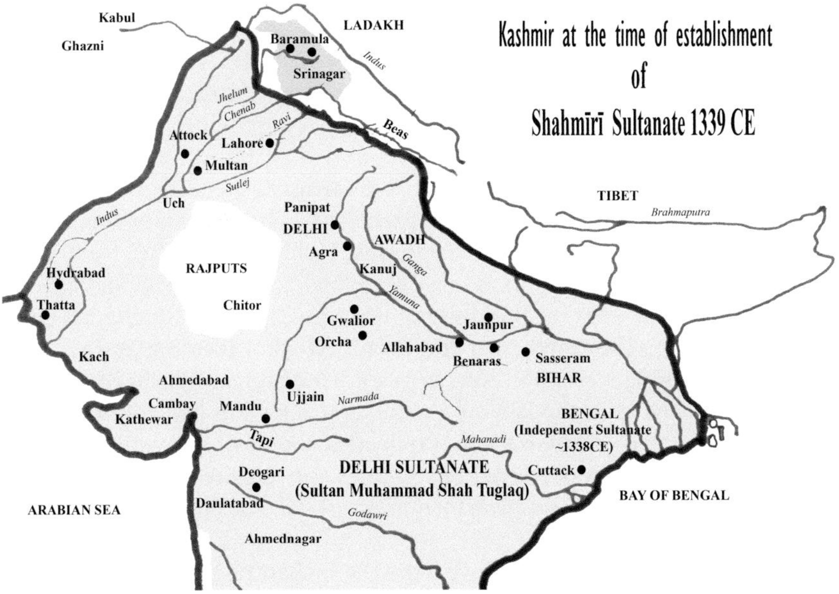

Figure 2.1 Kashmir at the time of establishment of *Shahmīrī* sultanate, © Hakim Sameer Hamdani.

immediate past. This change 'marked no revolution in the foreign relations of Kashmir or its internal conditions'[11], at least for the first century of Muslim rule in Kashmir[12].

The accession of Rīnchanā to the throne, his conversion and the establishment of Muslim rule in the region took place in the background of political instability and chaos that marked the closing period of Hindu rule in Kashmir – a period 'of progressive political disorganization and consequent economic decay'[13]. Ravaged by the invasion of the Mongols under Zulchu[14] in the springs of 1320 CE, the land was already suffering from a prolonged period of political turmoil and social instability since the death of King Jayasimha (r. 1128–55 CE)[15]. The Kashmir of the fourteenth century CE was far removed from the days of Lalitāditya (r. 725–53 CE) and Avantivarman (r. 855–83 CE) that had witnessed not only the consolidation of the country's boundaries but also great advancement in architecture and learning.

Nevertheless, Rīnchanā's conversion does not indicate an abrupt social transformation or import of foreign ideas – albeit of Islamic values, to replace local traditions. While contemporary discourse on this period would see the conversion of Rīnchanā as an event far outreaching its immediate historicity[16], even marking a paradigm shift, an analysis of the socio-political realities of the time would indicate on the contrary. A Muslim writer in the twentieth century CE drawing on social practices of fourteenth century CE, Kashmir could well wonder on the possibility how the consort of the first Muslim Sultan of Kashmir could be a Hindu[17], yet such a discourse is far removed from the realities of the time in which Rīnchanā ruled. The conversion of Rīnchanā does not mark a paradigm shift in the society; in fact, it marks a continuation of an older, established order, which in the wake of Zulchu's ravages, the Sultan sought to revive not to replace. Rīnchanā, though now a Muslim, was presiding over a court which was no different from that of his predecessors. A desire for stability on behalf of the ruler in the backdrop of continuing court intrigues were the hallmarks of court life, not a desire for religious supremacy[18]. The most important members of Rīnchanā's court remained Hindus, including his wife, Kotā Rani, as well as confidants such as Vyala, Bhimanaka, Lusta, Bashailakashura, Kumarabhatta, Avatara, or Buddhist as may the case with Rīnchanā's companion, Tukkā[19]. The only other important Muslim member at the court aside from the king was a non-Kashmiri soldier of fortune, Shāh Mīr, whose loyalty to Rīnchanā in the face of a near fatal rebellion had resulted in his rise to prominence[20]. Even in hagiographical accounts of later generations of Muslim writers, which perceived the Sultan's conversion as an act of divine intervention, no large-scale transformation of the society or mass conversion to Islam is reported[21].

It is also from this period that we trace the earliest physical representation of Muslim religious architecture in Kashmir. Within the city of Srinagar, on the right bank of Jhelum river (in an area that is today referred to as the 'Aālī Kadal'), Rīnchanā constructed the first mosque of Kashmir. The mosque forms a part of a series of religious and secular buildings[22] that were constructed by Rīnchanā within the *moḥala* of Rīnchanāpūrā, a *moḥala* that he had established on his accession to the throne [Plate: 2]. In addition to the mosque, the Sultan, during his brief rule of two years and six months, also constructed the first *khānaqāh* of Kashmir for Būlbūl Shāh[23]. Writing in 1614 CE, a native historian remarks upon the prosperous conditions of the *khānaqāh*[24]. The *khānaqāh* of Būlbūl Shāh was endowed with the revenue of various villages, enabling it to organize a free *langar* (kitchen) for the poor and the travelers. Creation of endowments *(wakf)* for sustaining of major religious institutions like the *khānaqāh* was important for maintaining the financial sustenance of these institutions. Richly endowed by kings, nobles and wealthy traders, they acquired an independent financial status with a certain amount of immunity from political interference throughout the reaches of Islamic civilization. Providing services to the needy, thus attracting a wide audience, the institution of the *khānaqāh* emerged as the nascent center from which Muslim missionary activities were carried. This role of the *khānaqāh* as a major public institution was a common feature that would prevail throughout the medieval history of Kashmir. *Khānaqāh* are traditionally associated with the various Sufi orders that spread across the Islamic world. Usually translated as hospices for religious mendicants, these *khānaqāh* (*rībat* in Arabic) evolved into huge establishments comprising rest rooms (*sarā'ī*), hammams, the main meeting space (*tekke)*, kitchen *(langars)* etc[25]. The institution of *khānaqāh* and the *langars* also seem to have played a role in the rivalry that existed between different Sufi orders competing for devotees. In Kashmir, the role of *khānaqāh* as a source of Islamic preaching far out-spanned the reach of the more traditional mosque or *maktab*. This is also reflected in the architecture, wherein the care taken in the construction of the *khānaqāh*, both in terms of detailing as well as financial resources, involved overshadows that incurred in construction of mosques. To a large extent, the institution of *khānaqāh* sidelined the more traditional mosque in Kashmir, way down till the contemporary period. The *khānaqāh* of Būlbūl Shāh was repeatedly rebuilt and no traces of the original structure or its spatial layout exist either in textual or visual references or even in terms of site archaeology.

Rīnchanā's death was followed by a period of cooperation and intrigue between the two principal protagonists of the court, both vying for power – Kotā Rani (r. 1338–39 CE) and Shāh Mīr. Assuming the regency in the name of her young son, Haidar Khan, Kotā Rani, a formidable woman, tried to keep close to the center of power while yielding of the numerous challenges she faced at the court. Though she married Udyanedeva (r. 1323–38 CE), the power remained in the hands of Kotā Rani, who along with Shāh Mīr rallied the people of Kashmir to face the invasion of Achala[26]. Shah Mir's act of providing shelter to the needy people during the threat of Achala had also endeared him to the public, as against Udyanedeva, who fled the country leaving both his country and queen in the lurch[27].

Upon Udyanedeva's death, Kotā (r. 1338–39 CE) ascended the throne of Kashmir and established herself at Anderkote, the second women ruler[28] of Kashmir after Diddā. Aware of the lingering threat from Shāh Mīr, who was also serving as the guardian of her children from both Rīnchanā and Udayanedeva, she appointed her minister, Bikhshana (Bikshana Bhattā), as her chief minister, resulting in the open revolt of Shāh Mīr. Invested in her fort at Andekote, the queen finally agreed to the terms of Shāh Mīr, which also included her marriage to the victor. Shāh Mīr's victory was followed by either murder or suicide of Kotā Rani[29]. The new king, Shāh Mīr[30], ascended the throne of Kashmir under the title of Shams-al Dīn (1339–42 CE), the founder of the Shahmīrī dynasty – the Sultans of Kashmir who ruled for the next two centuries, from 1339–1555 CE. Though the passing away of Kotā Rani would represent the end of 'the medieval Hindu royalty of Kashmir',[31] yet the new dynasty in its initial days was marked by a continuation of old social structure[32] and the symbols it embodied can also be examined and evaluated by available archaeological evidence from the period[33]. It was from this society that the Islamic architecture of Kashmir borrows, adopts and inherits its image, a society where:

> Conversion from one faith to another left the old manners, the customs and even the superstitions of the people intact[34].

The initial formative years of the new dynasty spanning over a limited period of almost three decades, culminating in the reign of Sultan Shahāb al-Dīn (r. 1354–73 CE) falls into two distinct phases: that of the founder of the dynasty, Shams-al Dīn and his two sons, Jamshid (r. 1324 CE) and ʿAlā'-al Dīn (r. 1342–54 CE) spent in trying to bring a sense of stability to the land and the 19 years of conquest and expansion under Shahāb al-Dīn[35] .

This period is of gradual and intermittent introduction of new institutions and building typologies in the society, not of a sudden and abrupt transformation. Shams-al Dīn was succeeded to throne by his elder son, Jamshid, who was deposed within months of his accession by his younger brother, 'Alā'-al Din. In an anecdotal account from 'Alā'-al Dīn reign, we are informed about three of the close companions of his son and future sultan, Shahāb al-Dīn (r. 1354–73 CE), Chandaradamara, Udsheh Rawal and Iktuji (or Aktajii)[36] – the names are by themselves indicative of the continuation of the members of the old regime in position of power. It was during 'Alā'-al Dīn's reign that the great Shivite *yogni*, Lalleshwari, or as she is commonly known, Lʿalā Ded (b. 1335 CE) came to prominence[37]. Remembered for her *vakhs*, the earliest surviving poetical compositions in Kashmiri language, the words of this ascetic articulated a need to break the mores of established orthodox traditions[38] while also forging a link between past Buddhist and emerging Muslim trends in a search for a universal transcendent reality.

In popular folk traditions within the Muslim community, Lʿalā Ded would be linked with two prominent Muslim saints of her time, Mīr Sayyid Ali Hamdani (1314–84 CE) and Shaykh Nūr-al Dīn (d. 1415 or 1438 CE)[39]. One a Persian missionary in Kashmir, the other a native of the land, the two would, over the years and centuries, characterize the way that Islam came to be defined in Kashmir. While the work of the Persian shaykh, Sayyid Ali, would replicate that of majority of Muslim missionaries of that period, Nūr-al Dīn's life shows the strength of the popular folk version of the religion – the little traditions, which would inspire and draw countless Kashmiris into their fold. Muslim historians and hagiographers would, over the centuries, bridge any notion of tension between the two streams of Islam in Kashmir; in fact, they would try to link the two, but the work of both these men indicates to the contrary. The influence of Sayyid Ali and Nūr-al Dīn will be studied in the next chapter, a period which also marks the beginning of iconoclastic activities in Kashmir and the emergence of an orthodox Muslim polity.

Interestingly, we find that from Rīnchanā's conversion till the rule of 'Alā'-al Dīn, for a period of 24 years, barring the semi-historical Būlbūl Shāh, no account exists of a Muslim missionary in Kashmir[40]. No report or evidence of a Sufi shaykh or preacher visiting the land, of an exchange of embassy with neighboring Muslim rulers, especially the Sultans of Delhi. Kashmir, at this point, still remained a virtually unknown, isolated land from its surroundings. And the journey to region through tortuous mountain paths and defiles for spreading the faith remained an unattractive proposition, especially in a land lacking resources of patronage, wealth or even a renowned king. Before the conquests of Shahāb al-Dīn, Kashmir was the forgotten land. The marital prowess of Shahāb al-Dīn brought fame and renown to the name of *mūlk-i Kashmir* – and in its wake, followed a host of Muslim missionaries.

Like Lalitāditya, most of Shahāb al-Dīn's[41] time was spent on the battlefield, keeping him 'away from Kashmir as he visited it sparingly'[42]. Uniting the land, Shahāb al-Dīn is reported by native Kashmiri historians to have conquered Pakhli, Multan, Kabul, Ghazni, Qandhar, Gilgit, Dardu, Ladakh, Lahore and the plains of India up till Sirhind in Punjab, while modern scholars' opinion being that his conquest was on a more modest scale, extending from Gilgit and Dardistan in north to north and western Punjab, including Peshawar, and also the hill states lying to the south of Kashmir[43]. It is also reported that a battle with Fīrāz Shāh Tughlaq[44] was averted by concluding a treaty of peace, as well as a matrimonial alliance between the Sultans of Delhi and Kashmir. No matter what the historic extents of Shahāb al-Dīn's actual conquest may have been, his exploits brought Kashmir to the notice of men of faith, of letters and sword from nearby Muslim lands searching for new regions of patronage, and marked the beginning of a significant change in the religio-cultural discourse of the land. While in his early days, Shahāb al-Dīn is said to have been repulsed by the idea of melting a brass image of the Buddha for minting money, towards the end, Muslim historians say, he had the temple of Bijbehara demolished[45]. In his conquest, the sultan was helped by the Chandra Damara, Laula Damara, Lohara, while the administration was looked upon by Kotabhattā and Udayashri, with his queen Lakshmi also serving as a close confidant before being eclipsed in that role by her own niece, Lasā, during the sultan's last days[46]. Unlike Jonaraja, some Muslim historians[47], basing their works on the statement of the author of *Tārīkh-i Kashmir*, ascribe the Sultan's victories to a Muslim commander and missionary, Sayyid Hasan Bahādur[48], a cousin of Sayyid Ali, yet this is implausible. Even the author of *Bahāristān-i Shāhī* or Haidar Malīk do not make any reference to Sayyid Hasan Bahādur being involved in the conquest or the fact that he had even arrived in Kashmir during Shahāb al-Dīn's reign. On the other hand, even in the absence of any evidence, the conjecture that the Sultan during his campaigns outside Kashmir may have come in contact with a more orthodox set of ideas resulting in the demolition of the Bijbehara temple cannot be ruled out. While Jonarāja does not speak about the demolition of Bijbehara temple, the report is found both in *Bahāristān-i Shāhī* as well in Malīk's account, lending it some credibility.

Tied down as he was with his military campaigns, Shahāb al-Dīn during his nineteen years of rule did manage to establish the towns of Lachhmi nagar[49], Shahāb al-Dīn porā and the *moḥala* of Shahābpur[50] in the capital, Srinagar. At Shahābpur, the sultan is also said to have constructed a Jamia Masjid, of which today we find no trace. It is also from this period that a mosque at Pampore, commonly attributed to Sayyid Ali Hamdanī also dates. The rule of Shahāb al-Dīn's successors is noticeable for the beginning of a gradual and steady arrival of Muslim missionaries, theologians, artisans, etc. in the court of the Kashmiri sultans bringing in their wake established socio-cultural practices, notions of art and architecture, and a drive to Islamize Kashmir. Though Shahāb al-Dīn had set on to conquer lands outside of the natural boundaries of his isolated mountainous kingdom, his success would result in a reverse – an inflow of men from distant land, who would in turn attempt to transform Kashmir.

Architectural traditions inherited by the sultans of Kashmir

The mosque as well as the *khānaqāh* that Rīnchanā built at Rīnchanāporā would be the first such buildings to be constructed in Kashmir, and establish the image of Muslim faith in the region. Unfortunately, as with most other religious buildings associated with formative period of Muslim rule in Kashmir, the mosque was rebuilt at a much later date and in the process, losing its original character. The Muslim community of Kashmir at the period, aside from the Būlbūl Shāh, was limited to Rīnchanā, a few converts at the court and above all, some Muslim soldiers in the service of the Kings of Kashmir. Given the circumstances, Muslim rule in Kashmir continued with the established architectural traditions of the land as with most other customs of life. As Waldrep in his critique of modernism puts it 'our sense of place is strongly related to social identity dominated over the architectural space'[51], we can apply a similar analogy positing that the pattern of Muslim society interwoven as it was with native Kashmiri identity helped in contextualizing the Islamic religious architecture of Kashmir.

The architectural traditions that Muslim rulers of Kashmir inherited were a synthesis of local customs and materials as well as foreign influences as varied and diverse as that of China or Gandhara, influences generated at the courts of the Guptas or the Parthians[52]. Much of this was because, though isolated within the protective fold of its mountain ranges, Kashmir had at various periods been subject to foreign rule from the Indian mainland as well as invaders who came in from Central Asia.

The study of medieval arts of Kashmir is influenced by two dominant trends regarding the origin and the influences that were responsible for the development of this art form. Cunningham and following him, Fergusson and Smith, while bringing to fore the distinct character of Kashmiri Hindu Art, traced its roots to the arts of Gandhara and its Greco-Roman traditions. On the other hand, we have scholars like Goetz[53], who would argue for a localized adaption of style which incorporated elements from Gandhara as well as Gupta, Byzantine, Chinese, Sasanian, even Bengali features in what can best be described as an architecture of assimilation of disparate elements and traditions. Kak who also favors the theory that mediaeval Kashmir art was deeply influenced by the Buddhist art of Gandhara to an extent that 'excepting the natural and unavoidable differences in material used, the two are practically identical'[54].

Yet for Goetz, this assembly of different individual elements belonging to architectural traditions with different temporal context did not result in 'an eclectic conglomeration of incongruous forms' but as 'representative of a new style [...] one of the great masterpieces of Mediaeval Indian art'[55]. It resulted in an architectural tradition where Marshall would trace out direct Gupta influences and Goetz features of Roman influence that did not fit in with Gandhara[56].

These traditions included not only the monumental stone temples, *vihāras*, *chatiyas* and stupas but also a well-developed vernacular architecture of wood. For Goetz, the medieval Kashmir represent an 'increasingly isolated outpost of Hindu civilization'[57], which nevertheless provided the patronage and refuge for not only the artisans and crafts men from a crumbling Gupta empire but also acted as a repository of cultural influence drawn from traditions as distinct and different as that of the Khushans, Sasanians, Byzantine, China as well as those of the Pallas, Rashtrakutas and the Chauhans[58]. This vast and disparate field of architectural traditions spanning over centuries and vast geo-cultural distances, resulted in the evolution of an architectural style, wherein various disparate elements were fused together in building tradition never seen before, a tradition that remained uniquely Kashmiri. The origin of Kashmiri architecture lies in this process of assimilation and selection from plurality of traditions. In this tradition of buildings, there is no origin of the form, rather an acceptance of elements and their reproduction resulting in a style. The process represents a borrowing – a borrowing of motifs, and concepts, borrowing which according to Juneja:

> [...] are centrally shaped by historical processes: a process of selection is invariably at work which determines what is borrowed and what is left out[59].

Yet, the possibility of a native prototype especially in the wooden architecture of the region cannot be ruled out. Goetz also speaks of a certain flourishing of wooden temple architecture in the second half of the tenth century CE, during the relatively stable rule of Queen Diddā (r. 958–1003 CE), in face of limited resources[60]. Given the climatic conditions and the availability of wood as easily available building material, we cannot rule out the possibility of existence of wooden architecture in the sacred domain even before the tenth century CE. Such a hypothesis is also substantiated by the preference of wooden construction in the vernacular architecture of the region, a preference that percolates down to our own times.

Examples of this Kashmiri style can be seen in the buildings of Lalitāditya (r. 724–760 CE), Avantivarman (r. 855883 CE), Samkaravarman (r. 883–902 CE) and those of the kings of Lohara dynasty from Samgramaraja (r. 1003–28 CE) to Harsha (r. 1089-1101 CE). Goetz has pointed out three distinct periods of developments of this Kashmiri style, from Lalitāditya's reign till virtually the end of Hindu rule in Kashmir, ranging from an initial monumental, coarse and impatient form of Lalitāditya [Figure 2.2], to a richer, refined and elegant form of the Utpala dynasty before the decadence that set in with the Lohara dynasty[61]. In spite of a brief artistic outpouring under the first kings of the Lohara dynasty, at the time of the advent of Islam in Kashmir, 'it's Hindu art was already dead'[62].

To a large extent, this phenomenon is also indicative of the nature of Kashmiri society, where new ideas, traditions were assimilated in a historical memory of the land, representing a sense of Kashmiri identity and continuity. The persistence of this phenomenon in the narratives that the people of this land developed for themselves as well its manifestation in the artistic and intellectual traditions of the land is what represents a perennial transcendent cultural uniqueness, defining Kashmiri sense of identity.

This can also be seen in the way Kalhānā internalizes the advent of Maurya rule in Kashmir, by reinventing the great Mauryan Emperor Ashoka as a native Kashmiri king, whose greatest merit was in founding the city of Srinagar[63]. Interestingly, in this semi-historic Kashmiri tradition, a son of

Figure 2.2 Martand sun temple with the peristyle showing Greek influences, Martand: 2013, © Hakim Sameer Hamdani.

Ashoka, Jaluka, is said to have freed the land from *mlecchas* (foreigners). Though no definite identification has been provided for these foreigners, some scholars have assumed them to be Greeks[64]. This historical isolation of Kashmir from actual history itself, as witnessed in Kalhānās rendition of the Mauryan rule, would result in a reading of past by native writers, where 'no lasting impression was left even by those periods when the Valley was under the sovereignty of great foreign dynasties'[65]. While such a reading would obscure actual history and historical events, it would and did create a narrative of Kashmiri identity, be it that of *Land of Sarada* in medieval period of Hindu ascendency or of *mūlk-i Kashmir* during the rule of Muslim sultans.

Given its physical isolation, Kashmir remained inward-looking[66], in spite of occasional invasions, in spite of occasional forays of conquests outside its natural boundaries. And, Kalhānā's work in its memory, in its remembrance of past, is a process at indigenizing encounters with outside forces. When Kalhānā, in the words of Krishna eulogizes Kashmir as the incarnation of Parvarti, he not only symbolizes the sacredness of the land but also establishes the narrative related to the making of this divine heavenly place. A making, which is deeply ingrained in the entire chronicle helping to create at both a political history and cultural image of the place and its inhabitants. It is to this unique ability to internalize every outside contact, that Kashmir owes it culture of assimilation and syncretism, both in art and architecture and the making of the society in general.

Such a spirit of syncretism is also seen in the internal functioning of the Kashmiri society in the medieval period, especially in the relation between two main forces of the society, Hinduism and Buddhism. Though historically there were also periods of tensions and conflict[67], yet the spirit had endured in the past with Hinduism and Buddhism co-existing peacefully for centuries. Numerous instances are to be found in the history of Kashmir when kings, queens and even courtiers bestowed their patronage upon edifices built for both the faiths, a spirit best exemplified at the erstwhile royal capital of Parihaspora built by Lalitāditya. Parvarasena II consecrated temples not only to Shiva, Vishnu and numerous other goddesses in the capital city of Parvarpura that he had built, but also allowed his uncle to construct the *vihāra* of Jayendravihara in the city with its statue of the Buddha[68]. Similarly, while Randitya and his principal queen, Ranarambha, built numerous temples and *mathas* (institute of teaching, also monastery), one of his wives had the statute of Buddha installed in the *vihāra* (monastery) of Bhinna[69].

While in certain cases it involved simple transformation of a stupa into a temple, such as at Huvishkapura, where the Kushan king's stupa was reconstructed as Vashnivite site in the eighth century CE[70], in certain cases it also involved acceptance of ideologically disparate architectural elements such as at Loduv where a small square temple located within a pond has an circular internal plan, used as the sanctum sanctorum [Figure 2.3]. The austere, plain external appearance of the temple along with its circular plan indicates a

Figure 2.3 Loduv temple: the circular sanctum of the temple indicates its pre-Hindu origin. The mosque in the vicinity reflects the continuing 'narrative of sacredness' associated with place, Loduv, 2012, © Hakim Sameer Hamdani.

Buddhist origin which was later on rededicated as a temple in spite of the vary unorthodox plan form.

Nascent Islamic religious architecture of Kashmir

If the peculiarity of Islamic architecture was its early concern for monumentalization of even secular settings[71], in Kashmir the same is not true even for the more religious architecture – an architecture that provides the greatest symbolic context – and thus would benefit from an architecture where scale reinforced the meaning of the symbols. A survey of existing surviving Islamic architecture from this period would indicate builder's preoccupation with underplaying the cultural significance of these structures in a manner that could be perceived them to be alien to the land. The appropriateness of early Islamic architecture lies in how it merges with existing cultural landscape to a degree wherein it borrows not only its language from the local traditions but also de-scales itself so as not to confront the monumental edifices it tries to replace. Seen in the light of what was built before, the religious Islamic architecture of Kashmir emerges as a deliberate attempt of vernacularization of existing architectural language, an attempt to re-humanize the architecture.

This chapter, based on study of early Muslim religious architecture in Kashmir, involves a survey of extant structures or buildings from the period and correlates it with contemporary textual sources, primarily historical and hagiographical accounts to address the methodological and historical evolution of an architectural style. By placing the architecture within their immediate and historic context, linking the building to its surrounding, the study links the religious architecture of Islam in Kashmir to the land itself, a representation of the 'Hegelian notion of essentialism, where art is an expression of the innermost spirit of the people or nation'[72]. Each building or site is studied to account for how this architectural style evolved over a period of time.

Unfortunately, the study is constrained by a severe lack of reference material, primarily relating to archeology, as well as archival material in the form of textual references. Most of the buildings or structures constructed in this period have disappeared, what survives is individual buildings or sites, that too reconstructed partly or wholly down the times, making any architectural reconstruction virtually impossible. Textual references related to the period are mostly anachronistic in nature, with the earliest written source separated by nearly half a century from the actual events. Some of the more elaborate accounts in fact date to the sixteenth century CE, or even later, especially those which provide a brief outline of architectural developments associated with construction of Muslim places of worship. The absence of significant archaeological material, specific textual sources dealing with architecture, or any other visual material serves as a major limitation in our study of this period. It limits the extent of evaluating and testing textual references on the subject against available archaeological evidence. This is largely compensated by the existence of an extensive field of architectural remnants from the pre-Muslim period, in the form of ruins as well as virtually intact architecture from the Hindu period, making it easy to trace and link specific architectural elements and features found within the Muslim religious architecture to forms that existed before the advent of Muslim rule in Kashmir. Thus, the vast archeological traces dating to medieval Kashmir form the archival pool from which to draw the antecedents and parallels for Muslim architecture in Kashmir.

The image: Islam between Delhi and Kashmir

More than a century before the first Muslim Dynasty of Kashmir was set up; Quṭub-al Dīn ʿAibak, a military slave of Muhammad Ghouri, captured Delhi from the Rajas of Chauhan dynasty in 1193 CE. The subsequent rule of ʿAibak (r. 1206–1211 CE) as the first sultan of Delhi is best remembered for construction of Delhi's first masjid-i jamī: Quwat-al Islam (Might of Islam) mosque in the former citadel of the Chauhans at Rai Pithora [Figure 1.1]. The mosque built on the remains of a demolished temple out of material sourced from ruins of Jain and Hindu temples symbolized not only the imperial aspirations of a new young dynasty, but also marks the victory of a new faith Islam, given its architecture if not the name which is of later-day origin[73]. The building, though built by Indian builders and masons, nevertheless employs dominant visual elements that were part of the architectural predilections linked with the Turko-Persianate world. This involves both the classical hypostyle plan around a central courtyard as well as the monumental arcade of pointed arches, giving the entire edifice a recognizable form. A form visually distinct from its immediate surroundings even though incorporating many of the local motifs in the overall assembly. Though the arches are corbelled, the structural system is trabeated, yet the mosque represents the establishment of a distinct new architectural vocabulary. Like all imperial manifestations, Quwat-al Islam mosque marks a break with the past, while setting a new image for the future. The construction of Quṭub Minar, a massive victory minaret in the vicinity of the mosque, marks this break as well as the victory of Islam and the associated socio-political order much more visibly. It also brings to fore the hegemonic nature of the new order, wherein art-architecture was also an instrument of legitimizing power and a new social order.

Historically, the court of Delhi remained the most important neighboring power center for the Muslim rulers of Kashmir way down till the sixteenth century CE, when Kashmir became a part of the Mughal Empire ruled from Delhi and Agra. The influence of the Delhi court was not limited to politics and occasional matrimonial alliances alone, but some of the Muslim saints and missionaries who arrived in Kashmir were also a part of the Delhi court or linked to it. Additionally, though in comparison to Delhi, Muslim rule was established quite late in Kashmir, yet many of the emigrant Muslim elites in Kashmir belonged to the same cultural and racial grouping as in Delhi-Turks and Iranians or people from areas with heavy Persian influences like Khurasan, etc. In both the instances, at the courts of the Sultans of Delhi as well as Kashmir, the architectural sensibilities of this group of non-local ruling class were broadly governed by the cultural traditions of the Persianate world. In Kashmir, just as in Delhi, artist or builders had access to both local 'pre-Islamic' traditions and those drawn from outside, provided by their Muslim patrons. Yet, in spite of these similarities, the reception of Islam in both these regions was widely different – most notably witnessed in the sacral architecture of Islam in Kashmir. In Delhi, the relation, interaction between the old and the new is that of two politically antagonistic cultures, not so in Kashmir, where it represents not a simple fusion but a continuation of an existing form, in an architectural language little changed from the past.

The mosque of Rīnchanā at Rīnchanā-pūrā

The first mosque in Kashmir, of which we have both a textual reference and physical remnants, is that of Rīnchanā. Given the sultan's Buddhist ancestry, the mosque is also referred to as the *Budh Masjid:* the Buddhist mosque. At the time of its construction, the mosque catered to the needs of the Sultan, his spiritual preceptor and other new converts to Islam. Additionally, the mosque was also used by a small number of non-local Muslims residing in Kashmir. In the immediate vicinity of the mosque, lies the *moḥala* of Maleech Mar[74] which many contemporary, local historians posit as the residential quarter linked with the earliest of Muslim community that settled in Kashmir. The etymology behind the naming of *moḥala*, as well as situating the first mosque of Kashmir in its neighborhood, strongly suggests the presence of a small, non-native Muslim community in the land.

Writing in the seventeenth century CE, Malīk opines that the original mosque, which he refers to as a *Jumma Masjid* – the Friday mosque, after being burnt down was rebuilt on a smaller scale. Malīk's report is also supported by a contemporary of his, the writer of *Bahāristān-i Shāhī*[75]. Yet, both the reports sound highly improbable. The small size of the mosque that exists today at the site fits in with what we know of mosques, which were constructed in the early decades of Muslim rule in Kashmir. Catering to the needs of a small community of believers that existed, in a land still struggling to recover from the socio-political turmoil left in the wake of Zulchu's invasion, the construction of a large Friday mosque seems highly improbable. It is only in retrospect, writers opined a larger size for the building, given the importance associated with it, as the first mosque of Kashmir[76].

The inference that the existing dimensions of the reconstructed mosque correlates with the original size of the mosque is also supported by Islamic rules relating to the establishment of a mosque. Though nothing in Islamic law or scripture would define or dictate the architecture of what a mosque can or cannot be, yet once a piece of land is endowed (*wakf*) as a place of worship, such an endowment remains sacrosanct, at least in the spirit of the religious law – sharia. Hence, a piece of land marked as a mosque will remain a mosque – no other usage of that land is possible. One may add to that piece of land a structure by future endowments, but cannot take away from it[77].

From historical references as well as site archaeology, it is obvious that the mosque of Rīnchanā was constructed in stone, the preferred building material of the ancient builders of Kashmir [Plate. 2]. The present mosque comprises a square single-story structure measuring around 7.7m × 7.6m, located on top of a high stone retaining wall overlooking the Jhelum [Figure 2.4]. Though the mosque was considerably repaired in the last decade of the preceding century, the footprint of the original mosque survived the reconstruction, referred to by Malīk.

Essentially, the building is simple cuboidal structure made of large stone blocks unevenly arranged in a manner that would indicate that the stones were acquired from an existing site rather than specifically fabricated for the structure. The use of stone as a building material is repeatedly seen in

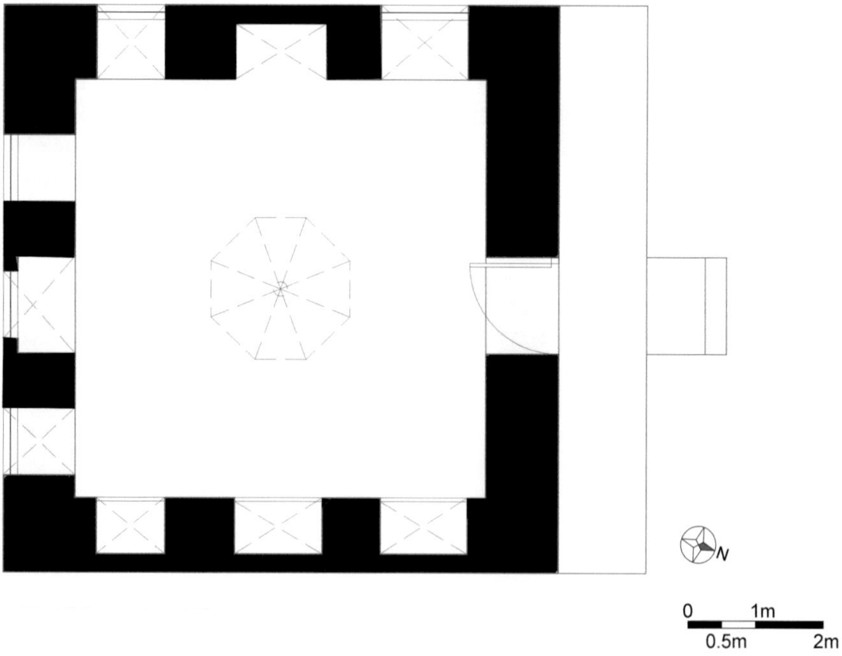

Figure 2.4 Mosque of Rīnchanā: plan with the entrance door on the northern side, © Hakim Sameer Hamdani.

the early Islamic religious architecture in Kashmir and challenges narratives that would indicate that the Muslims sultans opted for wood based on a cultural affinity with the building traditions of Persia and Central Asia or that the craftsmanship associated with stonework was no longer available in Kashmir.

The entrance to the building is on the north-west through a centrally placed door opening, from a low-height rectangular door opening. Internally, the mosque comprises of a single small chamber with a low-height ceiling, entirely redone during the recently undertaken renovations. The *miḥrāb* opening is located in the south-western wall, and marks a fairly accurate approximation of the direction of the *qiblā* by the builders – a technical feat that is missing in some of Kashmir's major mosque built later on, including the Jamia of Srinagar (c. 1402 CE).

This main entrance façade of the building is totally devoid of any architectural embellishment and lacks the columned porch, an essential of the temples of medieval Kashmir. Two small rectangular openings on the rest of the walls is what defines this simple structure. The *miḥrāb* niche is again devoid of any decorative feature. Based on archival images dating to early part of the twentieth century CE, we can summarize that the original roof comprised a *chār bām* (pyramidal roof) with wooden plank roofing. Given the uneven texture of the stone masonry used in the superstructure, it seems that the building was originally plastered externally. Traces of plaster can also be seen in old image of the mosque.

Though it is possible that this small and simple building may have lost its architectural and decorative elements in time, yet the surviving structure does bring to fore the basic architectural quality of early Muslim religious buildings in Kashmir – their simplicity and lack of a monumental scale. The extreme simplicity of the mosques, in a geography that was used to monumentalize religious edifices, the use of local materials and local techniques in its construction is a testament to how Muslim religious edifices during the early period of Muslim rule were built upon a paradigm of assimilation rather than that of conquest and dominion.

Mīr Masjid at Pampore

Aside from Rīnchanā's Masjid, the only other mosque surviving from the fourteenth century CE is the Mīr Masjid at Pampore[78]. The mosque lies in close vicinity of the temple of Padmasvami Vishnu that was erected by Padma[79], a minister of Lalitāditya, at the start of the ninth century CE, and is commonly associated with the *Kubrawī* Shaykh, Mīr Sayyid ʿAli Hamdani or alternatively with his son Mīr Sayyid Muhammad Hamdani (d. 1450 CE).

The mosque at Pampore is the best representation of the synthesis that marks the Islamic religious architecture of Kashmir. Much more than the mosque of Rīnchanā which was constructed earlier, the building at Pampore represents the unfolding of the narrative that would define Muslim sacral architecture in Kashmir. The inspiration for this small building can be found both in the older stone architectures of the region as well as its wooden architectures. As such the building also represents the oldest surviving example of wooden architecture in Kashmir. As a material abundantly available in Kashmir, wood was the most prominent construction material of Kashmir, which it remained till quite recently. Unfortunately, given the perishable nature of wood as a building material and the numerous conflagrations that have periodically plagued villages and towns across Kashmir, no wooden structure from the pre-Muslim period survives in Kashmir[80]. The 'mansions which reach to the clouds'[81] of Parvarasena's city of Parvarapora could only have been built of wood. Yet, even in case of residential architecture, the oldest surviving examples of wooden architecture in Kashmir dates back to the latter part of nineteenth century.

Fortunately, outside Kashmir survives two of the earliest representations of Kashmiri wooden architectures, a Buddhist temple at Alchi, Ladakh and the temple of Mrikula Devi at Udaipur in present-day Himachal Pradesh. Both the buildings at Alchi and Udaipur are a part of Kashmir's cultural outreach in the wake of Lalitāditya's conquest[82]. Both the temples fall in the post-Lalitāditya period and were constructed before the thirteenth century CE. While no authoritative dating for the buildings has been provided, the temple at Alchi is said to have been constructed between ninth and thirteenth century CE, while the temple of Mirkula Devi was expanded in the eleventh century CE incorporating influences and motifs from Kashmiri architecture.

In the temple of Mirkula Devi, Kashmiri influences have been dated to the time when Suryamati, the Queen of Anantadeva, (r. 1028–1063 CE)[83] 'renewed a ruined Surya temple of the late-Gupta period'[84]. The present structure with its distinct external resemblance to the hill temple architecture found in western Himalayas dates back to the sixteenth century CE, when it was rebuilt by Raja Pratāp Singh. Nevertheless, the wooden façade of the cella, the *garbhagriha,* covered with motifs that can be traced to Kashmir was preserved and re-erected in its place during the reconstruction. All over the façade carved engravings of seated deities can be found in a background uniquely Kashmiri, comprising the traditional trefoil arched niche[85] supported on pilasters and surmounted with the invariable pyramidal roof. The portrayal of the roof as in case of an actual building is a stepped pyramid. A pair of geese can be found adorning the upper elongated part of the pyramidal roof, geese that can be found at the temple of Payar (eleventh century CE) surmounting the capitals. The design of the cella with its small square plan, the detailing of the image of a Kashmiri temple with its pyramidal roof, trefoil arch with pilasters (or columns) all point towards the main characteristics of the stone temple architecture of Kashmir, reenacted here in wood. Another feature at Udaipur which replicates the traditional stone architecture of Kashmir is the design of the ceiling, comprising three overlapping squares formed by rotation, which is a replica of the ceiling at

Pandrethan temple at Srinagar, albeit the wood again replacing the stone as the medium of executing the design. Significantly, the temple of Pandrethan has been variously dated between the reigns of Partha (906–21 CE) and Jayasihma (1128–49 CE) and in case of former would have served as the inspiration for the wooden ceiling at Udaipur. Many of the motifs that we find carved in wood at Udaipur are simple recreations of what was found in the stone temple of Kashmir, be it the full-blown lotus in the ceiling, or the various geometrical and floral patterns.

Constructed in the second half of fourteenth century CE, the mosque at Pampore provides not only the missing link between the wooden and stone architecture of Kashmir but also serves as a historical antecedent on which to base our understanding of the evolution of the sacral architecture related to Islam in Kashmir.

The mosque is located within an old *moḥala*, on one of the inner roads leading into Pampore, and is preceded by a small open forecourt on its main eastern façade. In plan, the building, just like Rīnchanā's mosque, comprises a square single-story structure measuring 8.19m × 8.10m [Figure 2.9]. The small size of the mosque is in keeping with the mosque design from the early period of the Muslim rule, reflecting on the size of the community. The main entry to the building was on the eastern façade facing the *qiblā* wall, from a portico much like that in the Hindu temple. Internally, the mosque comprises a single chamber measuring 6.3m × 6.2m. Unfortunately, the entire building had been covered with wooden paneling at the time of study, making an appreciation of original architectural features impossible. What can be said with certainty is the ceiling is supported on a series of wooden joists which start from the same level as the eaves, this accounts for the low ceiling height of the building. The structural system followed at Pampore, just like that at Rīnchanā's mosque, is trabeate construction with an irregular, un-coursed load bearing stone masonry. Given the small size of the mosque, the builders found no need to add wooden column supports in the mosque interiors, the entire roof being supported on the thick masonry walls.

The entrance portico of the mosque is designed as a trefoil arched opening resting on two fluted stone columns [Figure 2.5]. The use of detached columns for the trefoil arch was seen in the heydays of medieval temple architecture and had been replaced by rectangular pilasters and shallow profile as we move closer to the thirteenth century CE. From the solitary available archival image of the building façade before the expansions and the subsequent demolition of the mosque, it seems that the twin columns, though following the same design, were dissimilar. One of the columns was longer than the other, and without the standard stone base. The rest of the feature including the square capital resting on a ribbed astragal and the shallow flutes of the column shaft are similar to what is found at many sites including the Avantiswami temple. That the stone columns were transported from the nearby site of the Padmaswami temple is a distinct possibility, which has also been opined by Kak in his brief note on the temple[86].

Figure 2.5 Shāh Hamdan mosque, main eastern elevation: image of the mosque from early 20th century, Pampore, early 20th century, © ASI.

The full-blown, well-proportioned arch of the portico which goes all the way up till the roof level, serves as one of the main decorative features of the building and would be replicated again, in the mosque of Madnī (c. 848 AH/1444 CE) as well as in the construction of an earlier mosque in the vicinity of Madnī's mosque [Figure 3.5]. Aside from absence of any sculptural decorations, what sets aside the portico of the Pampore mosque from that of a stone temple is the absence of an entablature. Framing the low-lying entrance doorway, the spandrel of the arch forming the portico is a combination of brick masonry with embedded wooden members. A pair of small, almost square-shaped windows on all the walls, barring the western *qiblā* wall, provided light for the dimly lit inner prayer hall. Drawing his inspirations from the stone temples of yesterdays, which were devoid of openings, the builder's hesitancy, unfamiliarity with how to articulate this architectural element in the overall façade, becomes obvious in the main eastern facade.

An obvious way of placing the openings, given the columned portico, would have been to work from the outside, with window openings placed centrally within the available wall surface. Yet, by designing the openings on the inner wall, on a proportion of ABABABA (wall pier: window) the window openings get placed too close to the stone columns, resulting in a lack of balance in an otherwise symmetrical façade. Though not perfected, this small detail gets substantially resolved by the time of construction of Madnī's mosque a century later. The *miḥrāb* niche projects as a rectangular offset on the western façade, which ends in a prismatic top. A single well-dressed stone, placed in the middle of the rectangular *miḥrāb* offset, highly reminiscent of the torus molding that we find in the plinth of the temple, serves as the main decorative element of this projection.

Aside from the trefoil-arched portico, the most significant architectural feature employed in the detailing of Pampore mosque is the heavy wooden eaves, corbelling out from the lintel level all the way up till the starting point of the roof [Figure 2.6]. The richly carved eaves, bearing a series of floral and architectural motifs derived from the wooden architecture of the region,

Figure 2.6 Temple at Alchi: the woodwork at Alchi represents the oldest surviving example of Kashmiri wooden architecture, Alchi: 2011, © Hakim Sameer Hamdani.

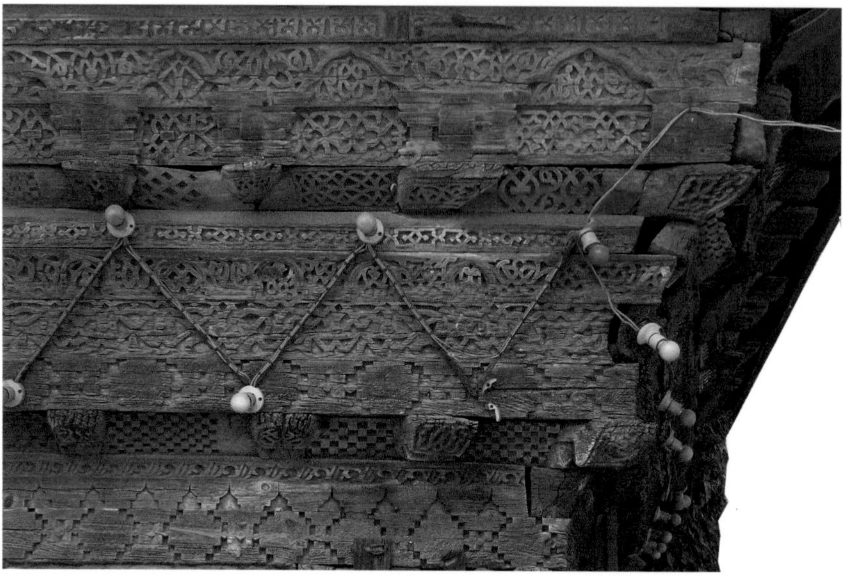

Figure 2.7 Shāh Hamdan mosque: details of wooden eaves resembling similar detailing at Alchi, Pampore: 2007, © Randolph Langenbach.

comprises alternative rows of wooden members projecting from the wall. The ornamentation is decidedly of a non-Islamic inspiration, thus making the structure a part of the initial stages of development of the Islamic architecture of Kashmir. The eaves at Pampore [Figure 2.7] can be posited as being part of an older established architectural tradition, on comparison with a similar feature at Alchi temple [Figure 2.6].

Both at Alchi as well as Pampore, the external surface of the beams comprising the eaves is decorated with motifs depicting vegetal scrolls as well as patterns based on a chess board pattern. We also find carvings, reminiscent of a stylized version of arch in the beams, a feature that can also be seen in door lintels of medieval Kashmiri stone temples. This would indicate that there was a field of communality between wooden and stone architecture practiced in medieval Kashmir. Regarding the square shaped chess board pattern to be found in Alchi as well as Pampore, it is significant that one of the earliest depictions of this motif is to be found at the Mauryan site of Sarnath, in brick masonry [Figure 2.8]. Given Kashmir's past cultural and political exchanges with the Mauryan empire, it is possible that the inspiration for this motif is of Mauryan origin.

The motifs used in the eaves were also replicated in the heavy wooden frames of the window openings. Though these frames are no longer extant at the site, based on archival images of the building we can observe the stylized floral motifs that are carved in the rebated window frame and draw their inspiration from native Kashmiri medieval architecture.

Figure 2.8 Sarnath: square motifs arranged in a diagonal pattern provided the inspiration for similar motif in wooden architecture of Kashmir, Sarnath: 2018, © Hakim Sameer Hamdani.

The entire structure is surmounted by a low-lying pyramidal roof – the quintessential *chār bām*. The traditional Kashmiri roof, as seen in stone temples of medieval Kashmir, is a pyramidal arrangement in multiple tiers with gables in the middle. The presence of pediments enclosing the trefoil-arched opening or portico is the most conspicuous building feature of the roof line. The pediment and its placement on the center of the building façade clearly points to its Greek origin. This roof form is uniformly followed in designing of Muslim places of worship during medieval Kashmir, with the gabled roof assuming the shape of a vertical spire *(brangh)* placed on top of a square or octagonal pavilion which performs the same function as that of a *minar*. At Pampore, the *brangh* is missing, which makes its presence in the mosque of Madnī [Plate 4].

Based on the archival images predating the demolition and new construction on the site, it can be surmised that the building façade was covered with lime plaster – and finished in *gaāch*, the traditional final layer of white gypsum plaster. The presence of moldings in the plaster, especially around the trefoil arch, indicates the decorative nature of the plaster. The plastering of the external façade helped in hiding from view the ill-looking masonry, and also presenting a finished state of the building.

Given the symbolic nature of the Pampore mosque, as a new typology associated with a new religion and a new polity, it is highly significant that no attempt has been made to monumentalize the structure. The placement

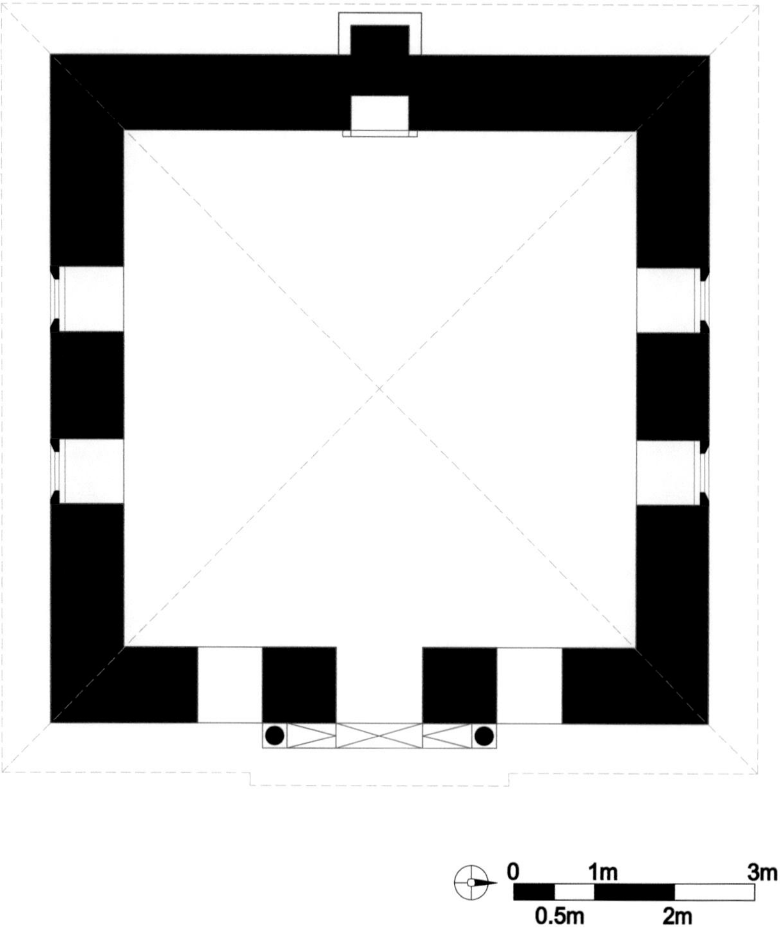

Figure 2.9 Mīr Hamdan mosque, plan of the mosque, © Hakim Sameer Hamdani.

of the building on a raised plinth, as was the tradition with the stone temples of Kashmir, would have significantly helped in this. Given that the all the architectural elements used in the designing of the mosque can be directly traced to the temple architecture of Kashmir, the absence of a plinth does again indicate a desire to de-emphasize the scale of the building, a desire to fit in rather than attempt at establishing the supremacy of a new faith. The placement of a building on high podium is an architectural technique we find in the designing of most buildings of Muslim origin in the Indian sub-continent, whether of religious or secular origin. In the buildings associated with Delhi Sultanate, this technique is a major departure from Persianate building traditions inherited by the Sultans.

The mosque of Pampore which can be tentatively dated to later part of the fourteenth century CE is conspicuous for the absence of any non-Kashmiri building element or decorative feature. Even the pointed arch, traditionally to be found in mosques constructed in adjoining parts of the Indian plains at this period, finds no mention in this fourteenth-century Kashmiri mosque. The mosque at Pampore, just like Rīnchanā's mosque, brings to fore the Kashmiri specificity of not only the Muslim religious Architecture of Kashmir in the fourteenth century CE, but also of Islam in the land.

Ziyārat–i Shāh Mīr at Anderkote

Aside from the two mosques at Srinagar and Pampore, the only other building forming a part of the religious architecture linked with early *Shahmīrī* sultans is located at Anderkote, the capital of the last Hindu ruler of Kashmir, Kotā Rani. For it is here that we find a small non-descript shrine; the *Ziyārat-i* Shāh Ṣāhab. For the locals, Sultan Shāh is a part of the long list of Muslim saints who were responsible for the spread of Islam in the region. What is purported to be the shrine, is in fact the tomb of the first *Shahmīrī* sultan of Kashmir, Shams-al Dīn, the Shāh Mīr who wrested the throne of Kashmir from the hands of Kotā Rani at Anderkote. Malīk calculates the reign of Shams-al Dīn to have lasted for three years and five months, but of his actual reign he gives no details.

Writing earlier Jonarāja would have Shams-al Dīn rule for five years, years which from the meager account provided by him were mostly spent in consolidating his power[87]. Yet, neither in Jonarāja's nor in Malīk's account do we get even the faintest suggestion of realignment of the old forces of power, in an attempt to restore the Hindu rule, nor do we see in the new rule, a significant shift – even the establishment of a new political order. The dynasty and the power that Shams-al Dīn established does not reflect in its initial years a hegemonic shift of power, ideas or even the social structure of the region. In the passage of dynasties, it marks the onset of another new dynasty, where Islam the religion and the vocabulary associated with the religion played a minor, if any, role at all. Interestingly, in this period, we hardly find a mention of a Muslim missionary, preacher or saint, who either visited Kashmir or was associated with the court of the Sultan of Kashmir. It would only be later, when Muslim rule was well established in Kashmir, that Muslim historians would perceive Shams-al Dīn's arrival in Kashmir as a part of divine intervention to establish Islam in Kashmir[88]. In Shams-al Dīn's rule, we find no clue, no evidence of this transformative nature of society that future Muslim writers would credit him with[89]. Stability of the land and his rule were the principal *rasion de etre* of the Sultan's rule.

On his death, the Sultan was buried at Anderkote, a place that marks both the beginning and the end of his rule as the Sultan of Kashmir[90]. Unfortunately, none of the older histories of Kashmir make any reference to his tomb or even the place of burial.

The patronage of the tomb must have fallen to Shams-al Dīn's younger son; Alā'-al Dīn. Over the centuries, as the once important fort of Anderkote slipped into oblivion from the political history of Kashmir, the memory of the Sultan who lay buried there was also lost. Reinvented as a saint in the local folklore, the tomb would be transformed into a village shrine, drawing the occasional devotee to offer his prayers and seek the blessing of the shrine. A ritual, that continues in contemporary Anderkote.

The shrine itself is located within a walled cemetery, which in addition to the building also has some isolated stone columns and stone cenotaphs scattered around, coeval to the original construction. The cemetery is itself part of an open green area which is again used as a public graveyard. The shrine of Shams-al Dīn is located in the north-western corner of the cemetery.

The shrine, or rather the tomb, of Shams-al Dīn comprises a small square structure measuring around 5.4m × 5.4m, raised on top of a low-lying stone plinth of 7.4m × 7.7m [Figure 2.10]. The plinth with its ancient looking stone blocks is coeval with the actual construction. The semi-chiseled unfinished nature of the plinth stone is a clear indication that the plinth is not a part of existing temple converted or designed on a Hindu foundation[91]. The superstructure is a recent reconstruction, and the date of the reconstruction is incised in the mud plastered wall of the building interiors as 1396 AH/1976 CE. Located within the walled compound of the tomb are numerous stone cenotaphs, in dilapidated condition, hidden under a dense vegetation of trees. The construction of a permanent masonry structure over the remains of the dead while widespread in the Islamic world was without a precedent in Kashmir. Writing more than a century later, about this phenomenon, Shrivara remarked:

> The Mausulas always take care about the structures over their graves and pay money to the architect[92].

The small square masonry chamber serving as the shrine is located centrally on the stone platform. A narrow corridor (1m wide) acts as an outer circumambulatory space. Internally, a small wooden partition wall filled with *pinjrākārī* (lattice work) encloses the actual burial chamber, again a square 1.82m × 1.82m with a narrow surrounding circumambulatory. The chamber is approached from a centrally located door on the southern façade,

Given the fact that the masonry walls are more than 1m wide and show no signs of sag or structural distress, it is understood that the walls are located on top of a supporting foundation, which would indicate that though the walls are a reconstruction, the plan including the position of the walls is reflection of the original design. Supporting evidence can be found in an archival image of the structure dating back to early part of the twentieth century CE in work of Sufi[93]. In the grainy black and white image, large blocks of stone masonry of the chamber wall can be observed, supporting the idea of the walled chamber being a part of the original design. Interestingly, while the present structure has two small ventilators on all the four walls, in the image, no opening can be observed, at least in the main

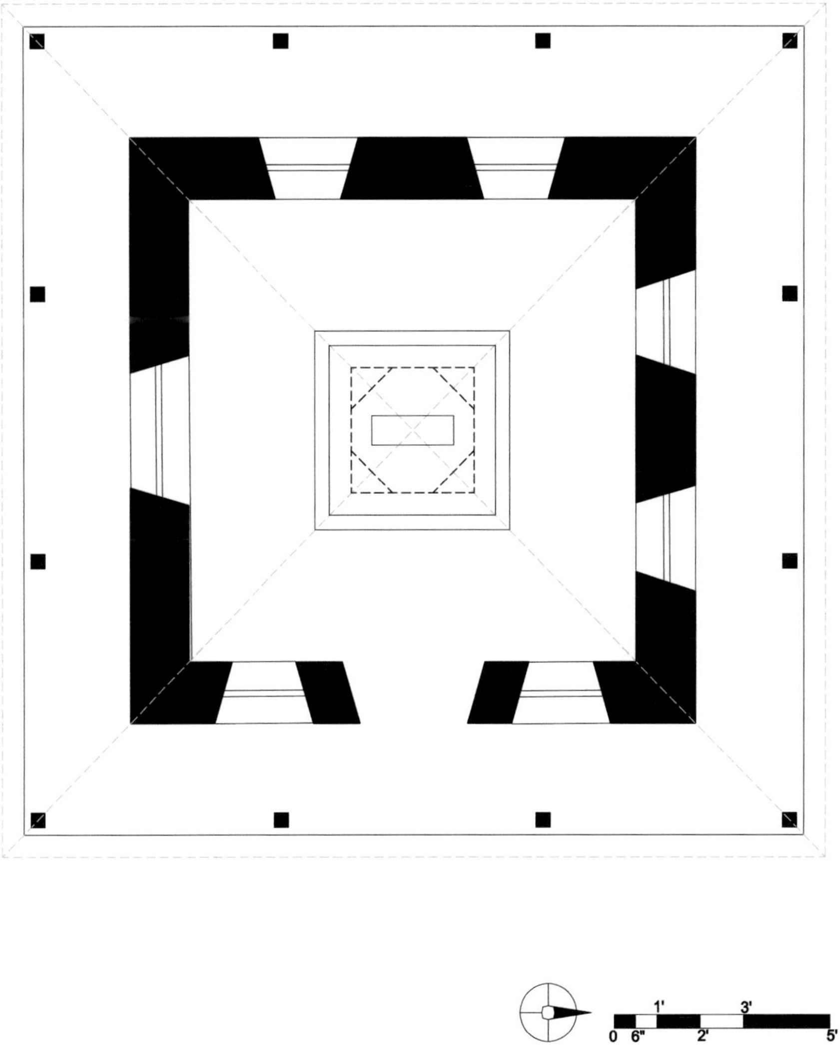

Figure 2.10 Shrine of Shāhmīr at Anderkote, plan of the shrine, © Hakim Sameer Hamdani.

southern façade. This is similar to the plan form of the temple where the only opening in the *garbhagriha* (cella) is that of the doorway. The irregular appearance of the stone masonry in the superstructure indicates that the walls must originally have been plastered over. While in most cases of medieval temples, with their massive fine, well-dressed coursed masonry, the external stone surfaces were left untouched, both Kak and Goetz speculate about the possibility of painted gypsum plaster on the walls, especially for the sculpture[94]. In case of early Muslim monuments, the plaster work would suffice to cover the ill-looking masonry, providing a cost effective and timely manner for dressing a building.

The overall plan of the tomb reflects simplicity of design which was to act as a prototype for future Muslim shrines in Kashmir. Stylistically, the tomb of Shams-al Dīn, like the earlier Kashmiri temples, comprises a single masonry chamber: the *ḥujrā* with an additional wooden screen around the actual grave. Like the *garbhagriha* of the temple, the *ḥujrā* is usually square, a reflection of the basic square form. The centrally located portico of the temple is transformed into a linear porch running all around the building. As with the temple, a single doorway suffices in both cases[95]. In so much as Kashmiri temple is a continuation of the earlier Buddhist monastery: the *vihāra*, the plan of this early Muslim monument follows that of the Hindu temple.

The spatial layout of the shrine indicates that in the view of its builders, the cenotaph was intended to serve for a circumambulatory rite – the *tawaf*. Interestingly, this is a ritual innovation as *tawaf* is legitimized for Kaaba alone. Yet, down the centuries, across the spiritual landscape of Kashmir, *tawaf* around cenotaphs of Sufis and saints has remained an accepted part of Muslim society. But with a significant departure. The *tawaf* around Kaaba takes a counter-clockwise direction, while in Kashmir, the *tawaf* is done in a clockwise moment. The difference may in part be seen as a continuation of the age-old tradition of *parikrama* (circumambulation) that is undertaken in the clockwise direction both in Buddhist and Hindu cultures. Additionally, it would also help in differentiating between a sanctified *tawaf* of Kaaba from a more questionable circumambulating around graves of saints.

While the custom of circumambulating the grave linked with Sufi saints is also prevalent within the mainland India, the spatial layout of the interiors of Kashmiri *ziyārat* (shrine, also *rūżā, āstan*) marks a significant departure. Unlike its mainland counterparts, in a Kashmiri shrine the grave is never on public display. Invariably, the chamber containing the grave, the *ḥujrā*, is screened off physically by a wooden screen with in-fills of decorative wooden *pinjrākārī*. This physical as well as visual inaccessibility helps in projecting an aura of remoteness and mystery heightening the spiritual aura of the space.

Between the *ziyārat* of Shāh Mīr and its antecedent in the medieval stone temples of Kashmir, in spite of similarities in spatial layout, there remains a significant difference. Foremost, again like at Rīnchanā's mosque is that of scale. As the oldest surviving example of Muslim shrine (tomb) architecture in Kashmir, the structure does not make any claim for monumentality. Though the structure is raised on a platform, but the height of the platform pales in comparison to what was undertaken before. In fact, by doing away with the pretension of scale, the tomb almost borrows back to the older tradition of the Buddhist *vihāra* with its 'unpretentious flight of steps'[96]. At Anderkote, even the unpretentious flight of steps is also done away. In comparison to the medieval temple of Kashmir, the unassuming plinth of the tomb of Shams-al Dīn makes any portrayal of power impossible. There is no conscious attempt to monumentalize the last resting place of the Sultan, whose descendants would rule Kashmir for more than two centuries. The structure makes no attempt to portray a sense of Muslim esthetics through an all-powerful visual image. In fact, there is nothing Islamic at the site, barring the orientation of the grave which follows the traditional north-south orientation and the shape of the stone cenotaphs.

No attempt has been made to glorify or monumentalize the burial place of a man whose rule would for a later generation of Muslim historians portray the establishment of Muslim supremacy in Kashmir.

If the medieval arts of Kashmir came into vogue 'under the psychological pressure' of a victor – Lalitāditya, to outshine those societies culturally superior to his own, which he had conquered[97], the Muslim architecture evolved from a desire to be as inconspicuous as possible in its new setting. Contrast this with what had been undertaken by Muslim conquerors at *Quwat-al Islam* mosque or at the *Adai din ka Jhaunpra*, where architecture propagated the hegemonic transfer of power. If the early architecture of Delhi Sultanate provides an example of how 'invading cultures interact'[98], that of the Muslim sultans of Kashmir exemplifies an altogether different interaction – an interaction between cultures which were not antagonistic but responsive.

Though a new dynasty, a Muslim dynasty, was established in Kashmir in the fourteenth century, the overwhelming local environment remained unchanged, and it was in this environment that long formed building traditions continued to provide the precedents for the new buildings typologies that were now introduced to cater to the needs of the emerging Muslim community.

Conclusion

During these early years of Muslim rule, the architectural proclivity of the Muslim rulers was limited to meeting the functional requirements of a small Muslim community rather than undertaking ambitious projects of monumental glory.

The formative years of Islamic religious architecture in Kashmir echo the experience of Islam itself in its initial years in the Arabian heartland – where the new architecture of the religion had evolved from what was available locally in the immediate surroundings of the community. Yet, an overview of lands bordering Kashmir in the fourteenth century CE that were a part of Muslim polity would indicate that while localized, indigenous, regional elements would manifest itself in the Islamic religious architecture, the overall iconography of the new architecture being set up was rooted in a hegemonic non-nativeness of the invading culture. On the other hand, in Kashmir, both Islam the religion as well as the power of Muslim rulers established its roots in a multi religious milieu. In these early decades of Muslim rule in Kashmir, the entire experience of Islam and Muslims in the region was an internalist experience with minimalistic outside contact. And in the strong nativist memory of Kashmir, the Muslim Sultans and the Muslim community established an existence which imbibed a strong consciousness of distinctive Kashmiri rather than Islamic character. Thus, we find in the emerging Islamic religious architecture of the fourteenth century CE, a continuation of old signs and symbols while adhering the dictates of the new religion against any figurative depiction.

Notes

1 Kalhānā, *Rajatarangini,* 353, 357.
2 The Kings of Kashmir at this time were closely linked with Hindu Shahiya dynasty. Thus, Queen Diddā, who ruled Kashmir, descended on her maternal side from the King Bhima of the Hindu Shahiyas of Kabul, Kalhānā, *Rajatarangini,* 104, 248–266. After the collapse of the Hindu Shahiya kingdom, some of the Shahiya princes found refuge at the court of King Ananta (1028–63 CE). Both the kingdom of Kashmir and that of the Hindu Shahiya were greatly influenced by the artistic traditions of Gandhara, the heart of both the Kushan as well as Parthian Empire.
3 Kalhānā, *Rajatarangini,* 107.
4 P N K Bamzai, *Cultural and Political History of Kashmir* (New Delhi: MD Publications, 1994), 15.
5 Of special interest are the scenes depicted on the *dhotī* (long loincloth) of the statute of Bodhisattva Avalokiteshvara at Sumstek.
6 Kalhānā, *Rajatarangini,* 64.
7 Ibid, 19.
8 On his conversion, he adopted the name of Ṣadr-al Dīn. The fifteenth century CE Hindu historian, Jonarāja, refers to him as Shri Rīnchanā, while writing in 1620 CE, Malīk calls him Rinchu, see Haidar Malīk, transl. Razia Bano, *Tārīkh-i Kashmir: History of Kashmir*, (Delhi: Bhavna Prakashan, 1991), 50.
9 Sufi, *Kashīr*, 81–83.
10 Malīk, *Tārīkh-i Kashmir,* 40.
11 Kalhānā, *Rajatarangini,* 130.
12 Sufi, *Kashīr,* 77.
13 Kalhānā, *Rajatarangini,* 130.
14 Jonāraja writes about the aftermaths of Zulchu's invasion:

> Kashmira became almost like a region before the creation, a vast field with few men, without food and full of grass, Jonarāja, transl. J C Dutt, *Rajatarangini: Kings of Kashmira,* a translation of Sanskrit work, (Srinagar: Gulshan Books, 2009), 294.

15 Hasan, *Kashmir Under the Sultans,* 34.
16 Muzaffar Khan, *Kashmiri Muslims*, 2 vols. (Srinagar: Humanizer Publications, 2012), 173–78.
17 Sufi, *Kashīr,* 127–28.
18 Jonāraja, *Rajatarangini,* 295.
19 Ibid, 294, 297, 298.
20 Ibid, 296.
21 What can be established is that Rīnchanā was followed in his conversion by his brother-in-law. The possibility of some other members of the King's entourage also embracing the new religion seems reasonable, but this number could not

have been significant, for neither Malīk nor Dedhmārī reports about en masse conversion. The only account which speaks of large scale conversion is that of the Mufti Muhammad S'ādat, who writing in the twenty first century CE, spoke about 10,000 new converts, Sufi, *Kashir*, 83.

22 This includes the palace of Rīnchanā.

23 *Bahāristān-i Shāhī*, transl. K.N. Pandit, (Srinagar: Gulshan books, 2013), 19.

24 'As a result of the abundance of goodwill and purity of disposition of this dervish, the *khanqah* continues to be in a prosperous state even to this day', *Bahāristān-i Shāhī*, 19.

25 For a discussion on the Muslim religious places related to various Sufi orders in the wider Indian context, see Edward W Troll, ed., *Muslim Shrines in India* (New Delhi: Oxford University Press, 2004). R M Eaton provides a understanding of the Muslim culture and construct of the Sufi sacred space in medieval India, see R. M. Eaton, *Essays of Islam and Indian History* (New Delhi: Oxford University Press, 2010).

26 Sufi, *Kashīr,* 127–29.

27 'Strange that this believer in Allah became the savior of people', Jonāraja, *Rajatarangini*, 297.

28 Third, if we account for the rule of the legendary Queen Jasohmati, who on the death of her husband King Damodar held power for her infant son, Gonanda I.

29 Kak, 28; Malīk, *Tārīkh-i Kashmir,* 41.

30 See, Kak, *Ancient Monuments of Kashmir*, 28.

31 Ibid, 29.

32 Malīk, *Tārīkh-i Kashmir,* 39.

33 '[...] no one was able to promulgate the Sharait of Islam because majority of people were infidels. The few Muslims here and there were Muslims in name only', Malīk, *Tārīkh-i Kashmir,* 39.

34 Kak, *Ancient Monuments of Kashmir*, 30.

35 Malīk, *Tārīkh-i Kashmir,* 52.

36 Jonāraja, *Rajatarangini*, 300–01; Malīk, *Tārīkh-i Kashmir,* 51.

37 Sufi, *Kashīr*, 135.

38 According to Zaffar, L'alā opposed the ritualistic tendencies of Saivistic *Trikamatwhih* as detailed by Abhinava Gupta, which were celebrated by the religious class presiding over their enactment, M H Zaffar, 'Lal-Ded: The Mystic of Kashmir', *Sutra Journal*, March, 2016.

39 The given name of Shaykh Nūr-al Dīn was Nūndā, which is translated as 'fortunate one', Malīk, *Tārīkh-i Kashmir,* 101. The transformation of Nūndā into Shaykh Nūr-al Dīn is a reflective of how later-day Muslim historians and *tazkira* writers attempted at reworking the early history of the region in what they perceived as a more acceptable Islamic image, an urban Persianised image linked with the court culture.

40 Later historians have made a reference to the visit of Makhdūm Sayyid Jalāl-al Dīn Bukhārī (d. 1384 CE) to Kashmir in 748 AH/1347 CE. The story is highly allegorical.

41 'When he became king, the country ceased to remember the prosperity and the dangers, the pleasures and afflictions of the time of Lalityaditya', Jonāraja, *Rajatarangini*, 301.

42 *Bahāristān-i Shāhī*, 25.

43 Hasan, *Kashmir Under the Sultans,* 50–51.

44 Ibid, 51.

45 Jonāraja, *Rajatarangini*, 305.

46 Ibid, 302, 303.

47 See, *Bahāristān-i Shāhī.*

48 Sayyid ʿAli, transl. G R Bhat, *Tārīkh-i Kashmir* (Srinagar: Center of Central Asian Studies, 1994), 1, 2.
49 Named after his Queen, Lakshmi.
50 Over the time, the name got corrupted to its present day form of Shāmpūr.
51 Shelton Waldrep, *The Dissolution of Place: Architecture, Identity and the Body* (Farnham: Ashgate Pub Co, 2012), 2.
52 Goetz, *Studies in the history and Art of Kashmir,* 6.
53 Ibid, 50, 57, 58.
54 Kak, *Ancient Monuments of Kashmir*, 54.
55 Goetz, *Studies in the History and Art of Kashmir,* 61.
56 Ibid, 38.
57 Ibid, 76.
58 Ibid, 75.
59 Monica Juneja, ed., *Architecture in Medieval India: Forms, Contexts, Histories* (New Delhi: Permanent Black, 2001), 42.
60 Goetz, *Studies in the History and Art of Kashmir,* 73.
61 Ibid, 71–75.
62 Ibid, 75.
63 In addition, Ashoka is said to have built numerous stupas and *chatiyas* while also rebuilding in stone the temple of Vijayesvara (Bijbehara) and the temple of Ashokesvara, Kalhānā, *Rajatarangini,* 19, 20.
64 Kalhānā, *Rajatarangini,* 21.
65 See Stein's note in Kalhānā, *Rajatarangini,* 30.
66 Such a reading does not negate what I have written earlier about the flourishing of a certain cosmopolitan culture that marks Kashmir. What I would argue is that the natural setting of Kashmir helped in localizing every foreign influence and experience. Thus the Shahmīrīs and after them the Chaks could both be argued to be non-native dynasties who 'went native' upon their arrival in the land.
67 Ksemagupta (r. 950–58CE) burnt down Jayendravihara, removing the image of Buddha taken from the *vihara* and confiscated its revenue to build a temple, Ksemagaurisvara consecrated to Shiva, Kalhānā, *Rajatarangini,* 248.
68 Ibid, 102, 103.
69 Ibid, 113.
70 Kak, *Ancient Monuments of Kashmir*, 152.
71 Grabar, *What Makes Islamic Art Islamic*, 248.
72 Juneja, *Architecture in Medieval India*, 2.
73 Sunil Kumar has convincingly argued that the politically charged name '*Quwat-al Islam*' is of a later-day invention. While questioning the interpretation of the mosque's construction, built in three different phases, as a singular symbol of hegemonic authority, he nevertheless does interpret the first construction at the site as such. Regarding the adjacent *Quṭub Minar,* whose ground floor also dates from this period, he refers to it as a 'memorial of victory', see Sunil Kumar, 'Qutub and Modern Memory,' in *The Partitions of Memory: The Afterlife of the Division of India*, Suvir Kaul, ed. (Delhi: Permanent Black, 2001), 43.
74 Saima Bhat, 'Islam's First Kashmir Address', in *Kashmir Life*, May 23, 2018.
75 Malīk, *Tārīkh-i Kashmir,* 40.
76 Ibid. Additionally as the only mosque at its time, the building would have served both the functions, of offering of five daily congregational prayers as well as that of the Friday. The present mosque at the site, also known as Jamia Masjid, would be the site of the palace that Rīnchanā constructed at Rīnchanāporā. See, Dedhmārī, *Waqāt-i Kashmir,* 78.

77 This idea is explained in the local vernacular by the saying that a mosque extends from *farash ta arash* (earth up till the heaven).
78 The mosque is presently in an advanced state of deterioration.
79 Ruins of the temple in the shape of a plinth can still be seen at site.
80 For the capital city of Srinagar alone, we have a record of nineteen major fires, see Khuihāmī, *Tārīkh-i Hasan*.
81 Kalhānā, *Rajatarangini,* 104.
82 Goetz describes the conquest in these words:

> [...] whose armies had swept from the frontiers of the Abbasid Caliphate to Orissa, Southern India, Bombay, Kathiawad, Rajputana, Tibet and Mongolia'

Goetz, *Studies in the history and Art of Kashmir,* 66. The view of Goetz reflects a degree of romanticism on Lalitāditya's military prowess, sustained by his understanding of the pivotal role he played in development of Kashmiri style.

83 For detailed account of King Ananta, see, Kalhānā, *Rajatarangini,* 278–305.
84 Goetz, *Studies in the History and Art of Kashmir,* 74.
85 The trefoil arch which is quite clear in the first row of niches above the doorway becomes disfigured to a segmental arch in the second row.
86 Kak, *Ancient Monuments of Kashmir*, 116.
87 Jonāraja, *Rajatarangini*, 300.
88 Dedhmārī, *Waqāt-i Kashmir,* 70–71.
89 'Shah Mir's accession is particularly notable for the fact that it marks the establishment of Muslim authority in both its religious and secular aspects in Kashmir', Sufi, *Kashīr*, 132.
90 Hasan, *Kashmir Under the Sultans*, 241.
91 Some see the beginning of Muslim architecture in Kashmir as, 'conversion of Hindu temples [...] built in place of one designed for Hindu foundations', Christopher Tadgell, *Architecture in Context* (London: Routledge, 2008), 492.
92 Shrivara, *Rajatarangini*, 356.
93 Sufi, *Kashīr*, 134.
94 Kak, *Ancient Monuments of Kashmir*, 63.
95 The presence of a single doorway can be found in temples like at Avantipura, which Kak groups together under the sub-style of *vimana*, while those grouped under the *mandapa* style have four doorways in the four cardinal directions. Of the latter examples can be found at Pandrethan and Payar or the miniature temple such as that in Pattan, see, Kak, *Ancient Monuments of Kashmir*, 66.
96 Kak, *Ancient Monuments of Kashmir*, 62.
97 Goetz, *Studies in the History and Art of Kashmir,* 55.
98 Juneja, *Architecture in Medieval India*, 40.

3

ESTABLISHMENT OF A STYLE: 1389–1586 CE

> [...] Shamsdena (Shams-al Dīn) was gracious, Alabhedena (Alā'-al Dīn) was politic, Shabhadena (Shahāb al-Dīn) was a hero, and Kudvadena (Quṭub-al Dīn) was wise. Sri Shekandhara (Sikandar) was the favourite of Yavana noble, Alishaha ('Ali Shāh) was liberal, King Shri Jaina (Zain-al Ābidīn) loved all branches of languages and was well versed in the literature of languages and King Haidharashaha (Ḥaidar Shāh) was an expert in performance of lute. But the present King (Hasan Shāh) is a master of music [....].
>
> Shrivara, **Rajatarangini: Kings of Kashmira, a translation of Sanskrit work**, 370.

This chapter analyzes and interprets the changes that took place in the socio-cultural landscape of Kashmir in the aftermath of Sultan Shahāb al-Dīn's expansion of the geographical boundaries of Kashmir. The arrival of Sufis and missionaries from Persianate world in Kashmir, post-Shahāb al-Dīn's conquests, was a result of not only the religious fervor and piety of these immigrant missionaries, but also the new-found acclaim of Kashmir, as a powerful court and possible sources of patronage.

The chapter explores the wider consequences of this influx as well as the emergence of conflict between native Muslim community and non-local missionaries of faith. The architecture produced in this period was representative of a society undergoing gradual transformation, a transformation reflective of a changing political and cultural milieu. Yet, in spite of political and cultural changes, the Muslim society also continued to adhere to values of co-existence and continuity, established earlier during the formative period of Muslim rule in Kashmir.

How the changing social dynamics within the Muslim community of Kashmir altered the cultural and architectural outpourings will be explored in this chapter as we examine various shrines, mosques and *khānaqāhs* constructed in this period. We will also examine cases where the older architectural forms based on native, pre-Islamic architectural traditions continued to receive patronage both from the court as well as the native Sufi order of the *Reshīs*. Drawing upon a multitude of building typologies linked with various Sufi orders and sectarian denominations within the Muslim community, we will study the dynamics of image that was projected and the cultural forces that formed a source of their inspiration as well as financial patronage for these projects.

Consolidation of Sultanate rule: Political expansion and immigrant Sufis

The conquests of Shahāb al-Dīn bought Kashmir much needed acclaim, for with the accession of his successor Quṭub-al Dīn (r. 1373–89 CE) numerous Sufi saints started to arrive in Kashmir, the most prominent being Mīr Sayyid ʿAli Hamdanī (714 AH/1314 CE-786 AH/1384–85 CE). In the medieval history of Kashmir, Sayyid ʿAli emerges as a major iconic figure leaving his mark on the socio-cultural life of the land. Spiritual preceptor of a major Sufi order in Iran, the *Kubrawis*, Sayyid ʿAli ran into conflict with Tīmūr (r. 1370–1405 CE), the founder of the Timurid empire[1]. The arrival of Sayyid ʿAli marks the first instance of an organized Sufi order making its presence felt in Kashmir. The personal presence in Kashmir, of such a trans-regional figure as Sayyid ʿAli accounts in part for the widespread prominence that future generation of Muslim writers would ascribe him in promoting Islam in the region. Sayyid ʿAli was accompanied by a large entourage of relatives, disciples, friends, some of whom settled down in Kashmir[2]. They in turn would help in propagating the narrative of Sayyid ʿAli as a path-breaking Sufi saint who travelled all over Kashmir, working miracles and engaging in mass conversions. Amongst the disciples were also artisans and craftsmen who found new venues of patronage in the court, resulting in infusion of new ideas and crafts.

Yet, Quṭub-al Dīn, like his brother and the former sultan, Shahāb al-Dīn, had been raised in a cultural milieu uniquely Kashmiri, which affronted Sayyid ʿAli's notion of faith, culture and orthodoxy[3]. The Sultan followed the customs of the land, wore clothes that were in vogue amongst his people, clothes that future generation of Muslims writers would characterize as non-Islamic[4]. Quṭub-al Dīn, from the brief accounts that we have of his rule, comes across as a cultured and humane king, concerned for the welfare of the general population[5]. When the land was visited by repeated famines, he is said to have performed a *yagna* (ritual sacrifice) to ward of the calamities, which also provides an interesting insight on the continuing role of Hinduism in the society[6]. The respect he showed Sayyid ʿAli was not a resolve to Islamize the society, a fact that Sayyid ʿAli realized soon. The sharia-minded Sufi did not stop at his initial limited success but insisted on a more orthodox functioning of the court and the society[7]. Dismayed by the Sultan's indifferent response to his suggestions, Sayyid ʿAli left Kashmir after completing a *chillā* (solitary retreat for 40 days) in Srinagar[8]. Drawing on his own Muslim-ness, Sayyid ʿAli and after him his son, Mīr Sayyid Muhammad Hamdanī (1372–1450 CE) would equate their own cultural practices as being representative of an authentic version of Islam. Culturally, this would mean following the practices of a part of the Islamic heartland, spread over Iran and Transoxiana[9] – a region to which Sayyid ʿAli and his order belonged. It was also the region that would provide a majority of Sufis, scholars, theologians who migrated to Kashmir in the coming decades[10].

The influence of orthodoxy that Sayyid ʿAli had tried to promote was realized under the reign of Quṭub-al Dīn's son and successor, Sultan Sikander (r. 1389–1413 CE) stylized by medieval historians as *būt-shikan* (idol breaker). And the man who played a prominent role in the young sultan's turn to the orthodoxy was Sayyid ʿAli's son, Sayyid Muhammad Hamdani, who arrived in Kashmir in 796 AH/1393 CE, spending 22 years in the valley. It is interesting to note that both the missionary and the sultan were in their early youthful years. Was the success of Sayyid Muhammed's effort a result of this youthful camaraderie with the Sultan[11], we can only venture a guess.

In contrast to the non-local Sufi orders, like the *Kubrawīs*, that were slowly being introduced into society, the *Reshīs* emerged as representative of a native, indigenous loosely grouped order of mendicants, representing a folk tradition of Islam in the region. An order that was in its 'pantheistic beliefs also [...] influenced by Advaita Saivism'[12].While the origin of the *Reshī* movement or order is lost in obscurity, some even claiming a beginning that predates Rīnchanā's conversion[13], it was only with Shaykh Nūr-al Dīn (Nund resh)[14], that they came into prominence during the early part of the fifteenth century CE[15]. The reclusive, vegetarian, wandering saints of the *Reshī* order, many of whom remained celibate, were representative, just like their name, of an older spirit, of wandering *bikshus* and *reshīs*.

Yet, in renouncing the world, these *Reshī* saints marked a break with tradition prevalent amongst both the Kashmiri Hindus as well Muslims. Ranjit Hoskote argues that the practice of renouncing the world was not a prevailing social reality of Kashmiri Hindu community in the immediate period preceding the advent of the order[16]. And celibacy was condemned in Islam, in prophetic traditions. It is safe to posit that the some of the customs adopted by the *Reshī* may have been sourced from remaining Buddhist influences in the Kashmiri society.

What also emerges is the adoption by the *Reshīs* of customs and the language that belonged to the common people – the local vernacular, not the Persianized customs and the Persian language that was being introduced at the court. In the verses of Shaykh Nūr-al Dīn, survives the earliest, extant critique of this new transformation being introduced into Kashmiri society in the name of Islam.

Though a later generation of Muslim historians would portray a seamless process of Islamization of Kashmir during this period, yet there are many apparent contradictions in such a generalized reading of history[17]. The Shaykhs surviving poetical works are replete with criticism of the educated, scholarly non-Kashmiri ruling elite at the court – the *mullā*'s[18].

While no authoritative dates exist for the period when the Shaykh flourished, the life of the saint was contemporaneous with the reign of Sultan Sikander. As such, the Shaykh would have been an eyewitness to the steady arrival of foreign missionaries at the court and the commencement of iconoclastic activities in the land. This period has been glorified by most Muslim historians of the medieval period as the golden days of Islam in the region. Yet, the Shaykh's verses do not celebrate the events or the times. His poetry does not serve as an endorsement of the acts of the Sultan, especially verses such as:

> In these evil times, I crossed [the lake] like a swan[19]

More importantly, there is hardly any recorded or authenticated tradition of the Shaykh's visit to the capital, Srinagar[20]. A significant aspect of Muslim rule in medieval Kashmir is the centrality of Srinagar in the political discourse of the region. While many of the Sultans established towns and quarters outside of Srinagar, yet the city continued serving as the capital city, throughout this period. An analysis of the various foreign Sufis who visited Kashmir from the reign of Quṭub-al Dīn down till that of Zain-al Ābidīn reveals that of a total of approximately 92 individuals, 60 are buried in various *moḥalas* of Srinagar city[21]. While such a breakdown does not rule out that as missionaries many of those who are buried in Srinagar, would also be engaged in proselytizing outside the capital, it does nevertheless indicate the urban character of the various Sufi orders. Additionally, the principal *khānaqāhs* associated with Sufi orders like the *Kubrawī*, *Qadrī*, *Naqshbandī*, *Suharwardī*, *Nūrbakshī* etc., were all located in Srinagar. Proximity to court, as a source of seeking patronage and influence, was a defining element in the way the various foreign Sufi orders operated in Kashmir[22]. As opposed to this, most of the sacred spaces associated with *Reshīs* are located in areas that come across as isolated and secluded spots of the then-rural Kashmir. In fact, a large number of the shrines built to commemorate these spaces date from a nineteenth and early twentieth century CE. Unlike, the proselytizing non-Kashmiri Sufis and theologians who were connected with the court, the Kashmiri *Reshīs* followed a path of wandering amongst the common population and away from the court. They did not seek to establish *khānaqāhs,* as a center of preaching and attracting devotees, *khānaqāhs,* which were central to functioning of the city based on established Sufi orders.

Another interesting characteristic of the *Reshī* order is the ease with which members of this order appropriated ancient sites linked with both Buddhist and Hindu past. We can see examples of this at Loduv, at Bamzu, Aeshmuqam, Tapil as well at numerous other sites. This they did by not desecration of a site, but by ensuring a continuity of its reverence, inserting personal experiences, personal narrative in the history of the site and what it represented. Writing in the early part of the seventeenth century CE, when Kashmir was a part of the Mughal Empire, Bābā Nasīb-al Dīn Ghazī characterized the importance of the *Reshīs* to Kashmir in these words:

> [...] This peace-loving paradisiacal Kashmir has through the wealth of the action of the *Reshīs* been bestowed with many rituals [...]. The land of Kashmir is like a fort, the strength of whose towers is dependent on dwellings of its *Reshis*'[23].

The influence of Sayyid Muhammad and his orthodoxy resulted in Sikander's banning of all forms of music (except the use of drums and fife by the army), use of wine, gambling, dancing of women[24]. He was the first Sultan who made use of sharia law, imposed *jaziya* on non-Muslims and introduced the post of qazi to oversee the administration of the sharia[25]. And also engaged in widespread demolition of temples and images[26]. While medieval Muslim hagiographic and historical accounts may have exaggerated Sikander's destruction of non-Muslim religious sites in a classical representation of religious piety, the tendency of some writers in the twentieth century CE to shield the Sultan from these iconoclastic activities is not historically correct, especially given the evidence from the period coming from writers of different religious backgrounds[27].

While Sikander's rule shows a consistent increase in the role of non-Kashmiri missionaries at the court, a considered policy of conversion through coercion at the behest of the court, it also represents a dichotomy between the formal, orthodox and the popular representation of Islam in the region. The rule of his son and eventual successor Zain-al Ābidīn (r. 1420–70 CE) would result in setting up of a court that would be representative of the most transcendent, ecumenical, interactive and pluralistic as well as inspiring period of Kashmiri society under the Muslim rule. In the overall medieval history of Kashmir, Zain-al Ābidīn emerges as a much-celebrated ruler[28]. Cultured, humane, tolerant; patron of art and architecture and men of learning; Zain-al Ābidīn is unlike any of his predecessors or successors that ruled as the Sultan of Kashmir[29]. In posterity, Kashmiris would remember him as *Budshāh* (supreme king).

Most historical references maintain that Zain-al Ābidīn invited various craftsmen from all part of Islamic world, especially Iran and Central Asia[30]. His entire reign, whether it be his appreciation of arts or patronage of learning, shows a marked determination of assimilation – of different cultures and cultural influences in a manner that was celebratory of all the differences rather than discriminatory or hegemonic. As the king, he patronized Muslim as well as Hindus, and their traditions of learning[31]. The great Hindu epic, Mahabharat, was translated into Persian as was *Rajatarangini*, the chronicle of pre-Muslim kings of Kashmir[32]. While the role of Persian as the court language was not diminished, the use of Sanskrit would continue way down till the end of the Kashmiri Sultanate.

The cultural syncretism that is reflective of Zain-al Ābidīn's rule is significantly different than that of the rulers who preceded Sultan Sikander. Before Sikander, it was primarily due to the cultural and physical isolation of the land. The fame of Shahāb al-Dīn's conquest resulted in the gradual break of this isolation. The destabilizing conditions of regions to the west of Kashmir, especially in Khurasan and Fars as a result of military exploits of Tīmūr contributing to dislocation of communities of missionaries, preachers and artisans also resulted in ending this isolation. And as Kashmir, fully recovered from the ravages of Zulchu's invasion, welcomed these immigrants, it resulted in the introduction of processes of religious and cultural hegemony under Sultan Sikander. The syncretism of Zain-al Ābidīn's reign is a reversal of this process. It is also a period where the forces of orthodoxy and cultural domination started undergoing a process of transformation themselves – becoming more Kashmiri.

The syncretism of Zain-al Ābidīn was broadly continued under his successors[33], though the political authority of the throne was gradually eroded under a series of weak and ineffective Sultans and the increasing power of powerful clans of military leaders. Zain-al Ābidīn was succeeded to the throne by his son, Sultan Haidar (r. 1470–72 CE). The reign of Haider and his successor, Sultan Hasan Shāh, (r. 1472–84 CE) set the seeds for the disintegration of the Shahmīrī rule, with the sons, and later on grandsons of Zain-al Ābidīn, vying for throne against each other, supported by rival group of powerful nobles. This period also represents a steady increase in the power of the Baihaqī Sayyids. The Baihaqī Sayyids made their presence felt in Kashmir during Sikander's reign, when the future sultan, Zain-al Ābidīn was married into the Sayyid family[34]. This was followed by a series of inter-marriages between the Shahmīrī and the Baihaqī families resulting in Sayyid Hasan effectively ruling Kashmir for his infant grandson, Sultan Muhammad Shāh (r. 1484–86 CE). The rise of Sayyid Hasan and his powerful family revived efforts at Persianization of the court, which can be inferred from the Sayyids' neglect of, '[...] men learned in the vernacular and in *Samskrita* [...]'[35]. The behavior of the Sayyids, their cultural chauvinism and high handedness resulted in a revolt of Kashmiri nobles, an overwhelming majority of who took to the arms against the Sayyids[36]. From an examination of available sources, we can also observe the gradual eclipse of Hindus from position of importance following Sultan Hasan Shāh. Hasan Shāh was the last Muslim sultan during whose reign, we find references of prominent Hindu public figures[37].

The defeat of the Sayyids resulted in the ascendancy of Kashmiri nobles, the most prominent of which were the Chaks, the Magres, the Malīks and the Rainas. And it set in motion a series of events wherein the groups would oppose and support each other in a race for power and prominence. The rise of the nobles was also representative of the loss of power and prestige of the institution of the Sultan.

More everlasting than the continuing presence of the Baihaqī at the court was the arrival in Kashmir of the *Nūrbakshī* shaykh, Mīr Shams-al Dīn ʿIrakī in 1487 CE. The *Nūrbakshīs* were a messianic offshoot of the *Kubrawīs*. Significantly, in addition to the proselytizing zeal of the *Nurbakshīs* was the distinct Shi'a coloring of the order which resulted in opening sectarian divisions within the Muslim community, adding another dimension to the ongoing climate of intrigue and plots amongst the nobles vying for power. The conversion of the powerful Chak clan to the Shi'a faith, the dissension within the older *Kubrawī* order in their reception of the *Nurbakshīs* and the reaction among more orthodox group of Sunni nobles, preachers and Sufis left their mark on the affairs of the land. And in the continuing political turmoil, the *Reshīs*, with their apolitical outlook, alone remained largely unaffected by these happenings. The pluralistic nature of Kashmiri society in early sixteenth century CE, which Mīr Shams-al Dīn sought to change, can be viewed in the words of his biographer:

> Such atheistic and idolatrous practices continue to be observed in the houses of scholars, theologians and leading personalities of this land (Kashmir). They observe all the festivals and feasts of infidels and polytheists. The family members of the elders and leading persons of this land, especially their womenfolk, do not do anything without the permission of the infidels and permission of astrologers. In fact, in all activities of daily life like eating, drinking, sleeping, rising from sleep, travel and rest, astronomers and polytheists have a role to play[38].

This period of strife and dissension in Kashmir runs parallel with the commencement and consolidation of the Mughal Empire in India, established by Emperor Babur (r. 1526–1530 CE). While the Kashmiri nobles continued to vie against one another, plotting and counter-plotting, they also managed to unite in face of an external threat, which from now on would be the ever-looming presence of the Mughal Empire, and their ever-increasing interest in Kashmir. This unity against outside aggression is reflective of a Kashmiri-ness, of a unique Kashmiri identity that manifested itself at crucial moments of Kashmir's history.

Kashmir's first brush with the Mughals occurred in 1527 CE when Babur sent a contingent of Mughal troops with Sikander to help him acquire the throne from his cousin, Sultan Muhammad Shāh. The Kashmiri nobles united against the invading army under the leadership of Kājī Chak (d. 1545 CE)[39]. The second incursion of Mughal troops occurred soon after when they came to the aid of Kashmiri rebels seeking to overthrow Kājī Chak in 1528 CE. After successfully deposing Kājī Chak with the help of the Mughals, the Kashmiri nobles rewarded the Mughal army with presents, requested them to leave the valley. Both Sufi[40] and Hasan[41] highlights the care the nobles took to ensure that they would not be seen as collaborating with foreign invaders, given the distrust the foreigners would invoke amongst the Kashmiris. Soon after another, bigger Mughal contingent invaded Kashmir in 1531 CE under the orders of Emperor Humayun's (r. 1530–56 CE) brother Kāmran Mīrzā, the governor of Punjab. Initially successful, the Mughals managed to cross the mountain passes and reach Srinagar, before being forced to withdraw under a united Kashmiri front, again led by Kājī Chak[42].

While these initial inroads by the Mughal were successfully resisted by the Kashmiri nobles once they united in the face of the invaders, these failed attempts also resulted into a continuing interest of the Mughals in the land of Kashmir. This interest was temporarily offset by the troubles the Mughals were facing in the Indian heartland after the accession of Humayun.

In January 1533 CE, Mīrzā Haidar Duglat, the maternal uncle of Humayun, acting as the commander of Sultan Sʿaid Khan of Kasghar, invaded Kashmir after conquering Ladakh and Baltistan[43]. Surprising the ill-prepared Kashmiris, Mīrzā Haidar occupied the capital and other parts of the land. In face of the invader and his marauding army[44], Kashmiri noble once again united[45] and forced the Mīrzā to conclude a treaty of peace and withdraw from Kashmir in 1533 CE[46]. Interestingly, in their resistance against the Kasgharī army, the Kashmiri nobles also found it prudent to obtain religious decrees from the ulama, sanctifying their resistance as a jihad[47]. The need for a fatwa is indicative of the importance religion had assumed in the affairs of the state.

The unity forged amongst Kashmiri nobles was short-lived. In 1540 CE, Mīrzā Haidar appeared once again in Kashmir, leading Mughal forces sent by Humayun to aid Kājī's opponents. On reaching Srinagar, they set up Nāzuk Shāh as Sultan, though the power remained with Mīrzā Haidar during his eleven-year rule, from 1540 CE till his death in 1551 CE. Initially, Mīrzā ruled Kashmir in the name of Nāzuk Shāh, and on Humayun's return to India in 1545 CE in the name of the Mughal Emperor. Soon, however, Mīrzā's rule descended into open conflict with the Kashmiri nobles, after he slighted them, concentrating power in his own hands[48]. In his attempts to unify the country behind his rule in face of his foreignness, he turned to religious orthodoxy verging onto open sectarianism. Mīrzā's rule is the first instance during Muslim rule of Kashmir when an attempt was made to promote sense of political unity in the land based on a confessional identity. The single-mindedness of the Mughal conqueror on the issue finally proved his undoing, when the Kashmiri nobles in spite of their differing sectarian identities united once more against a foreigner, resulting in Mīrzā Haidar's death and the return of nominal sovereignty to *Shahmīrīs*.

The accession of Ghazī Shāh Chak (r. 1555–63 CE) resulted in the establishment of the short-lived Chak dynasty, who ruled Kashmir for 31 years before it was annexed by Akbar in 1586 CE. The rule of the Chaks was marked by a fierce resistance to the encroaching Mughal Empire to retain the independence of this mountainous kingdom. All the six Chak Sultans had to deal with internal dissensions and repeated

Mughal intrusions. In defiance of the Mughal Emperor Akbar, the later Chak Sultans also adopted the title of *Pādshāh* (Great King) as opposed to the traditional title of Sultan. The Chak rule in Kashmir coincides with a period of steady expansionism of the Mughal Empire who, under Akbar, made repeated and determined attempts at conquering Kashmir[49]. Given the interest exhibited by the Mughals in Kashmir since the time of Babur, its incorporation was seen by the Mughals as the logical culmination of an empire-building process.

Cultural and architectural traditions

The nearly one and a half century in the aftermath of Shahāb al-Dīn's rule represents both the highpoints of Kashmiri Sultanate as well as its unraveling. It also represents the consolidation of the architectural traditions associated with Muslim faith in Kashmir which were first established in the sacral Islamic architecture of Kashmir in the first three decades of Muslim rule as we have seen in the previous chapter. It also marks the gradual introduction of Persianate influences in the region following the advent of Sufis and missionaries from these areas.

The architecture of this period follows two distinctly different traditions – a continuation of the indigenous system of wooden and masonry construction already established and a style of masonry construction with domes and arches as seen in funerary architecture as well as in the construction of at least one specific mosque from this period, derived from Timurid architectural practices. While continuing to patronize the local building traditions, at least two successive Sultans, Sikander and Zain-al Ābidīn, made a conscious endeavor to promote a sense of cultural unity with the Persianate-Islamic world. Mīrzā Haidar, who was well versed in the artistic and cultural traditions of the Timurid court, recorded his appreciation of the vibrant craftsmanship available in the sultanate of Kashmir in these words:

> [...] In Kashmir one meets with all those arts and crafts which are, in most cities, uncommon [...] In the whole of Mavara-un-Nahr, except in Samarqand and Bukhara, these are nowhere to be met with, while in Kashmir they are even abundant[50].

It is in the genre of funerary architecture that we see earliest example of Persian influence in Kashmir, in the designing of the mausoleum of Sultan Quṭub-al Dīn [Figure 3.1]. The mausoleum, which was built by the Sultan at Langaratta in Srinagar, is the earliest example of a coming together of two different architectural traditions, in a curious style, which is not of fusion but of hesitant experimentation. The mausoleum was constructed in vicinity of tomb of the *Kubrawī* saint, Pīr Hājjī Muhammad Balkhī, who on Mīr Sayyid ʿAli's departure served as the spiritual mentor of the

Figure 3.1 *Mazar* of Sultan Quṭub-al Dīn, trefoil arched opening in the eastern façade, Srinagar: 2015, © Hakim Sameer Hamdani.

Quṭub-al Dīn. The building finds mention in a number of overviews of Muslim architecture in Kashmir. Cunningham identifies the building as the site of the ancient stone temple of Vishnu Ranasvamian, founded by King Ranaditya but confuses the mausoleum with the shrine of Pīr Hājjī which is also located within the same compound[51]. Goetz[52] also identifies the site with the shrine of Pīr Hājjī, though he associates the ruins to a far later date – eighth century CE.

The building plan itself comprises a regular octagon with the inner diameter of 12.1m with rectangular offset projecting in the four cardinal directions. With dressed stone masonry up till plinth level (1.94m) on the outer façade, the structure comprises an inner core of rubble masonry in lime mortar. The superstructure is also in rubble stone masonry, which probably was plastered on the external façade. The projection on the western side also forms the entrance to the structure and is framed by a trefoil stone arch – an arch sourced from an older temple site. The rear projection facing the gateway also has a similar stone panel with three arch openings which seem to have been originally filled in with masonry. Based on a centralized octagonal plan, it is not clear whether the structure was ever completed as a building or merely comprised the existing stone masonry plinth with a screening compound wall. The plan suggests a

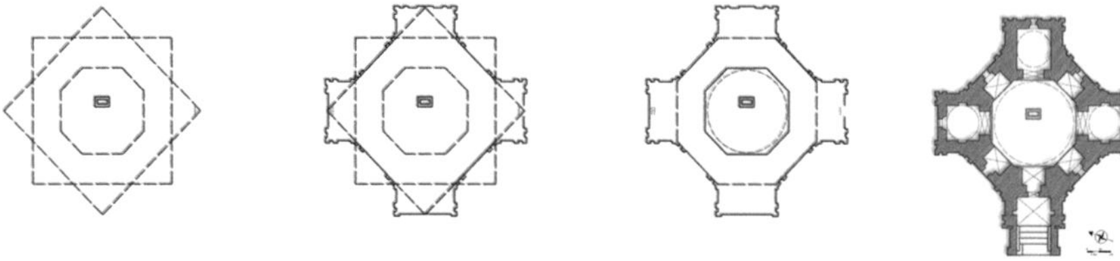

Figure 3.2 Centralized octagonal plan: both at the *Mazar* of Quṭub-al Dīn and Dumath, the octagonal plan is achieved through rotation of a square, with rectangular projections along the main cardinal directions, © Hakim Sameer Hamdani.

domed roof, but we find no description of the building in the local vernacular sources. Importantly, the building is the first instance of a centralized, octagonal plan introduced to Kashmir, which also served as the prototype for *Dumath*, the mausoleum Zain-al Ābidīn constructed for his mother [Figure 3.2]. The building also finds a mention in Tadgell's overview of the Islamic architecture, though he confuses the *Dumath* with the tomb of Pīr Hājjī Muhammed[53].

The cenotaphs, located not at the center but rather oddly along the periphery, also indicates that the space was intended to be used economically for future burials. This is a feature that also gets repeated at the *Dumath*. Most probably, the structure was never completed and only an enclosure wall was constructed on top of the plinth much like the royal cemetery of the *Shahmīrī* sultans, *Mazar-i Salātīn.*

The earliest example of a centralized plan in the Islamic world is the Qubat-al Sakhra: dome of the Rock (c. 695 CE) at Jerusalem which, because of its association with *Mi'rāj-al Nabī* (The Night of Prophets Accession), had acquired a highly symbolic image[54]. Because of the functional requirement of the Muslim prayer to accommodate linear rows of worshippers, such a design was deemed inappropriate in the designing of mosques. Thereafter, centralized plans based on circle and octagons found favor in the designing of mausoleums. Over the centuries, this plan became a common form for designing of mausoleums within the Islamic world[55]. In South Asia, the earliest example of an octagonal plan is the celebrated shrine of Rukn-i 'Alam at Multan[56] constructed in 1340 CE, followed by the mausoleum of Khān-i Jahān (c. 1369 CE) at Delhi. It is no small coincidence that almost a decade after the octagonal plan was used in Delhi, we find this form adopted in Kashmir. This happened in the wake of a steady influx of missionaries, artisans, craftsmen and builders from the west who imbibed the court with a distinctly Persianized flavor. The continuous import of talent of individuals and families during this period from the Persianate world resulted in gradual displacement of native non-Muslim population and its influences at the court. Over the centuries, local histographers would ascribe cultural and intellectual achievements of Kashmir during Sultanate rule to this émigré group, linking every major art and craft to a foreign origin: real or imagined.

The migration of skilled artisans and craftsmen (including architects) in search of higher social and financial rewards also helped in disseminating of established artistic and architectural ideas throughout the world of Islam[57]. That the form was associated with the construction of royal mausoleums and not tombs of the saints is also significant along with the fact that this experiment was limited to that single period of Muslim rule in Kashmir when the political stability and the financial resources of the state were assured.

The structure also brings to fore the way Muslim rulers of Kashmir reused materials as well as the building traditions they had inherited from the Buddhist and Hindu past. This is an important part of the evolutionary process of Muslim architecture in Kashmir, which has been mostly judged on the basis of accounts that came into vogue with writers from the colonial period. Most of these writers had their own preferences, to see architecture along with politics and culture being compartmentalized into isolated phases of Buddhist, Hindu and Muslim rule. Such a narrative also seeks to empower a paradigm of interaction of warrior elites destroying all examples of indigenous culture. The underlying theme being that all of these early Muslim buildings were constructed on top of destroyed Hindu and Buddhist sites. This is the hypothesis that is expanded by Kak, when he mentions the *mazar* of Quṭub-al Dīn as well as the plinth of the *Dumath* as being remnants of a Hindu temple. The assertion that these structures are based on prevalent 'square temple plan with the angles cut off and replaced by rectangular projections'[58] is not supported by any historical reference or archaeological evidence as seen in any stone temple of medieval Kashmir. The structure with an internal diameter of 12m could only have been spanned by a dome in the absence of any column support. The architectural and structural knowledge associated with this feat was something that came with Muslim artisan and builders of Central Asia as can be seen in Zain-al Ābidīn's *Dumath* and was not in vogue during pre-Muslim rule of Kashmir. None of the older stone temples of Kashmir had a corresponding span; at Martand, the grandest of the temples, the inner span of the sanctum is a mere 2.62m. Even at the *chatiya* at Parihaspora built by Lalitāditya, with a roof spanning 8.22m × 8.22m, sanctum was supported on four columns[59]. Kalhānā's description of the temple of Ranasvamian is also devoid of any reference to its peculiar shape or more importantly its span, which would have also resulted in an inspiring scale for both the inner chamber, the main sanctum, as well as the external appearance of the building. Where Kak is correct is in summarizing that material for the mausoleum was transplanted from a Hindu site[60]. This would also be seen in the construction of the *Dumath*.

The construction of the *Dumath* underlies the Timurid influences that the court of Kashmir was steadily imbibing [Plate 3]. The main features of the Timurid buildings with their monumental scale are the massive entrance portals, domes supported on high drums and a multi-colored façade decoration in mosaic tiles. The use of *naqāshī*, papier machie, *muqarna* was also employed in the decoration of internal surfaces in Timurid architecture. The *Dumath*, with an inner diameter of 6m, is a continuation of the octagonal plan that was first witnessed at Quṭub-al Dīn's *mazar*. Constructed on top of a dressed stone plinth in the local traditions, the superstructure is entirely in brick masonry, a technique that had been first employed in the construction of the Jamia Masjid of Srinagar. The building façade in each of the main eight faces along with the smaller side niches contains a blind pointed arch with smaller square window and ventilator panels infilled with brick *jāllī*. In continuation with the local building traditions, wooden lintels have been used to span the window openings.

The *Dumath* also retains the earliest extant example of glazed tile work employed on a building façade in Kashmir. Glazed and molded bricks in blue (turquoise) colors are 'studded at intervals in the exterior walls, the semi-circular brick projections on the drum of the main dome and the molded brick string courses and sunken panels on the drum of the cupolas'[61].

Glazed tile work along with *faience* mosaics has remained as one of the most distinct methods of façade decoration in Islamicate architecture. Though the technique of glazing was used by Assyrians, Egyptians as well as the Achaemenians, it was within the Islamicate culture and especially the Iranian-Central Asian region that the use of tile decor reached its visual splendor. Within the Islamicate world, the first reference to the use of glazed wall tiles is at Samarra, Iraq, in the new *Dar-al Khalīfa* (capital) of the Abbasid Caliph Al-Mu'tasim (r. 833-42 CE)[62]. The use of terracotta tile work in Ancient India has also been proven in various excavations dating from the Kushan period, though based on a limited color palette. In India, we find the use of glazed tile in Tughlaq architecture: turquoise and cobalt glazed square tile at Begampuri mosque (c. 1343 CE), Delhi. Coming back to Kashmir though, no example of glazed tile work predates the construction of *Dumath*, yet the use of terracotta tile work has been excavated at Harwan. Historically, the area is identified with the place where the Kushan king, Kanīshkā (125CE), convened the Fourth Buddhist Council. Coeval to the construction of Dumath, we find the use of under-glazed painted tile in the Jamāli-Kamālī shrine (c. 1536 CE) at Delhi. While the use of turquoise and green glazed tiles points towards Timurid influences, the motif employed in the tile could be of native origin, inspired by the stylized lilies or floral scroll as seen in the Kushan tiles of Harwan.

The *khānaqāh*, mosques and shrines of the sultanate: From the *sufa* to the *khānaqāh* at Alā'-al Dīnpūrā

The outpouring of architectural proclivity that took place during the reign of Sultan Sikander had its beginning in a modest enterprise, the construction of a *khānaqāh* at Alā'-al Dīnpūrā in remembrance of Mīr Sayyid ʿAli

Hamdanī. The Sayyid during his brief stay in Kashmir resided in a *sarai* at Alā'-al Dīnpūrā. Early Muslim historians record that the sultan (or Sayyid ʿAli himself) constructed a *ṣufa* for offering prayers in vicinity of the *sarai*[63]. Interestingly, we see that *ṣufa*, as a built element became a permanent part of the architectural vocabulary of the region. In Kashmir, the form that the *ṣufa* acquired, essentially comprise two to three feet high, open-to-sky rectangular or square platforms in ashlar (*devrī*) stone masonry. These *ṣufas* continued to be erected at sites of new *khānaqāh*, many of which exist today. During succeeding centuries, *ṣufas* became an integral part of the mosque design also, wherein it initially came to denote the open verandah preceding the mosque.

The use of the *ṣufa* was not confined to religious places alone. The writer of *Tuḥfatūl Aḥbāb* provides us with a brief description of how *ṣufa* was used, as a waiting space, both in the *sahn* (forecourt) of the sultan's palace and in the residences of the city elite. We hear about a large congregation that gathered on the *ṣufa* of Sultan Hasan Shāh's palace on his death[64].

At Alā'-al Dīnpūrā, it was only in 798 AH/1396 CE that Sayyid ʿAli's son, Sayyid Muhammad, got a *khānaqāh* constructed at the site of the *ṣufa*. The construction of the *khānaqāh* was undertaken by the reigning sultan, Sikander, and was completed in a year's time[65]. While no description of the *khānaqāh* from the period survives, we know that the building as a single-story structure that also included ancillary structure including a *langar*. Regarding the extent of the *khānaqāh*, the author of *Bahāristān-i Shāhī* writes:

> The foundation and the structure of the *khānaqāh* as laid by Āmīr Sayyid Hamdanī made it small and limited. Private houses of the inhabitants (of the locality) and the caretakers were so close to the walls of the *khānaqāh* that if a fire would break out in the locality, its flames would engulf the entire *khānaqāh*[66].

The *khānaqāh* was rebuilt during the reign of Sultan Zain-al Ābidīn[67] and again in 885 AH/1480 CE, 89 8AH/1493 CE and then vastly expanded during the reign of Sultan Muhammad Shāh on the advice of Mīr Shams-al Dīn ʿIraki[68]. Private houses and land in the vicinity of the *khānaqāh* was acquired and added to the *khānaqāh* precinct, which was reconstructed as a double-story building. The expanded site in addition to the *khānaqāh* included a public kitchen (*langar khāna*), a pottage house (*āsh khāna*) and store house for paddy[69]. The present outer boundary of site conforms to the expansion that were undertaken by Kājī Chak.

The *khānaqāh* built by Sayyid Muhammad was endowed (*waqf*) by the Sultan with revenue of three villages. The endowment deed which is preserved in the *khānaqāh* provides an overview of the custodianship of the *khānaqāh*, its working and organization. A somewhat assured regular income devoted to the *khānaqāh* helped in maintaining the social activities of the institution, of which the free kitchen service was the most significant. In addition to being the setting for close-knit fraternity of Sufis belonging to a particular Sufi order, the *khānaqāh* also served as institutions of imparting learning (madrasa), socializing centers (*langar*) as well as taking upon the task of congregation prayers (*nimāz-i jamāt*) that was traditionally associated with a mosque.

The various *khānaqāhs* that emerged in Kashmir would rival mosque both as an institution as well as an architectural edifice throughout medieval times. With a dedicated and learned team of Sufi masters, trained both in the polemics of theology and Sufism, the *khānaqāh* provided an intellectual leadership that was still unavailable to the community at large, which controlled the local *moḥala* mosques.

Additionally, some of the *khānaqāh*s served not only as a hospice for Sufis but also as a rest house where the Sultans of Kashmir would lodge their guests. The *Nūrbakshī* shaykh, 'Iraki, on his arrival in Srinagar was initially lodged in the *khānaqāh* of Malīk Ahmad, a common practice according to the author of *Tuḥfatūl.*

The *khānaqāh* that Sayyid Muhammad built would, over the years and centuries, help in enshrining the memory of Mīr Sayyid ʿAli Hamdani as the *bāniy-e Islam* (founder of Islam) in Kashmir[70]. In this created image of the saint, Sayyid ʿAli would not only be associated with the propagation of a faith, but he would also be projected as the man behind every major art and craft form that emerged in the Kashmir of medieval times.

While in history we see no evidence of large-scale proselytism being undertaken by Sayyid ʿAli in Kashmir, yet given the cultural developments that followed in the wake of his son's missionary activities, he did attain success. As a result of Sayyid Muhammad's efforts, the cultural forces that Sayyid ʿAli attempted to introduce in Kashmir would make their way into the court life of the Kashmiri Sultans.

From an unassuming *ṣufa* to a *khānaqāh* and then as *Khānaqāh-i Mʿaulā* (The Great *Khānaqāh*), the hospice of Mīr Sayyid ʿAli Hamdani [Plate 10] would, in the words of the seventeenth-century CE Kashmiri historian, Dedhmari, emerge as the unrivalled structure of the city[71]. It would be intertwined not only with the religious landscape of the country but also become an integral part of the political tapestry of the land, both in its celebrations as well as dissensions[72]. In the sacred geography of Kashmir, an earlier Muslim *tazkira nigār* would describe the *khānaqāh* as having 'attained the position of the second Kaaba in this country'[73].

Given the social relevance of *khānaqāh* as an institution in medieval Kashmir, by the beginning of sixteenth century CE, almost all major Sufi orders with a visible presence in the Persianate world had also established *khānaqāhs* in Srinagar.

Khānaqāh-i Nūrbakshiya at Zadibal

Barring limited textual references, we have no way of assessing the architectural quality of the *Khānaqāh-i Mʿaulā* during the Sultanate period, as the present building dates from late Mughal period. This loss also affects our understanding of most of the mosques and shrines dating from the Sultanate period which were either lost in fire or have been rebuilt in succeeding centuries. Nevertheless, the establishment of a *khānaqāh*, its actual construction and functioning is detailed out by the writer of *Tuḥfatūl*, who provides us with a detailed account of the proclivities of Mīr Shams-al Dīn in Kashmir along with a description of the construction of the *Khānaqāh -i Nūrbakshiya* (c. 910 AH/1503 CE) at Zadibal on the outskirts of Srinagar. Mīr Shams-al Dīn was associated with the Timurid court of Sultan Husayn Bayaqara (r. 1470–1507 CE) and was highly dismissive of Muslim culture of Kashmir. The author of *Tuḥfatūl* records 'Iraki's contempt for the existing *khānaqāh*s of Srinagar in these words:

> [...] *Khānaqāh*s in the city (Srinagar) were useless and not worth the name; at best these were like a caravanserai or the traveler's inn. No hospice in the town was fit for lent (*chillā*) for the seekers of the path to divinity, even the Amiriyyeh hospice (i.e., *Khānaqāh-i Mʿaulā*).[74]

Thus, in his construction of *Khānaqāh -i Nūrbakshiya,* 'Iraki sought to promote esthetics of the Persianized Timurid court. The actual construction of the *khānaqāh* was preceded by clearing of a forested area near the Mahasen temple in Kamraj (North Kashmir). The forest had been left untouched, as the local Muslim community held it be inviolate on account of it being associated with temple. Given Mīr's predilection towards widespread iconoclastic activities, along with the felling of trees, he also had the temple burnt down[75]. The dismissal of the notion of sacredness associated with forest sets Mīr and many of the non-Kashmiri missionaries apart from the local order of *Reshīs*, who not only nurtured such beliefs but were also responsible for actively undertaking planting of trees of shade and fruit for wayfarers, something that is recorded in Mughal accounts of the land also[76].

While the wood obtained from the forest was transported to the city on the onset of spring, the excavation at the site were completed during the winters, a practice that is still common in the vernacular architectural traditions of Kashmir. The building was conceived as a two-story structure, measuring 24.6m × 24.6m, with each floor comprising a double height hall[77]. The author of *Tuḥfatūl* records that while the lower floor had a ceiling height of 9.8m, the upper floor ceiling stood 7.3m high, with;

> Each floor divided between a central open space and small cubicle for solitary exercises along the sides[78].

Even at this period, the construction of a two-story *khānaqāh* was seen as a novelty in Kashmir, as is clear from the writings of *Tuḥfatūl*[79]. Equally noteworthy for the author of *Tuḥfatūl* is the fact that the *khānaqāh* was constructed without the use of wooden columns. The interior of the *khānaqāh* were well-decorated, and the walls were painted with calligraphic renditions of Qazi Muhammad Qudsī's verses in *thuluth* script. The monumental scale of the *khānaqāh* would have made the building a noteworthy structure in the city. The preference of the builders for a masonry structure would indicate that in large parts the *khānaqāh* was built based on arcuate construction. While such a construction system was not unknown to Kashmiris, as we see at *Dumath*, the *Khānaqāh –i Nūrbakshiya* provides the first instance these construction practices being employed for a *khānaqāh*.

What is especially interesting in the account of *Tuḥfatūl* is the mention of gardens surroundings the *khānaqāh,* which itself was located within a walled courtyard. Traces of the courtyard wall still exist at site in the form of large stone blocks. The immediate courtyard surrounding the *khānaqāh* was lined with water channels and airy pavilions (*bāradarī*). This is the first known instance in Kashmir, where we find mention of use of a landscape element associated with water, in a Muslim religious place.

From the written accounts we have of the *khānaqāh,* it is safe to posit that the building, its layout and its size was indebted to Timurid architectural traditions. A large central domed space, surrounded by smaller rooms can be found at the shrine – *khānaqāh* complex of Shaykh Ahmad Yasavi (d. 1166) constructed by Tīmūr. And, the court of Husayn Bayqara, 'Iraki's patron, was also responsible for construction of numerous *khānaqāh's* designs that would have served as inspiration for 'Iraki in Kashmir.

In the *khānaqāh*, 'Iraki presided over a seamless interaction of activities and events where dreams would be interpreted, events foretold, penances and rituals observed, devotes met, all within the realm of spiritual sovereignty represented by the *khānaqāh*[80]. Interestingly, as opposed to other such institutions, the *khānaqāh* of 'Iraki remained open to the public only for the five obligatory prayers. For the rest of the times, entry to the *khānaqāh* was open only to prominent Sufis and close associates of the 'Iraki, excluding a sense of exclusiveness and distance from the general public. Heavily involved in court politics, on account of which he was also briefly banished from Kashmir towards Ladakh, 'Iraki in his public dealings also imitated many of the customs, associated with power. The *Tuḥfatūl* likens the *khānaqāh* with Kabba, and records an instance where 'Iraki once asked a disciple to forgo a trip to Mecca for undertaking the haj and replace it with symbolic circumambulation of the *khānaqāh*[81]. While the representation of *khānaqāh* as Kaaba of mendicants was already established in Sufi writings outside Kashmir, this is the first such reference we find in Kashmir.

Following his death, a shrine (*rūżā*) was constructed within the *khānaqāh* compound over his grave, which served as a family burial chamber. The entire edifice along with the *khānaqāh* was destroyed by Mīrzā Haidar during his rule.

Khānaqāh-i Naū of Baba Khalil-al Lah, Nawa Kadal

The only *khānaqāh* dating from the Sultanate period, of which traces survive today, is from the time of Chak sultans. Kashmir's architectural development under the Chak rule has been lost to obscurity. Only passing textual references exist about construction of various *rūżā*, *khānaqāh,* madrasa and masjids during this period. Absence of any surviving building from the period makes it difficult to analyze how far architecture in this period was molded on the older Shahmīrī traditions, and if any new experiments and stylistic innovations were undertaken. Though during their brief rule, the Chak Sultans were heavily involved in internal as well as external conflicts, yet they were also involved in sustained if limited architectural proclivity. This includes the construction of the *khānaqāh, sarai* and shrine of the *Nūrbakshiya* saint, Baba Hasan Ali, the reconstruction of the *rūżā* and mosque of Shaykh Nūr-al Dīn at Char and the establishment of the madrasa of Sultan Husayn Shāh at Dal Hasanyar and the *Khānaqāh* Bābā Khalil-al Lah at Nawa Kadal. Of these buildings only the ruins of the *Khānaqāh* Bābā Khalil-āl Lah exist today, in a state that help us in achieving an overview of how the contours of Muslim architecture had evolved during the Chak period.

The *khānaqāh* also known as *Khānaqāh-i Naū*[82] was constructed by the Chaks for Bābā Khalil-al Lah (d.1000 AH/1591 CE)[83], a Shi'a preacher intimately connected with the Chak court[84]. Unfortunately, no information is available about which of the Chak Sultans was responsible for the construction. The earliest record of Khalils's association with the Chak court is from the time of Sultan ʿAli Shah (r. 1570–1579 CE). During the reign of Sultan Yūsuf Shāh (r.1579–86 CE), Khalil-al Lah intervened at numerous times between the sultan and rebelling nobles. And it is from this period that we have the first textual reference to Khalil's *khānaqāh* as the site[85] used for holding parleys between Yūsuf Shāh and the nobles[86].

The ruins of the *khānaqāh* are located on the right bank of the river Jhelum near Nawa Kadal. A wide open *ghāt* leads from the river to the *khānaqāh*, which is located to the north of the *ghat.* The location of the *khānaqāh* within the center of the historic Srinagar city is representative of how prominent Muslim religious places in the city were constructed in close proximity to the river. Within the Srinagar city, today the ruins of *khānaqāh* represent the third such building to be found in vicinity of the Jhelum, the other two being the *khānaqāh* at Būlbūl lanker, and the *Khānaqāh-i Mʿaulā.*

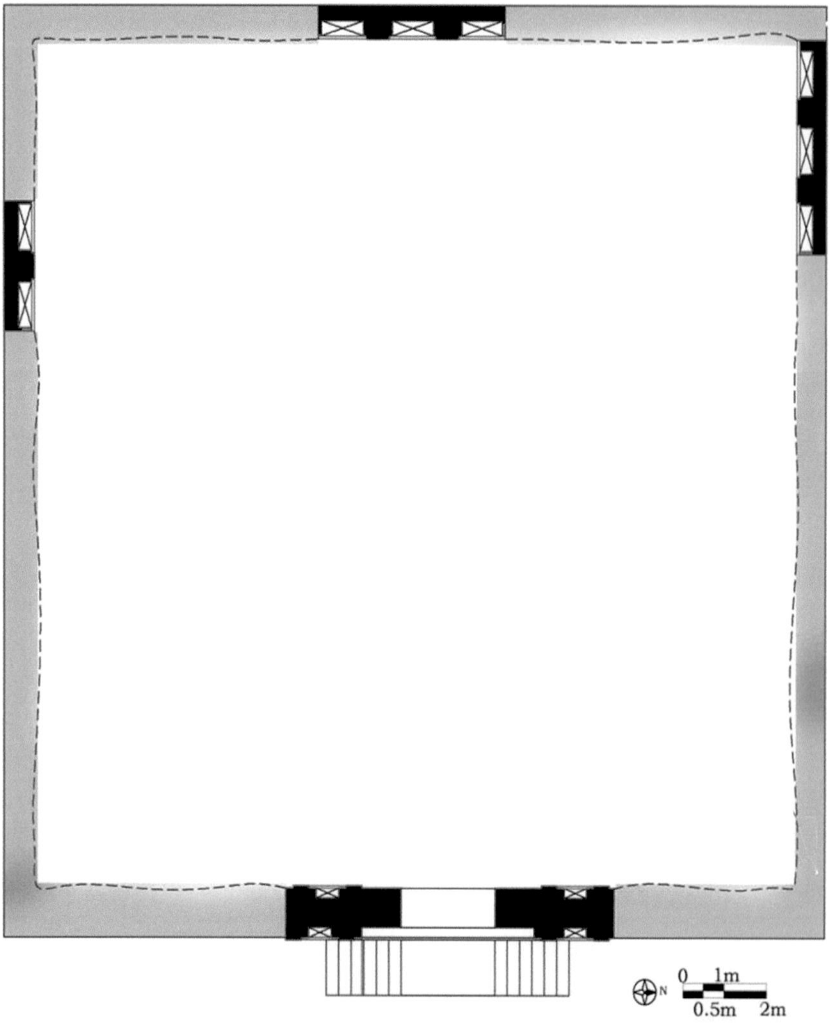

Figure 3.3 Plan of *Khānaqāh-i Naū,* © Hakim Sameer Hamdani.

The building plan comprises a square with an outer measurement of 20.3m × 20.3m, aligned so that the western wall is perpendicular to *qiblā* [Figure 3.3]. The superstructure which comprises brick masonry lies on a top of a high stone plinth (2.1m) made of large blocks of stone laid in regular courses. While the stone blocks fit well in the plinth, but a close examination reveals that the stones have been acquired from an older site, as some of the stone blocks are clearly remnants of a door frame[87]. At the time of its construction, the *khānaqāh* must have commanded a fine view of the river and the *ghāt*, and the high plinth of the building must have added to the sense of scale associated with it. Interestingly, the placement of a building on a high plinth or platform is an architectural scheme totally lacking in the older buildings and structures associated with Islam in Kashmir. Whereas earlier building related to Muslim worship in Kashmir try to merge the structure with the immediate surroundings, we find that in mosques and *khānaqāhs* constructed from fifteenth century CE onwards, there was a determined attempt to design the building on a more monumental scale. The *khānaqāh* at Nawa Kadal is designed on that principal of a building that stands apart from the surroundings and commands a visual prominence of the site, in this instance the river front. Given that river borne transport was the main means of transportation in the city way down till late nineteenth century CE, a visually dominating building along the river commanded the sight of every passerby, native as well as visitor. By building monumental commanding structures along the river front, Muslim builders and their patrons were not only catering to a need, but also creating an image – an image of a politically dominant Muslim community.

The entry to the *khānaqāh* is from a flight of steps leading to a centrally placed arched opening on the main eastern façade[88]. The 2.3m wide gateway opening is reminiscent of a central portal that was first seen at Jamia Masjid, Srinagar, but lacks both the dimensions and the bold projecting of the latter. The entrance gateway of the *khānaqāh* is designed as a shallow *pīshtāq*, decorated with a series of blind arches on the surrounding rectangular frame. Interestingly, the rectangular frame projects only slightly from the surrounding masonry walls of the *khānaqāh*, indicative of an architectural hesitancy related to the introduction of a new architectural feature.

The shape of the arches, whether in the main entrance gateway or in the wall arcade, is not the quintessential Kashmiri trefoil arch, pre-dating the Muslim rule in Kashmir, but the pointed arch favored in Persianate architecture. We find similar arches in the mosque at Zaina lank as well as the shrine of Malīk Jalāl-al Dīn Thakur, both constructed during the rule of Zain-al Ābidīn, which are also the earliest extant use of such an arch profile in Kashmir. At the *Khānaqāh-i Naū*, the arch over the entrance gateway is extremely shallow with a rise to span ratio of 1:3.

Internally, the *khānaqāh* would have comprised an enclosed space of 18.5m × 18.5m. Remnants of the brick masonry wall can still be seen on all four sides. From what remains of the wall, it is clear that the superstructure comprised a masonry arcade, with the arches opening on the western side facing the *qiblā* wall, having a masonry infill. While the inner walls comprise a series of arched niches, traces of arched projection can also be seen in the outer façade. The use of projecting brick band for surface decoration can be first seen at the mosque at Zaina lank.

Presently, the *khānaqāh* serves as an enclosed garden with no trace left of how the inner spaces might have been utilized. Till the time archaeological excavation is carried out at the site, our understanding of the inner spatial layout of the building and its structural system will be incomplete. Nevertheless, we can safely summarize, based on our knowledge of the *khānaqāh* at Zadibal, that the central space would have been surrounded by smaller chambers on the northern and southern side for solitary worship, the *chillā khāna*, which would also mark building as a *khānaqāh* linked with *Nūrbakshiya* order.

The *Khānaqāh-i Naū* falls within an evolving architectural style which was more and more Persianized. Stylistically, its form is a continuation of both the *Khānaqāh-i Nūrbakshiya* and the mosque at Zaina lank, both representative of non-native architectural form.

Mosque near Madin Ṣāhab and Malīk Ṣāhab

Some 100m to the south of the famous fourteenth-century CE mosque and shrine of Madnī are to be found the ruins of a medieval stone temple. The ruins are located in an area that was included in Naushera, the capital city built by Sultan Zain-al Ābidīn.

The plan of the temple consists of the square chamber (12.8 × 12.75m) forming the original plinth, with the entrance portico located centrally on the southern side [Figure 3.4]. Two stone pillars framing the entrance doorway, and part of the stone door frame, are still preserved at site. Significantly, there is an extension to the temples on the northern side measuring around 8.1 × 7.5m, an addition that marks the conversion of the temple to a mosque. The addition also helps in orienting the building along the more traditional north-south axis, functionally suited with the needs of Muslim worship, for a linear hall oriented parallel to the *qiblā* (western) wall.

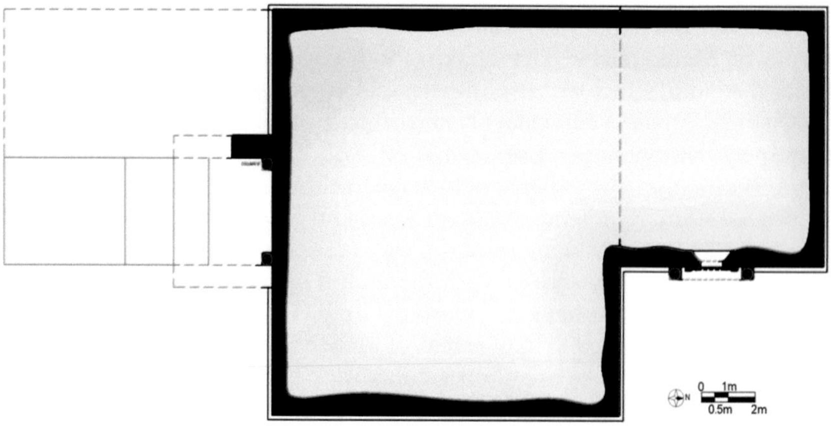

Figure 3.4 Plan of the temple, showing mosque extension, © Hakim Sameer Hamdani.

The eastern façade of the extension also served as the new entrance to this refurbished mosque, with a pillared portico preceding the doorway. The location of the new entrance doorway on the eastern wall facing the *miḥrāb* is also a preferred axis of approach as opposed to the cumbersome sideway entrance. Though functionally the new additions to the temple were more in keeping with a mosque design of a linear layout, yet the plan remained a misfit with its juxtaposition of two squares.

The extension is undertaken in material serviced from the site, with the plinth and the entrance portico replicating the same design as seen in the temple [Figure 3.5]. The construction of the extension again underlies the fact that the initial Muslim structures of Kashmir followed the tradition of building in stone, with detailing highly reminiscent of the local temple architecture. This is relevant while dating some of the older mosques and shrines of Kashmir, questioning the assumption that the transition from a Hindu to Muslim rule in Kashmir also resulted in a complete break of the existing architectural traditions. It is correct that the initial Muslim religious architecture of Kashmir does not display a finesse of detailing, even character and drive, associated with what was undertaken in the region in the past. But such a realization has to be tempered with both the realities of the society

Figure 3.5 Extension to the temple on the northern side. Note how the builders have tried to match the original texture of the structure in their reconstruction, Srinagar: 2018, © Hakim Sameer Hamdani.

in the medieval Kashmir under the Muslim Sultans as well as what they inherited in terms of architectural traditions and skills. Goetz has rightly determined the preponderance of wooden architecture in construction of temples as we come closer to the Muslim rule, a consequence of political dissensions and dwindling resources[89]. This resulted in a 'vernacularization' of the great monumental stone tradition of Kashmir, and it was this wood and stone architectural hybrid that served as the immediate 'living tradition' from which the Muslim builders of the fourteenth and early fifteenth century built upon.

The construction of the mosque must have been coeval with the establishment of Naushera as the capital city during early fifteenth century CE, and the subsequent dislocation of significant members of the court. This is also supported by the absence of any textual reference to Muslim presence in the area prior to the setting up of the new capital. The re-appropriation of a temple into a mosque can also be seen as representative of a substantial Muslim presence in the court, making use of available building material, in this case that of a temple, to put a place of worship in the new capital. Nevertheless, the limitations of the plan soon led to it being abandoned and construction of new place of worship – the mosque of Madnī.

Of the surviving building features at site linked with the extension, the most interesting element is the stone entablature on top of the doorway, which is also significant because of the use of Islamic epigraphy. This is the first such instance of decorating a building with a feature associated with Islamic iconography and uses the Prophetic tradition: those who construct the mosque of Allah, for them Allah constructs a house in heaven.

The inscription conveys both a sense of Islamic piety as well as a clear indication that a revered temple is now an equally revered mosque. Carved in low relief and making use of the highly recognizable *thuluth* script, the epigraphy introduces a Muslim message in a style particularly favored in monumental settings since the tenth and the eleventh century CE[90]. By placing the text in bold and an easily readable script at a prominent part of the building, it also undertakes to popularize an alien Arabic script associated with Quran to a Kashmiri audience undergoing through a conversion process.

The epigraph carrying the Prophet's Hadith is repeated in another mosque dating to the Sultanate period, situated at Safa Kadal (Srinagar). This small modest single-story mosque measuring 6.75m × 6.64m was constructed by Malīk Ahmad (d. 887 AH/1482 CE), the vizier of Sultan Hasan Shāh. On his death, Yatoo was buried in the premises of the mosque compound and today a shrine stands over it. Like many of the Muslim religious places of Srinagar dating from the Sultanate period, the mosque of Malīk Ahmad Yatoo is located on the banks of the Jhelum River and is built in the slope of the site. Consequently, two sides of the building serve as a retaining wall. The main entrance to this small structure is from the eastern side from a centrally located doorway looking onto the *miḥrāb*, flanked by a floor-length rectangular window on either side. Internally, the building comprises

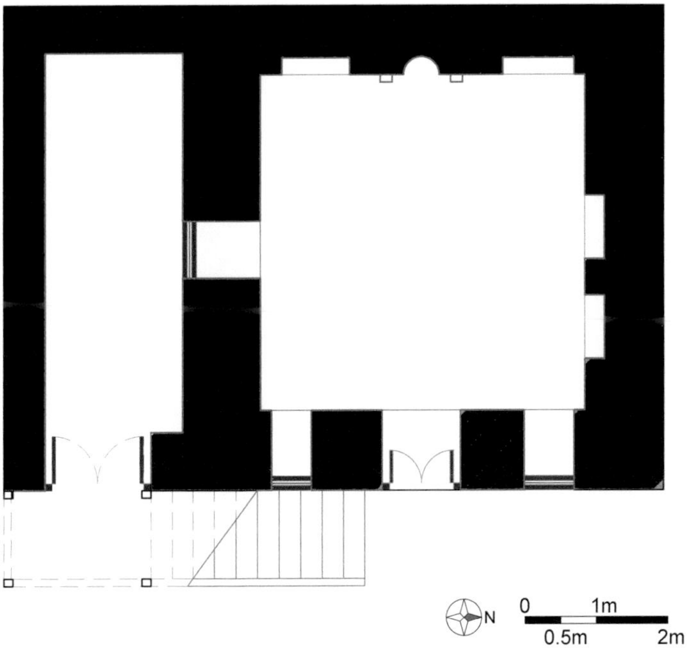

Figure 3.6 Malik Ṣāhab mosque, plan, © Hakim Sameer Hamdani.

of a single low-height chamber measuring 4.55m × 4.52m [Figure 3.6]. Architecturally, the most significant feature of this modest building is the stone entablature over the main door. Three separate inscriptions in Arabic are located within the elaborate stone entablature, interspersed with floral patterns. The inscription gives 878 AH/1473-74 CE[91] as the date of construction of the mosque [Figure 3.7]. Another inscription commemorates Malīk Ahmad as the patron while the main inscription over the doorway comprises the Prophetic tradition that is also seen at the mosque-temple structure near Madin Ṣāhab. All the inscriptions are once again in the *thuluth* script. Together, the mosque of Malik Ahmad along with the mosque at Madin Ṣāhab provides us with some of the earliest epigraphic evidence from the Sultanate period.

It is interesting that the earliest examples of Islamic epigraphy that we come across in Kashmir are based on the same Prophetic saying, mentioning the merits of constructing mosque. Such a public injunction is more in the nature of encouraging a sense of religious piety in the community rather than propagating the dominating message of a victorious religion. This is in sharp contrast to what occurred in the Indian mainland two centuries before, where 'one of the principal functions of Islamic epigraphs in late twelfth-century India was to warn the non-Muslim majority to accept Islam'[92].

Figure 3.7 Malik Ṣāhab mosque, entrance door to the building framed by a semi-circular pediment, Srinagar: 2017, © Hakim Sameer Hamdani.

The mosque of Madnī at Naushera, Srinagar

One of the other earliest examples of Muslim architecture in Kashmir surviving in totality is the mosque of Madnī at Srinagar. The mosque of Madnī is located on a slightly elevated piece of land and was constructed in 848 AH/1444 CE by a leading Muslim émigré from the Arabian Peninsula, Sayyid Muhammad Madnī [Plate 4]. The mosque is essentially part of a small complex comprising four self-enclosed structures not all of which date to the same period. In addition to the main mosque, this precinct includes a hammam and the tomb of the saint and also an entrance gateway which is the only surviving structure in Kashmir to retain fragments of the glazed tile

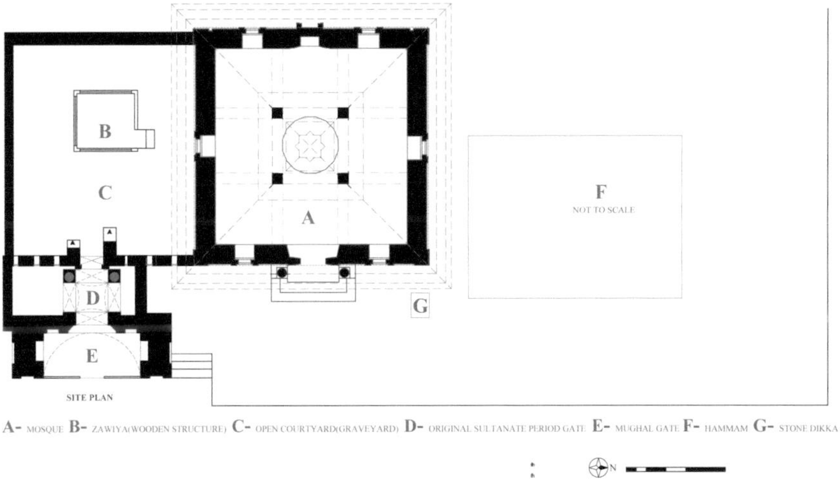

Figure 3.8 Mosque of Madnī, plan of the precinct, © Hakim Sameer Hamdani.

surface. While the mosque and the structure serving as the shrine date back to the fifteenth century CE, the gateway is a Mughal construction. Remnants of a nineteenth century CE hammam could be seen at the site till late 1980s, the present structure being a modern-day reconstruction [Figure 3.8].

Based on a square plan, the mosque of Madni measures about 11.58m × 11.88m. The basic design of this small mosque echoes the principles that were established in designing the Mīr mosque at Pampore. Dedhmārī mentions that the dimensions of the mosque were designed so as to correspond to the measurements of Kaaba[93], which seems to be the case, barring for a slight variation in one of the sides. As such, it would be the first recorded instance of an explicit symbolic imagery being used in designing and construction of a mosque in Kashmir.

The basic form of the Madnī mosque is of a low-lying cuboid with a stepped roofed and pyramidal spire. The roof with its pyramidal arrangement in multiple tiers of sloped roof with a square (or an octagonal) pavilion in the center makes its first presence in the mosque of Madnī. From henceforth, it would serve as the leitmotif of Muslim religious architecture in Kashmir. Apart from the presence of the pavilion, this roof profile is directly derived from a similar arrangement in the medieval stone temples of Kashmir, and with its soaring visual impact would remain the most distinct and defining feature of a Kashmiri mosque, *khānaqāh* or a shrine.

Internally, the wooden ceiling of Madnī's mosque is supported on four wooden columns that divide the plan into three bays of nine modules: the quintessential nine-bay plan. While the use of nine-bay plan is well represented within Muslim communities from tenth century CE onwards, the nearest early example being the mosque of Hājjī Piyāda (c. nineth century CE or earlier), the plan of Madnī's mosque owes its inspiration to native vernacular traditions of building with wood as seen at Alchi. The columns rest on plain stone base, the wooden capital bears a close resemblance to its Tibetan counterparts. The central module is covered with a sixteen-sided wooden pseudo-dome. The dome as well as the rest of the ceiling is covered with *khatmband*[94] work which has been painted. The *khatamband* work probably dates from the repairs carried out in the 19th century. Though many contemporary historians believe that the art of *khatamband* was popularized during the Sultanate period, but we have no textual or archaeological evidence for this assertion. The earliest example of *khatamband* work is to be found at *Khānaqāh-i Mʿaulā* which again dates from the Mughal period.

Of the original decorative features in the mosque, the wooden door and corbelled eaves are the most distinct and historically important. They represent the earliest surviving example of decorative wood work in Kashmir, whether of pre-Muslim or specifically of the Muslim period itself. Though the door, which has also been replicated in the old gateway of the adjoining tomb, is supposed to date back to Zain-al Ābidīn's time, it is by no means certain and could easily be a replacement from the Mughal period. Comprising two unequal shutters carved from a single plank of wood, each shutter in turn comprises seven panels decorated with foliate arabesque motifs, with each alternative panel raised. The door of Madnī's mosque has been stylistically compared to what is described as the door from the tomb of Mahmud at Ghazni[95]. Notwithstanding the actual source and date of construction, this doorway represents a highpoint of Kashmiri wood carving from the medieval times.

The building possesses a stone plinth, which has given rise to the idea that it was constructed on top of a Hindu temple. There is a possibility that some of the material from the nearby mosque/temple described before might have been used in the construction of the building. Nevertheless, the detailing and the construction, along with the symbolic reference to its size, are clear indications of the building's construction as a composed whole, and its resemblance to the mosque at Pampore is striking both in form as well as in some of the essential details.

The door to the building is framed by a trefoil-arched masonry porch supported on fluted stone columns. The columns as well as the stone entablature over the door are detailed in the traditional Hindu style, also reminiscent of the Pampore mosque. The only significant departure being the use of epigraphy in the entablature and in side panels inserted in the main eastern wall.[96]

The stone entablature is inscribed with the verses comprising the *shahāda* (profession of faith) and the name of the reigning sultan, Zain-al Ābidīn. The use of the trefoil brick masonry arch in the porch as well as in the window openings provides historical continuity with the building traditions of the past wherein it was a prominent architectural feature.

While in the Hindu model, the trefoil served a decorative purpose, the builders of the mosque utilized it as a true arch for spanning the openings and transferring of the load. Another subtle but significant difference lies in the silhouette of the arch, whereas the Hindu version has a circular profile, the one employed by the builders here has a pointed outline with a dip at the crown due to a slight outward curve. The window openings are framed by continuous band of brick pilasters and molded brick work at the top, the entire facade being originally plastered. The miḥrāb niche is again framed by a trefoil arch with the spandrels decorated with arabesque motifs also seen on the wooden door [Figure 3.9]. The exposed patchwork of brick and stone masonry visible on the building façade is of immense archaeological importance and brings to fore the way builders experimented with various materials and decorative features in their endeavor to establish a new architectural vocabulary. The mosque of Madnī also possesses a stone *dikkā* (bench), which would indicate that large congregational prayers used to take place here, outside the walled premises of the small stone building.

The shrine of Madnī comprises an open square courtyard (10.3m × 9.2m) appended to the mosque on the southern side. A 3.2m high stone wall encloses this area on three sides, with an entrance gateway located on the east. The gateway with its wooden door replicates the main entrance portico of the mosque, though on a smaller scale. The grave of Madnī which is located in the center is surrounded by numerous other graves belonging to members of his family. As a part of the reconstruction work undertakes in 1980s, a wooden sarcophagus has been erected on top of Madnī's graves. Oral traditions prevalent amongst the locals of the area indicate that the sarcophagus was a part of the original shrine design, which because of lack of maintenance had fallen prey to decay. A series of niches are located at the base of the stone platform supporting the cenotaph itself used for holding *tcheng* (clay lamps) much like the *chinī khānas*. Of special interest is the presence of stone *jālī* work in two small niches located in the lower hall of the eastern wall. These stone *jālīs* are the earliest examples of *jālī* work in Kashmir, whether of stone or wood. Featuring vegetal inspired motifs, they are different from the other surviving specimens of stone *jālī* at Mullā Shāh masjid, a seventeenth century CE Mughal structure which features geometrical design. The entire courtyard is paved with stone and also contains a stone drain for letting of surface water. Again, this is a feature that we find in many of the temple and *vihāras* quadrangles of the more ancient past and formed an essential device of draining accumulated snow or rain water.

The mosque complex of Madnī depicts the first known instance of symbolic imagery being employed in designing of a mosque in Kashmir. Constructed in the mid-fifteenth century CE, the ensemble of buildings at the site are representative of a cultural milieu that incorporated a multi-faith

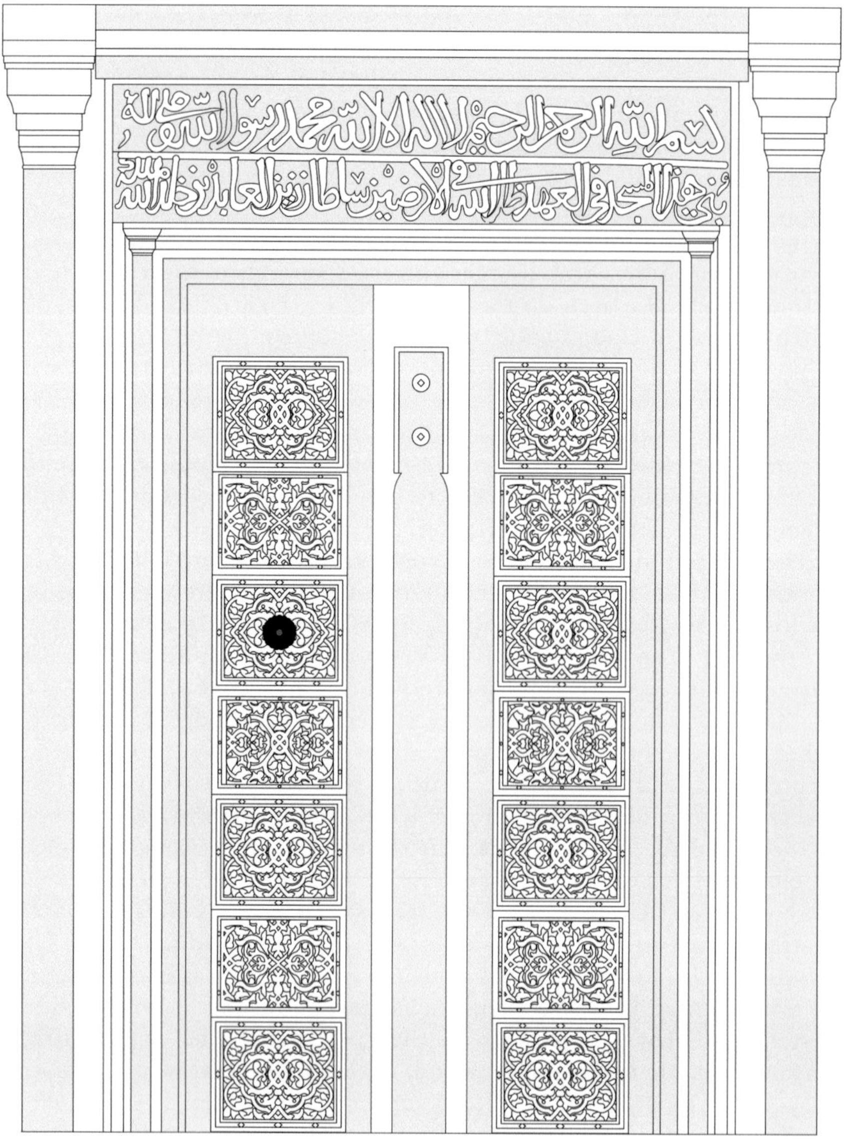

Figure 3.9 Mosque of Madnī: entrance doorway to the tomb. The wooden door of both the tomb and the mosque comprises a series of panels with arabesque (*islim*) motifs, Srinagar, © INTACH, Kashmir.

cosmopolitan society. Built for a non-native saint, the construction employs native architectural vocabulary which had, after more than a century of Muslim rule, firmly established itself as the language of Muslim religious architecture in the region.

Jamia Masjid and the introduction of *iwan*

The first successful attempt of building at a monumental scale under the Sultans of Kashmir is the construction of the Jamia Masjid at Srinagar. The mosque, in terms of its scale alone, is a worthy addition to the overall world survey of fourteenth-century Islamic architecture [Plate 5].

Of the various Muslim monuments of Kashmir, the Jamia Masjid of Srinagar is the most documented. A description of the building with its courtyard plan is found in all prominent architectural surveys of Kashmir as well as political histories of the region. A measured drawing of the building was also undertaken by the ASI in 1906–07 before undertaking repairs at the site during the early 1930s. The building and its repeated reconstruction also find a mention in the native Persian histories of Kashmir which have meticulously recorded each date of reconstruction and the individuals involved in these repairs. While the present structure[97]dates to the reconstruction undertaken by Aurangzeb in 1677 CE, the mosque in terms of its overall plan and style has remained true to the original design despite repeated reconstructions[98].

The construction of the Jamia at Sikandarpur (present-day Nowhata) was undertaken by Sultan Sikander, and the work was completed in 840 AH/1402 CE[99]. The construction of the mosque can be seen as an example of the sultan's religious fervor and zeal or more simply a practical need to accommodate a significant amount of worshippers. It is also indicative of the resources available with the Sultanate to undertake such a building activity.

The Jamia was constructed at the edge of the settlement, in between Quṭub-al Dīnpūrā and the western flanks of the Hari Parbat hillock. The construction involved cutting of the slope of the hillock so as to create a large, flat level land required for the construction of the mosque. The cut part of the hillock was retained by arched masonry wall which survived till early part of the twentieth century CE. The traditional approach to the mosque was from narrow streets leading into the city located to the west of the Jamia, with dense residential areas surrounding the mosque on its south, north and western side. Historically, to the east of the mosque, on the elevated slopes of the hillock were located two major Muslim cemeteries of the city, *Mazar-i Kalān* and Malkha.

The mosque with an external measurement of 117m × 115.7m, is built on the courtyard plan with four *iwans*[100] surrounding a central open courtyard (71.6m. × 76.2m) [Figure 3.10]. The main as well as the side prayer halls are based on the principal of a hypostyle hall, with a basic square module (~ 4.6m × 4.4m) defined by four columns, acting as structural supports. The principal western hall (113m × 19.0m) is four bays deep, with the main aisle (8.9m) opening towards the *miḥrāb* taking the shape of an *iwan* with a higher ceiling (15.5m) as compared to the rest of the hall (8.6m).

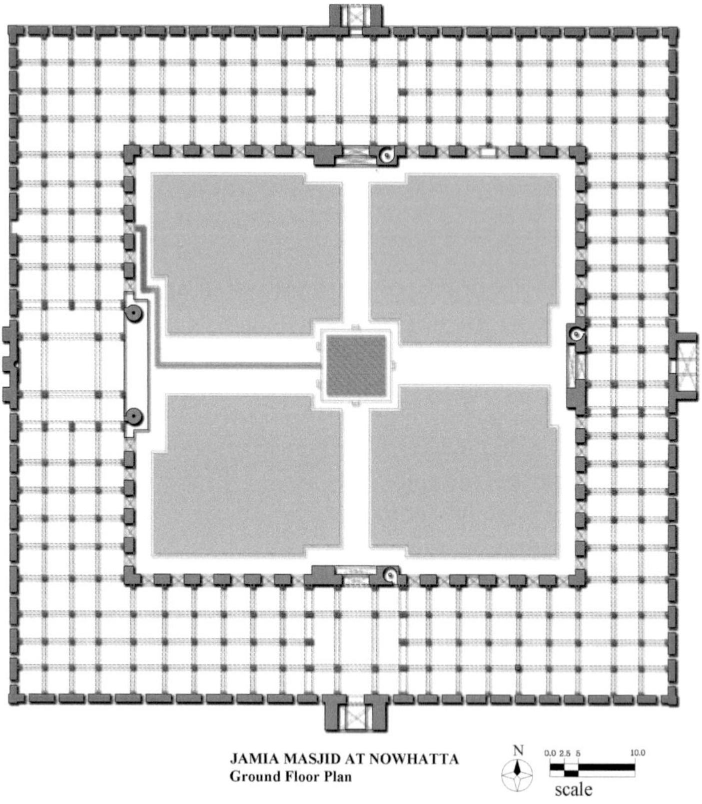

Figure 3.10 Jamia Masjid: Ground floor plan of the mosque with the centrally located *hauz* (pool) in the courtyard, © INTACH, Kashmir.

The four-*iwan* plan seen at Jamia Srinagar was introduced in the Islamic world in eleventh century CE, and is associated with the Seljuks, and had thereafter emerged as the most prominent and widespread form of the Friday or Jamia mosque in Iran. The plan remained an essential feature of what has been defined as the Iranian mosque, a form that did not remain confined to the land of its origin alone, but became an accepted model for areas as widespread and diverse as Transoxiana and India. The first four-*iwan* mosque in India, the Begampur Friday mosque (94m × 90m), had been constructed by the Tughlaqs at their capital, Jahānpanāh, in 1343 CE, virtually around the same time when the Shahmīrī sultanate was being set up in Kashmir. The adoption of this plan in Kashmir for the first time, which came nearly after a century of establishment of Muslim rule in the area, was complimented with the steady arrival of missionaries and artisans from the Persian-speaking world. The design of the mosque is also reflective of the architects chosen, Sayyid Muhammad and Khawjā Sadr-al Dīn Khurasanī, both being Iranians and the guiding factor behind the entire project along with Sikander, the *Kubrawī* shaykh, Sayyid Muhammad Hamdani.

It is interesting to note that, while the finest example of the *iwan*-courtyard mosque in Iran dating back to the Seljuk period, Masjid-i-Juma at Isfahan has a central courtyard measuring 59.74m × 70.1m; in comparison, the architects at Srinagar designed the mosque around an impressive central courtyard of 71.6m × 76.2m. While there is no implicit record of the desire to outsize the Isfahan mosque courtyard, yet the architects as well as Sayyid Muhammad Hamdani must have been well-aware of the fact that the Isfahan mosque comprised the largest courtyard mosque of Iran, their native land. The desire to outbuild it could certainly have been there. In fact, the author of *Bahāristān-i Shāhī*, while recording the construction of the mosque takes obvious pride in the size of his native mosque in these words:

> Throughout the lands of Hind and Sindh and the climes of Iran and Turan, one cannot come across a mosque of such grandeur and magnificence, though of course such grand mosques do exist in the lands of Egypt and Syria[101].

Unlike Iranian mosques where the side halls comprised arched arcade of masonry pillars supporting the domed or vaulted ceiling, the Kashmiri builders adopted a trabeated system wherein a flat, plain and unadorned wooden ceiling is supported on wooden beams and columns, the abundance of good quality deodar wood making the use of time-consuming vaults and domes unnecessary. One obvious drawback of this system lies in the narrow spacing between the wooden columns which obliterated the view of the worshippers from the *miḥrāb* as well as the *minbar*.

The use of wood can be explained by both the ease of construction using wood as well as its abundance. The feel of a forest of wooden pillars that is associated with the Jamia can also be observed in the Jamia Khiva[102] (c. dating from ninth century CE) with its highly ornamented wooden columns. Additionally, the designing of the wooden ceiling with its receding squares seen in the Khiva mosque can also be observed also in the ceiling of the entrance *iwans* in Jamia Srinagar. The similarity though is more of a coincidence, a result of working with similar materials. For the arrangement of the ceiling is a replica of what can be seen at the temples of Pandrethan and Udhampur temple, though unadorned with floral and human depictions that we find in these temples.

Where the Jamia of Srinagar departs from its Iranian or Central Asian prototypes is in the designing of the four entrance gateways located on the principal cardinal directions. In the Iranian mosque, the gateways are traditionally crowned with domes, vaults and *minars*, which act as the principal visual architectural elements defining the appearance of the building. In the Jamia at Srinagar, the dome, minaret and the vault are replaced by the quintessential *brangh* – the wooden pyramidal spire with projecting gables at the base. The *branghs* are in turn surmounted by the molded brass finial. The umbrella shape of the finial owes its origin to the *doūr*, the traditional Kashmiri earring. The same shape is repeated in the wooden pendant suspended from the corners of the building. Overall, it is the shape of the Kashmiri spire and its columned halls that remain as the most distinct architectural feature of this monumental building rooting it in the land of construction as opposed to the land of origin of the design. The Jamia of Srinagar with its soaring pyramidal *branghs* surmounting a restrained façade of harmonious arched arcade represents the one of the most successful examples in Kashmir's Islamic architecture. A composite design representing an amalgamation of heterogeneous elements, it exemplifies the marriage of an Iranian plan form to a native Kashmiri visual composition.

The mosque at Zaina Lank, Wullar Lake

The preponderance of architectural activity that is associated with Zain-al Ābidīn finds an interesting expression in the waters of the Wullar lake. It was within this vast lake that the Sultan constructed an artificial island named, *lank*[103] (island) which would in years become famous as Zaina Lank after the builder [Figure 3.11]. The ruins on the island all are representative of a diverse architectural vocabulary, bringing to fore the nature of this period – that of experimentation. The construction of the island palace was a novelty that aroused the curiosity and admiration of writers down the ages[104]. Significantly, the *lank* predates a similar occurrence in the plains of the sub-continent whether in the island gardens of the Mughals or even

Figure 3.11 Zaina Lank, western façade: the mosque and its immediate setting. The approach ghāt can be seen in the foreground, Zaina Lank: 2017, © Hakim Sameer Hamdani.

the island mausoleum of Sher Shāh Suri (r. 1539–45 CE) built earlier at Sahsaram. The closest parallel we find is in the funerary architecture of the Tughlaqs, the mausoleums of Ghiyās-al Dīn (d. 1325 CE) at Tughlaqabad set in an artificial lake.

The date of construction (847 AH/1443 CE) of the island as well as the ensemble of buildings raised on it is derived from the word *khurram*[105] (happy), that occurs in the last line of verse written by the sultan's poet laureate Mullā Ahmad. The island was a favorite retreating place for the Sultan. In his dying days, dissatisfied with the conducts of his sons and outliving most of his intimate courtiers, Zain-al Ābidīn turned into a recluse, and would often journey to the island for quite meditation[106].

The anecdotes relating to the construction of the island are well-recorded in traditional Kashmiri sources dating from the medieval period[107]. The *lank* was constructed in the waters of Wullar lake at the site of an earlier temple that had been inundated in the waters, and involved the raising of an artificial platform by submerging boats laden with stones derived from the earlier ruins[108] – boats built by master craftsmen from Gujrat with sails that were used in the enterprise[109].

The earliest detailed description of the buildings constructed on the island is to be found in the writings of ʿAli. He describes the island as a marvel of the time, comprising a four-storied palace, with stone and brick masonry in the first two floors, while the upper stories were built in wood[110]. He also refers to a *khilwat khāna* (solitary cell) on the island, where the Sultan used to meditate[111]. The use of wood in combination with masonry harbingers an architectural practice that found favor in the vernacular architectural of the area way down till early part of the twentieth century CE. Malīk also refers to the construction of the island which according to him included many buildings, including a mosque. The author of *Bahāristān-i Shāhī* also follows the description of Malīk, mentioning the existence of two buildings at the site, a palace and a mosque. He also refers to planting of mulberry, fruit trees and flowers on the island making it a picnic spot of unique beauty in Kashmir. The island was also visited by Emperor Jahangir who leaves us with a brief description of the *lank* and the buildings constructed on it. In his description, he writes about a mosque and three additional buildings that were constructed by the Chak sultans on other three sides of the *lank*[112].

Unlike many of the lesser Muslim monuments of Kashmir, we have a more detailed architectural description of Zaina Lank, in the writings of Bates and Kak. The *lank* is described by Bates as:

> [...] Quadrangle in shape measuring two acres; its longer side, north and south, are about 95 yards long, and its shorter, which are east and west, about 75 yards [...][113].

Bates also identifies two buildings on the island, the ruins of a square stone temple near the north-east corner measuring 10.36m × 10.36m and a single dome-shaped masonry building comprising a room measuring 4.87m × 4.87m. He also writes about the use of enameled tiles on the decoration of the façade of the masonry building[114]. In Kak's writing, we have the first recorded description of the island from a trained archeologist. Unfortunately, Kak's description of the various ruins existing at the site is at variance with their architectural functions. Thus, what Bates has described as the temple becomes a mosque for Kak and the domed masonry structure in Bates description is identified as a possible tomb by Kak[115].

The island presently comprises a linear terrace aligned along east-west axis [Figure 3.11]. The main approach to the island is from a flight of steps located on the western side. The site has been extensively restored by ASI (Archaeological Survey of India) and it is possible that the original contours of the island might have been altered within the process. The stone parapet wall outlining the island seems to be a new addition, as traces of blocked steps leading from the lake bed to the island can still be seen on the southern and northern side.

The island itself rises in three levels from what is the present lake bed, comprising two levels of stone pitched sides with a small landing in between, and the main top terrace forming the island proper[116]. The corners of the top terrace are defined by pentagonal shape, which may have served as the location of corner towers. The main brick masonry domed building is located on the western side of the terrace, slightly to the north of the central axis. The ruins of the temple with trefoil arches and stone columns can be seen along the northeastern corner of the island. Remnants of old stones could also be seen along the southeastern corner of the terrace. It is possible that archaeological excavations at the site might reveal footprints of other buildings at the site.

Regarding the arrangement and functioning of the various buildings on the island, based on its orientation and historical description, it is possible to identify the domed brick structure as a mosque. The building is oriented to the *qiblā* with a blind wall on the western side, in keeping with the requirements of a mosque. The stone structure located on the northeastern corner of the island is too small to classify as a palace. It would not be an unwarranted conclusion to infer that this incongruous structure was constructed as a temple on the island, though we have no textual reference for such a supposition. Such an arrangement would be in keeping with the highly ecumenical temperament of the Sultan. Additionally, the disparate arrangement of various buildings, their varied architectural styles can conceptually only be conjoined in the ideological moorings of their patron, who while promoting Muslim scholars also patronized Hindu and Buddhist men of learning.

The mosque existed till early part of the twentieth century CE, in its original form, but due to lack of attention from the Dogra rulers was allowed to fall in complete ruin. The building has been entirely reconstructed in recent years by the ASI, with only the stone plinth retained in its original form. Nevertheless, the building footprints have not been altered during the reconstruction. Fortunately, in addition to Bates' and Kak's description of the building from the Dogra period, we also have the only surviving image of the building[117]. I was also able to gain access to a few images of the building prior to its demolition, which were of immense help in comparing the original structure with changes affected during the reconstruction.

The mosque comprises a small square single-story domed building measuring 6.6m × 6.6m [Figure 3.12]. The building itself lies on top of a well-dressed stone plinth (0.5m high) with a rounded torus molding, reminiscent of medieval stone temples of Kashmir. The superstructure was entirely constructed of *budshāhī* bricks, which in the reconstruction has been replaced by modern brick tiles. Internally, the building comprises of a single domed room measuring 5.0m × 5.0m. The main entrance to the building is from a centrally located doorway on the eastern wall. The rectangular low-height door opening was originally framed within an arched masonry recess. The door is flanked on either side by a double row of shallow arched recess.

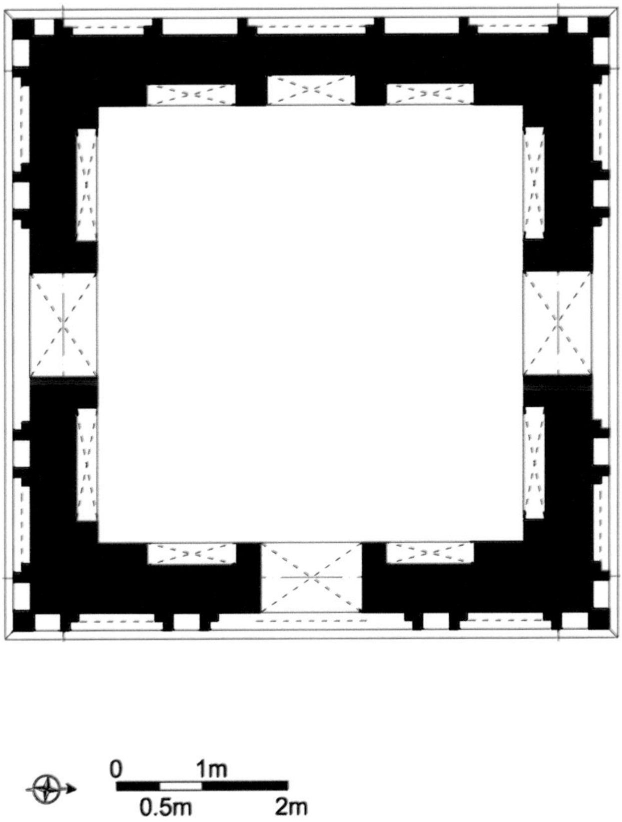

Figure 3.12 Zaina Lank, mosque plan, © Hakim Sameer Hamdani.

The use of double row of arched recesses is an architectural device which is also employed in the construction of the adjacent temple, though in this case, the arches are trefoil, flanked by miniature stone columns as seen in the stone temples of Kashmir. The use of double row of blind arched niches in both the temple and the mosque may have helped in establishing a certain visual similarity between the varied architectural styles of the two buildings.

The building façade was originally repeated on the northern façade, which also had a door opening at the center[118]. The southern and western façade resembled the main eastern façade with the exception of the central opening which was walled in. These blind arched recesses are formed by projecting brick pilasters, an architectural innovation dating from Zain-al Ābidīn's reign. This is a design feature we also find in the surface decoration of *Dumath* at Srinagar. The niches which were framed within a projecting rectangular masonry band virtually gave the mosque an appearance of a two-story building. The entire structure was surmounted by a low-height, almost hemispherical, dome at the center. The use of a hemispherical dome also figures prominently in Tughlaq architecture, as seen in the mausoleum of Ghiyās-al Dīn. Externally, the transition from the cubical base to the dome takes place without any visible zone of transformation. In the image of the building, we see no drum that would serve as the base for the dome. It is possible that the building had significantly degenerated by the time the image was taken in the twentieth century CE, yet the perspective offered does not indicate a drum supporting the dome. While it is not quite clear from the image we have of the building, it is possible that in addition to the central dome, the building also had smaller domed copulas at the corners. This is again an architectural element we see at *Mazar-i Salātīn*. The possibility of corner domes is again based on the intriguing detailing of the building edges. In the reconstruction, the building corners take the shape of octagons[119] which are indicative (if the reconstruction has followed original plan) of the presence of corner cupolas. The zone of transition is through the squinches, supporting the dome, as can be observed in the images dating back to the pre-restoration work carried in the building.

In his description, Kak has mentioned about the presence of projecting wooden beams defining the string course of the masonry top[120]. In the surviving images of the building, presence of wooden tie beam can be clearly seen but at the lintel level, rather than at the top of the building. Given the rectangular openings in the building façade with thick masonry walls (0.8m), the use of wooden beams as runners was an easy and more traditional Kashmiri way of spanning openings. In the local vernacular, wooden runners at floor level additionally also function as seismic band. Here it remains a simple carryover from the construction techniques employed by the architects in composite structures of masonry and wood

The mosque was externally provided with surface decoration, which according to Bates, comprised blue enameled slabs while Kak mentions about glazed and painted tiles[121]. It is possible that the building was covered with blue slabs while glazed tiles were only used in the horizontal and vertical bands separating the recessed arched panels. Unfortunately, no trace of either the enameled slabs or glazed tiles exists at the site.

The mosque with its overall massing and detailing of the façade bears a degree of visual resemblance to the *Alā-i Darwaza*[122] constructed by Sultan Alā'-al Dīn Khalji (r. 1296–1316 CE) in Delhi in 1311 CE. The resemblance between the two structures in spite of the vast difference in the scale and material is too remarkable to be dismissed as a coincidence. The external dimensions of the *Darwaza* at 7.22m × 17.22m vastly out-scales the diminutive mosque constructed by Zain-al Ābidīn, yet there is a similarity in the plan. Both the buildings are designed on a square plan with a symmetrical arrangement of niches (or windows at *Darwaza*) on either side of the central opening. The employment of masonry projections to create blind niches and projecting pilasters is a common feature in both the buildings, in spite of the difference in their purpose of construction; one designed as a mosque another as a triumphal gateway to a mosque compound. In addition, both the structures share architectural features such as the use of a low-height hemispherical dome, the symmetrical rendering of the building façade with a central arch surrounded by twin row of alcoves creating the illusion of a double-story structure and the use of horizontal and vertical bands of decorative cladding to create a polychromatic effect. Interestingly, the transition zone in both the buildings is achieved through the use of squinches.

Alā-i Darwaza because of its architectural quality is seen as a building bridging two different architectural traditions, an architectural fusion, and at Zaina Lank, the builders reproduced not only a part of the architectural style associated with the *Darwaza* but also the spirit. We know that in the construction of his boats, the Sultan employed the skills of Gujrati builders; it is all the more possible that in the actual designing of the mosque he was also assisted by builders who were well-versed with the architecture of the Delhi Sultans. Yet, in spite of the similarity between the two buildings, there is a major difference. *Alā-i Darwaza* was commissioned to proclaim Islam's triumph amongst a land of non-believers. The mosque at Zaina Lank is a part of an ensemble which portrays an equally powerful image, that of assimilation between two different faiths. There is another significant difference; *Alā-i Darwaza* is a part of public complex which at time was in the heart of the royal citadel. Zaina Lank on the other hand is part of the ruler's private realm, unapproachable physically and visually within its isolated lake setting.

In the cultural landscape of Kashmir, the island of Zaina Lank serves as a set piece, representative of a spirit of cultural assimilation and respect which in the Indian subcontinent was seen only in the sixteenth century at the court of the Mughal Emperor Akbar. Designed as an island palace of pleasure, the *lank* with its idyllic setting makes use of architecture as a symbol of religious tolerance that was associated with the Sultan. The contrasting architectural vocabulary employed may seem today like a medley of odd ideas, even ill-fitted visuals, this becomes more apparent due to the absence of any axial planning in laying of the various buildings. But, then our reading is also severely hampered by the absence of understanding of the buildings as they were originally constructed. Hopefully, in near future, a systematic excavation carried out at the site would provide us with a better reading of the site.

The designing of a small personalized mosque seems to have been widespread during the Sultanate period. And, it is during the closing part of Kashmiri Sultanate that we find another small mosque was constructed at Aham in North Kashmir, near the town of Bandipora. Local oral traditions as well as historical references associate the mosque with Shaykh Hamza Makhdūm (984 AH/1576 CE), a Suharwardī Shaykh who worked extensively across Kashmir for revival of Sunni faith in the face of court patronage of the Shi'as under the Chak Sultans.

The mosque at Aham sharief is said to have been constructed for the Shaykh in 963A H/1555 CE for enacting solitary penances and prayers, and assumes the shape of a small, square mosque. While the present structure dates back to the nineteenth century CE, following its reconstruction by a local merchant Khawjā Amān-al lah in 1294 AH/1877 CE, the reconstruction follows the footprints of the original, in terms of the plan. The association of the mosque with the severity of the spiritual penances undertaken there by the saint, the popularity of the saint in the community and hence the respect and sanctity reflected on the mosque ensured the preservation of the mosques layout during its reconstruction.

The mosque can be broadly seen as a small cell measuring 3.96m × 3.81m on the outside, with the inner chamber measuring 2.4m × 2.5m, constructed in sundried bricks. Entrance to the building is from a low-height door centrally, located on the eastern side-facing *miḥrāb*. While the *qiblā* wall has two niches on either side of the centrally placed *miḥrāb*, the other two building façade comprise a window each. The chamber has a low-lying ceiling (1.7m) supported on single wooden column, slightly off-centered. The size of the chamber, its low ceiling height, almost resembling that of a cave, is representative of the monastic lifestyle, which was a part of the overall personality of the Shaykh Hamza, who also happens to be one of the very few Kashmiri Muslim saints outside of the native *Reshī* order, who remained a celibate his entire life.

The personal life of the Shaykh with its simplicity mirrors the life of the *Reshī* saints, yet the Shaykh attempted at re-shaping the *Reshī* order into more orthodox mode. The austere and rustic appearance of the mosque at Aham sharief, its isolated location, resembles the traditions prevalent amongst the *Reshīs*, traditions that Shaykh attempted to change. As such, the building is reflective of the complexities of a society, which while holding to older traditions was also coming under the influence of more orthodox forces.

Figure 3.13 Makhdūm Ṣāhab shrine precinct, Srinagar: 2019, © Mukhtar Ahmad.

Also associated with the Shaykh is the vast shrine complex located on the southern foothills of Hari Parbat hillock in the heart of Srinagar city [Figure 3.13]. The precinct has been continuously expanded, built and rebuilt since the sixteenth century CE, and also houses the *rūżā* of Shaykh Hamza (c. 1601 CE). To its south, further down the hillock of Hari Parbat which during medieval period was renamed as Koh-i Maran, borders Malkah – the vast open cemetery located at the foot of the hill[123].

The various buildings within the shrine complex assume a distinct organic pattern of construction, with a linear placement of buildings governed primarily by need, and availability of constructible space on the narrow hillock rather than any consideration for achieving an intended spiritual or visual hierarchy of spaces and form.

Amongst the different buildings in the shrine precinct of Makhdūm Ṣāhab, the oldest and most modest surviving structure is of Zakir Masjid. As far as the dating of this building is concerned, we have enough textual evidences to indicate that the mosque was made specifically for Shaykh Hamza and was used by him exclusively during his lifetime[124]. The location of Shaykh Hamza's tomb in the vicinity of the Zakir Masjid is indicative of the esteem in which the mosque (and the site) was held by Shaykh Hamza's disciples[125]. A stone plaque inserted over the entrance door of the mosque gives its date of constructions as 1550 CE. Though the white marble plaque with its Urdu inscription is of recent origin, yet the stone reaffirms the historicity of the mosque, as the first place of seclusion of Shaykh Hamza. Historically, the mosque which cuts into the hillock on its northern side was the first building to be constructed at the site along the slope of the hillock. Today, this small building is lost in the maze of buildings that form part of the wider precinct of the shrine complex.

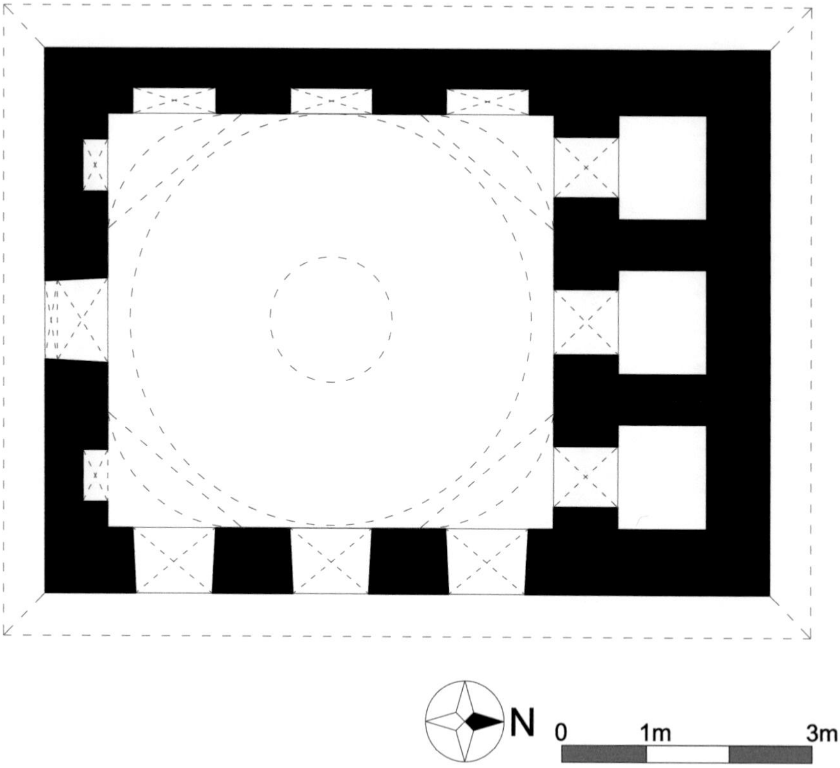

Figure 3.14 Zakir Masjid:plan, Srinagar: 2018, © Hakim Sameer Hamdani.

Zakir Masjid is designed as a small rectangular low-height single-story building with external dimensions of 8.68 x 6.35m [Figure 3.14]. The entrance to the small building is from the eastern façade with a central doorway flanked by unassuming rectangular window opening on either side. The western façade is similar to the main eastern elevation barring the replacement of the doorway with the *miḥrāb*. The southern façade of the mosque overlooking the rest of the shrine complex comprises a single rectangular window, internally flanked by an arched niche on either side.

Internally, the mosques comprise of a small domed chamber measuring 5.3m × 4.8m with three small cells (*hujra*) measuring 1.21m × 1.06m, located along the northern side for performing solitary penances. The most conspicuous feature of the building is the presence of a shallow *muqarna* dome built of concentric rings of flattened *muqarnas* [Figure 3.15]. The dome is supported on an arrangement of eight arches with the corner taking the shape of semi-domes. The *muqarna* ceiling of the mosque resembles a similar arrangement that can be seen in the tomb of Tambulan Begam at Allahabad dating to the Jahangiri period[126]. Regarding the dome of Zakir Masjid, Ebba Koch indicates seventeenth century CE as a possible date, which fits in with

Figure 3.15 Zakir Masjid: shallow domed *muqarna* ceiling, Srinagar: 2018, © Hakim Sameer Hamdani.

the native traditions that indicate that construction work was undertaken at the site by courtiers linked with Mughal court of Jahangir. Nevertheless, given the arrangement of the mosque's façade, it is certain that barring the dome, the rest of the superstructure is of older Kashmiri workmanship. The use of wooden lintels within shallow-arched opening, fitted with rectangular window openings in the mosques, finds parallel in pre-Mughal buildings of Kashmir. Examples of this nature are widespread, including at the *Khānaqāh-i Naū* and the shrine of Malīk Abdul Rahim.

The building is located on an elevation from the main shrine, preceded by an open courtyard serving as *mazar*. The mosque has been heavily restored, which includes the addition of a sloping roof, hiding the original profile of the roof. Internally, the mud plastered walls of the mosque are decorated with moldings, again in mud plaster. The detailing of the plaster finds parallels in the architecture of the nineteenth century and probably dates from the same period.

The arrangement of the mosque indicates its use for solitary rather than communal worship. Used rigorously by Shaykh Hamza, the mosque also served as a place for spiritual retreat for his intimate disciples. Today, the mosque is revered for its association with Shaykh Hamza, though no longer used for undertaking solitary retreats. The construction of the mosque dome by courtiers linked with the Mughal court is also indicative of the favor in which the saint was held by the Mughals, given the association of his disciples with establishment of Mughal rule in Kashmir.

ᶜAālī masjid at ᶜ*idgāh*, Srinagar

Though not much has survived of religious architecture from the Sultanate period, yet based on what is preserved, it is possible to form a reasonable generalization of this architectural genre. Barring the Jamia Masjid, we find no substantive example at monumentalization of religious places, with the notable exception of *khānaqāh*s. The various *khānaqāhs* that emerged in Kashmir would rival mosques both as an institution as well as an architectural edifice throughout medieval times. Aside from the Jamia Masjid at Srinagar, the only other major surviving mosque whose footprints can be traced to Sultanate architecture is a mosque located at ʿ*idgāh*, Srinagar: ʿAālī Masjid [Figure 3.16]. The building happens to be the second largest mosque of Srinagar, only surpassed in size by the principal Friday mosque of the city, Jamia Masjid.

The mosque is located on the edge of the historic Srinagar city, within the vast open ground of the ʿ*īdgāh*. According to Field ascompared to rest of the Islamic world,ʿ*īdgāh* are more widespread in thirteenth-fourteenth century CE, North India[127].Traditionally ʿ*īdgāh* are located to the west of the settlement, at Srinagar we find the choice of the site dwelled on the northern outskirt of the city. In Kashmir, the *īdgāh* at Srinagar was established during the reign of Sultan Sikander by Mīr Muhammad Hamdanī.

Historically, construction of mosque within a *īdgāh* is more of an aberration than a standard procedure. For traditionally, ʿ*īdgāhs* comprise vast

Figure 3.16 Aālī Masjid, south eastern façade: the wooden *dalān* is an eighteenth-century CE addition, yet the building retains its original spatial layout, Srinagar: 2018, © Hakim Sameer Hamdani.

open fields mostly located at the edge of a city or settlement where large crowds of people could congregate twice a year on the occasion of *ʿīd*. The only physical structure within this vast area comprises a freestanding wall with niches serving as the *miḥrāb*, also known as *nimāzgāh*. One hardly finds a permanent mosque located in a *ʿīdgāh* in other parts of the Muslim world but an elaborate structure comprising *miḥrāb* wall with domes and octagonal buttresses do exist from Tughlaq times[128]. The only possible reason that can explain the construction of the mosque is the severe winter of Kashmir, where a covered structure was the only possible mean of offering shelter to worshippers during snow or rain. And as all Muslim festivals, including the *ʿīd,* are based on a lunar calendar, there would be occasions when the *ʿīd* would fall within the severe winters of Kashmir, extending from November to March.

A stone slab located over the *miḥrāb* of the mosque dates the construction of the mosque to Sultan Hasan, the tenth Sultan of Kashmir and mentions the year of construction as 1471 CE[129]. The stone slab also bears the *shahāda* and the name of the mason, Kājī Hūstī. In the Muslim religious architecture of Kashmir, this is the first recorded instance wherein the name of the master-mason (architect) has been documented on the walls of the building.

Khuihami also writes that in 1075 AH/1664 CE, the mosque was expanded by the *naib subeadar* (deputy governor) Islam Khan during the rule of Mughal emperor Aurangzeb, while also clearing the adjacent areas of existing trees and planting *chinars* their instead. The mosque was burnt down in 1215 AH/1800 CE during Afghan rule before being rebuilt by an Afghan noble, Sardar Gūl Muhammad Khan, in 1300 AH/1882 CE[130].

The building is based on the rectangular plan with the main prayer hall measuring 61.2m × 20.5m oriented along the north-south axis and comprises 75 such modules [Figure 3.17]. Like the side halls at Jamia Masjid, Srinagar, ʿAālī Masjid is also based on a hypostyle plan, with a module of 3.65m × 3.65m grid supported on 4.5m tall wooden columns. The main module along the end and the central aisle leading towards the *miḥrāb* are slightly bigger than the rest. The modules are arranged in 15 aisles perpendicular to the *qiblā* wall, five bays deep. Hence, the entire space in the hall is defined by five rows of columns, repeating the same effect of a wooden forest as seen in the columned hall of Jamia at Srinagar [Plate 6]. The hall is preceded by an extended 9.5m deep portico (*dalān*) two bays deep running along the entire length of the building on its main eastern façade [Figure 3.18]. The addition of the linear wooden *dalān* running along the entire length of the mosque is a Mughal addition to the building from Jahāngīr's period. The dating of this building feature is confirmed both by textual references as well as stylistic examination.

In pre-Mughal buildings of Kashmir, wooden *dalān* as a building feature is conspicuously absent. It is only in the seventeenth century CE, during Mughal rule, that this feature was introduced in Kashmir, in designing of buildings within the Mughal gardens. The earliest archaeological evidence

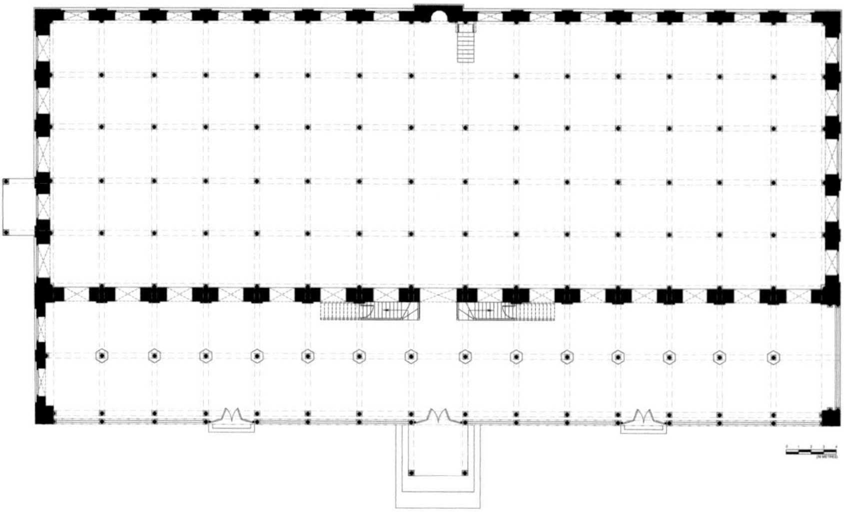

Figure 3.17 Aālī Masjid: Ground floor plan © INTACH, Kashmir.

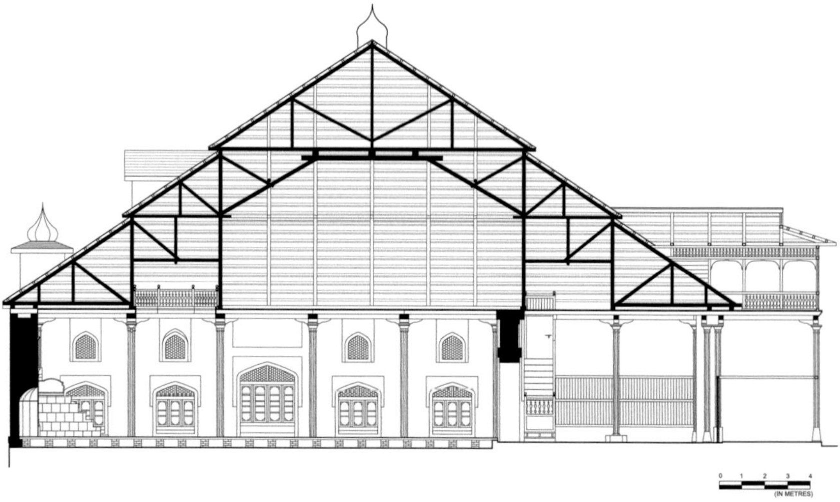

Figure 3.18 Aālī Masjid: longitudinal section, © INTACH, Kashmir.

of a wooden portico can be seen in the Mughal-era hammam at Shalimar. Positing on our existing understanding of wooden audience hall in Mughal period, it is reasonably to argue that this feature was transported from Safavids to Mughals, and then through the Mughals into Kashmir. The *dalān* of Kashmir can be seen as a reworking of the Iranian *tālār*.

The main approach to the mosque is direct and frontal on the eastern side. Unlike many other mosques in Srinagar which are hampered by the constraints of the site, rows of chinar trees, all but hide the main eastern façade from the view, especially during summer months, when they are covered with dense green foliage.

While the spatial layout of the building remained unchanged during the subsequent reconstruction of the mosque during the Afghan period, yet the superstructure, especially the articulation of the openings, is based on architectural traditions of the eighteenth century CE.

The architecture of 'Aālī Masjid shows gradual adaptation of external influences in designing of major public buildings in Kashmir in the fifteenth century CE, influences first witnessed at Jamia Masjid, Srinagar. Nevertheless, the very placement of a large mosque within a *'īdgāh* is a uniquely Kashmiri innovation determined by local geographical conditions and customs.

Iconoclasm and the *rūżā* of Sayyid Husayn Khurazmī at Srinagar

The life and work of Mīr Muhammad Hamdanī and the missionaries who followed in his wake marks a sustained attempt at changing the contours of community life of Kashmir. It marks a transition from a path of assimilation to a path of conversion and iconoclastic activities. Consequently, it is from this period that we have the oldest surviving trace of forced conversion of Hindu place of worship into a Muslim shrine – the *rūżā* of Sayyid Husayn Khurazmī at Srinagar. Sayyid Husayn was a companion of Mīr Muhammad, on whose advice he settled down at Munwar. The area of Munwar, which today forms a part of the old Srinagar city, was at that time an island within the marshes of Brar-i Nambal[131]. On the advice of Mīr Muhammad, Sayyid Husayn destroyed the temple that existed on the island, appropriating the site for his personal use and worship. From the brief details we have of Sayyid Husayn, it emerges that the Sayyid led a life of recluse on the island and unlike most of his contemporaries in the *Kubrawī* order, he never married[132]. In spite of being a recluse, Sayyid Husayn continued to maintain his link with the court especially the sultan, serving as the interpreter of Quran and Islamic injunctions for Sultan Sikander. On his death, Sayyid Husayn was laid to rest within the ruins of the temple that he had destroyed, marking the destroyed Hindu temple as a Muslim shrine[133].

The erstwhile island at Munwar is located to the southeast of Barar-i Nambal and comprises an open piece of land, almost rectangular in shape. The entire area is slightly elevated from the surroundings, which mostly comprises a residential area. The island-graveyard is oriented diagonally along the north-south axis, with the ruins of the temple located on its southern edge. It is possible that the present form of the graveyard does not follow the original contours of the island but is the result of shifting boundaries as residences were constructed in its vicinity.

The superstructure itself comprises a small single-story contemporary structure (4.4m × 3.85m) located on top of the old stone plinth of the temple. It is quite possible that the present location of the shrine corresponds to the profile of the original temple cell (sanctum) and the surrounding platform corresponds to the circumambulatory of the former temple. The plinth measures 11.5m × 11.5m (approx.), is oriented on the north-south axis and stands at a height of 1.5m (approx.) from the surrounding ground level[134]. The lower part of the plinth up to the torus molding has neither been disturbed nor altered. The upper part of the plinth comprising two courses of stone masonry finished with a molding[135] course seem to date from a later period, probably post destruction of the temple. The stone used in the upper courses have clearly been sourced from the temple ruins, but the absence of dressed ashlar masonry would indicate that this part of the structure was rebuilt at a later date. Nevertheless, the plan of the structure follows the tradition of medieval stone temples of Kashmir with the preference of the builders for a southern entrance. A series of steps lead down from the shrine-temple plinth to what would originally have been the disembarking point from the boat[136]. Traces of the original stone gateway and some of the stone steps can still be seen at the site on the southern corner on the site at this point[137]. In addition to the shrine itself, the plinth also contains three other stone cenotaphs of Muslim saints. Two of the cenotaphs are located on the southern side of the shrine and one on the east. Internally, in addition to the grave of the Sayyid Husayn, another grave can also be found in the burial chamber. The shrine of Sayyid Husayn marks neither a case of architectural experimentation nor adaptation or evolution. The various stone cenotaphs located on the plinth are the only representation of an artistic outpouring and mirrors similar creations happening in the Persianate world. The stone cenotaphs are made in shape of *kalamdān* (pen cases) and are inscribed with Arabic script in *thuluth*, unfortunately the script is not legible.

The destruction of the temple marks a conscious attempt by the non-native members of the emerging Muslim elitetocracy at managing a break from the local past. This included the earlier experience of Islam in the region, which was based on syncretism rather than iconoclasm. Burying the Muslim saint responsible for the desolation of the temple, on top of the ruins, visually mark the permanence of a new faith and its supremacy, a case of cultural appropriation. It could and would have also been seen as a deliberate act of desecration of a venerated sacred site, though no Muslim account describes it as such.

The phenomenon of iconoclasm, once started, would continue to be a part of the Kashmiri society, at times gaining new adherents and supporters, including court patronage. It would be a source of tension not only within the wider Kashmiri community but amongst Kashmiri Muslims themselves. The phenomenon would be limited not only to buildings – temples and other religious sites – but to various aspects of the culture and society at large.

The *mazar* of Malīk Jalāl-al Dīn Thakur at Nauhata, Srinagar

While the Munwar shrine represents a clear case of temple destruction, the *mazar* of Malīk Jalāl-al Dīn posits a different question. Was the construction of *mazar* another example of iconoclastic fervor or was it a case of appropriating an abandoned site. According to the historian Dedhmārī, Malīk Jalāl belonged to the clan of Thakurs whose ancestor; Malīk Hasan arrived in Kashmir during the reign of Zain-al Ābidīn. The honorary title of Malīk was conferred on the family by the Sultan[138] and quickly gained prominence at the court, with Malīk Jalāl marrying Lachma Khātūn, daughter of the powerful *vazir,* Malīk Saif-al Dīn[139]. Lachma Khātūn, who is said to have been a disciple of Mīr Muhammad Hamdanī, emerges as a notable figure[140] in the court life of fifteenth century CE Kashmir. She is credited with digging a water canal to bring the water of Sind River into the city. The canal fed the Jamia Masjid, before emptying in the Nalah mar[141]. Due to her religious piety and patronage of works of public welfare, Lachma Khātūn also finds a mention in Dedhmārī's list of Muslim saints.

Following the death of Zain-al Ābidīn and the ensuing war of succession between his children, the eight Thakur brothers retired from the court, settling down in different parts of the land. Malīk Jalāl withdrew to the *khānaqāh* he had built at Srinagar in the vicinity of the Jamia Masjid. On his death,[142] he was buried in the compound of the same *khānaqāh*[143].

The construction of *khānaqāh* was undertaken by Malīk Jalāl in close proximity of the Jamia Masjid on an elevated plot of land. The site chosen was originally part of a temple site. This can be clearly seen in the detailing of extant original gateway of the *mazar* with traces of human figures on the lintel and remnants of the enclosure wall on the south and western side of the site[144]. Comprising massive blocks of semi-dressed stone in regular courses, the enclosure wall would have served as the peristyle of the temple, a common and defining feature of medieval stone temples of Kashmir. Whether the enclosure was designed as a cellular peristyle[145] or simply as a defining compound wall cannot be established given the changes and loss of material. The *mazar,* which has now been rebuilt as a single-story building, was located in the middle of the quadrangle, which indicates that the remains of the temple were made use of for burial of Malīk Jalāl and other members of his family.

A close examination of the images, pre-dating the reconstruction at site, reveal that the entrance gateway was partially reconstructed on its conversion to a *mazar*. This was accomplished by constructing a brick masonry arch on top of the gateway, leaving the lower parts of the gateway up till the molded lintel course in place undisturbed. Unlike the trefoil arch of the Hindu temple, which had also been adopted into early Muslim architecture of Kashmir, a three-point arch was used in the gateway of the shrine. The shape of the arch derived from Timurid architecture had already been used in Kashmir in designing of mosques and mausoleums. Beside this slight modification of the entrance gateway, no other construction activities were undertaken either to embellish the *mazar* or make it visually more prominent. This is again a pattern which found much favor with the builders of the Sultanate period. We see a similar arrangement at *Mazar-i Salātīn* [Figure 3.19], the royal cemetery of *Shahmīrī* sultans

Figure 3.19 Entrance gateways: (t to b) i. Malik Jalal, ii. *Mazar-i Salātīn,* iii mosque of Madnī, and iv. Mīr Masjid (ASI).

where a stone compound wall and a similar gateway was constructed on an earlier temple site.

The appropriation of the temple ruins for reuse as a Muslim burial place gives rise to two distinct possibilities: either that an existing temple was destroyed and converted by Malīk Jalāl (or his disciples), or that the site had been abandoned before its conversion into a shrine. Unlike the shrine of Sayyid Husayn at Munwar, where a temple was first destroyed and then the ruins of the temple converted into a Muslim shrine, the same is not true for the *mazar* of Malīk Jalāl. Muslim hagiographic accounts of medieval times, which tend to highlight such iconoclastic activities as commendable act of faith and piety, are entirely silent on the issue, though they record the construction of the *khānaqāh* as well as Jalāl's burial in its vicinity. Secondly and more importantly, the construction of the shrine was preceded by the construction of the Jamia Masjid by Sultan Sikander. The desolation of temple would have taken place during Sikander's reign and not during the life of Zain-al Ābidīn, who was known for his religious tolerance. Again, it is hardly conceivable that with his strong iconoclastic temperament, Sikander would have allowed a temple to remain functional in the immediate vicinity of the main congregational mosque of Srinagar, a mosque built by him. Furthermore, the *mazar* of Malīk Jalāl was preceded by the construction of the *khānaqāh,* which itself is not a part of the temple quadrangle but adjoins it on the side. In the post-Sikandar period, we find instances of Muslim shrines and mosques coming up at the site of older temples and *vihāras.* While many temples were rehabilitated during Zain-al Ābidīn's reign[146], not all were. Many abandoned non-Muslim sites were reused by an expanding Muslim community for construction of its places of worship[147]. This is reflective of both a significant change in the society, with an increasing Muslim population as well as the limited availability of built-able land, especially in the old Srinagar, which remained confined between various physical limitations[148]. The phenomenon was repeated at the shrine of Rahim Ṣāhab in the sixteenth century CE, and closer to Malīk Jalāl's time in the construction of the *mazar* of Malīk Ṣaif-al Lah Dār.

The *mazar* of Malīk Ṣaif-ul Lah Dar at Watal Kadal

Malīk Ṣaif-ul Lah Dar was a prominent Kashmiri noble who briefly also occupied the post of *vazir* under Sultan Fateh Shāh[149]. Ṣaif Dar's rise to power took place in the days following the death of Sultan Hasan Shāh, when dwindling royal authority was accompanied by increasing clout of powerful nobles who consolidated their power by aiding rival royal claimants to the throne.

During his brief tenure as *vazir*, Malīk Ṣaif remained the real power behind the throne which soon alienated the sultan who conspired against him with other Kashmiri nobles[150]. In the ensuing turmoil, Ṣaif Dar was killed in a conflict that was orchestrated by Fateh Shāh to get rid of his powerful minister. On his death, Ṣaif Dar was laid to rest near Watal Kadal, in close vicinity of the Jhelum River. Aside from his partisanship of the cause of Fateh Shāh, the only other depiction we have of Ṣaif Dar is recognition for his religious piety, resulting in patronage of religious edifices[151]. A manifestation of this patronage is also reflected in the *mazar* of the vizier.

Similar to the *mazar* of Malīk Jalāl, the *mazar* of Malīk Ṣaif comprises a series of stone cenotaphs (scattered and damaged) located on top of a stone plinth base presently in an advanced state of decay. The plinth measuring 10.68m × 10.68m is a part of a larger plot of land which functions as a public graveyard for the residents of the local neighborhood. The plinth of the *mazar* comprises large blocks of limestone laid in ill-fitting courses. The presence of odd architectural elements such as segments of stone entablature and frieze within the stone courses of the plinth indicate that the materials used was sourced from an older site – that of a temple. This is further supported by the presences of two multi-faceted stone columns along with base and astragal molding, and the capital on the main southern façade. The columns and their location framing what would have been the entrance gateway is highly reminiscent of the traditional entrance portico of a medieval stone temple. Ancient-looking stone steps leading up to the plinth are also partially visible at site. The various stone cenotaphs are located along the north-western corner of the plinth. Possibly some of the stone cenotaphs, given their present positioning, have also been dislocated from their original location. The cenotaph of Malīk Ṣaif could not be located on the site, though a few Arabic verses in *thuluth* script could be deciphered on the surviving fragment of one of the cenotaphs. Traditionally, these verses are part of a prayer only found on cenotaphs of deceased belonging to the Shi'a community.

The general form of the *mazar* and the arrangement of stone plinth course are indicative that the present *mazar* was created on a site of an older temple. Given the time period we are looking at, it is certain that the temple must have fallen to disuse due to the iconoclastic tendencies of Sikander's reign, possibly also being damaged in the process. The form and the construction of the *mazar* is generic to a later generation, when following the death of Sikander, older religious sites mostly comprising temples were re-appropriated by members of the Muslim community, especially the court elite. This is unlike what happened in Sikander's time, when temple sites such as at Munwara and Bijbehara[152] were damaged and then immediately re-used as Muslim sites, whether as a mosque, khanqah or shrine. The *mazar* of Malīk Jalāl-al Dīn Thakur and Malīk Saif were not themselves a part of an iconoclastic project, but followed on such a program at a later date.

At both the *mazar* of Malīk Jalāl and Malīk Ṣaif, we see older pre-Muslim sites in the immediate vicinity of the city, along with the material remains of those sites being reused to create a physical edifice to monumentalize the memory of individual Muslims connected to the court. The construction itself does not reflect a coherent architectural vocabulary, being representative of a hastily reassembled edifice, constructed from readily available material. Yet, as a newly emerging built typology, both the structures draw on the image of *Mazar-i Salātīn*, but lack the workmanship that we see in the royal cemetery to give the structure a well-articulated form.

The *rūżā* of Rahim Ṣāhab at Soura

At Soura, on the outskirt of Zain-al Ābidīn's capital Naushara, stands a shrine popularly known as Rahim Ṣāhab Dumath, dedicated to the *Suharwardī* Sufi, Malīk Abdul Rahim Nachū[153]. The allusion to the shrine as Dumath is a clear reference to the mausoleum of Zain-al Ābidīn's mother at *Mazar-i Salātīn*. In Kashmir, *dumath* is the term used for big terracotta urns, especially those used for storing rice and other food grains. The shape of the lower half of the urn evokes a visual resemblance to the profile of the dome and hence the analogy.

Malīk Rahim is said to have been a disciple of Shaykh Hamza Makhdūm, yet most hagiographic accounts related to Shaykh are silent about Malīk Rahim or his supposed relation with the Shaykh. This includes the fairly authoritative account of Bābā Dāwūd Khākī[154], an intimate disciple of Shaykh Hamza. According to the nineteenth century CE writers, Malīk Rahim constructed a place of worship at Soura, where he used to retire for prayers. On his death, Mālik Rahim was buried within the same building – the *Dumath* at Soura.

Architecturally, the shrine represents an odd medley of two dissimilar esthetics that developed simultaneously during the reign of Zain-al Ābidīn. The main part of the structure up till the roof bears resemblance to the local brick and stone style as seen at Madnī's mosque while the dome draws from the traditions of *Dumath* and Zaina Lank mosque. While we have no account of the actual construction of the shrine, stylistically the building appears to date from the latter part of the Sultanate period, representing an odd combination of two styles that flourished during fifteenth century CE. The placement of the building in the later part of the Sultanate rule would also fit in with the narrative of the shrine being constructed by a disciple of Shaykh Hamza.

The shrine itself is a small, almost square, structure measuring 6.35m × 6.28m, with the main entrance from a rectangular portico 4.2m × 2.59m located on the eastern side [Figure 3.20]. The 1.8m deep portico is coeval with the shrine, though today a small room measuring 3.86m × 2.75m, preceded by a small 1.1m deep *dalān* leads up to the portico. The room and the *dalān* are wooden extensions that were undertaken during the twentieth century CE. According to the local residents, this extension of the shrine was undertaken to accommodate devotees on the occasions of the saint's *ʿurs*, for performing prayers. The plinth of the extension nevertheless is coeval

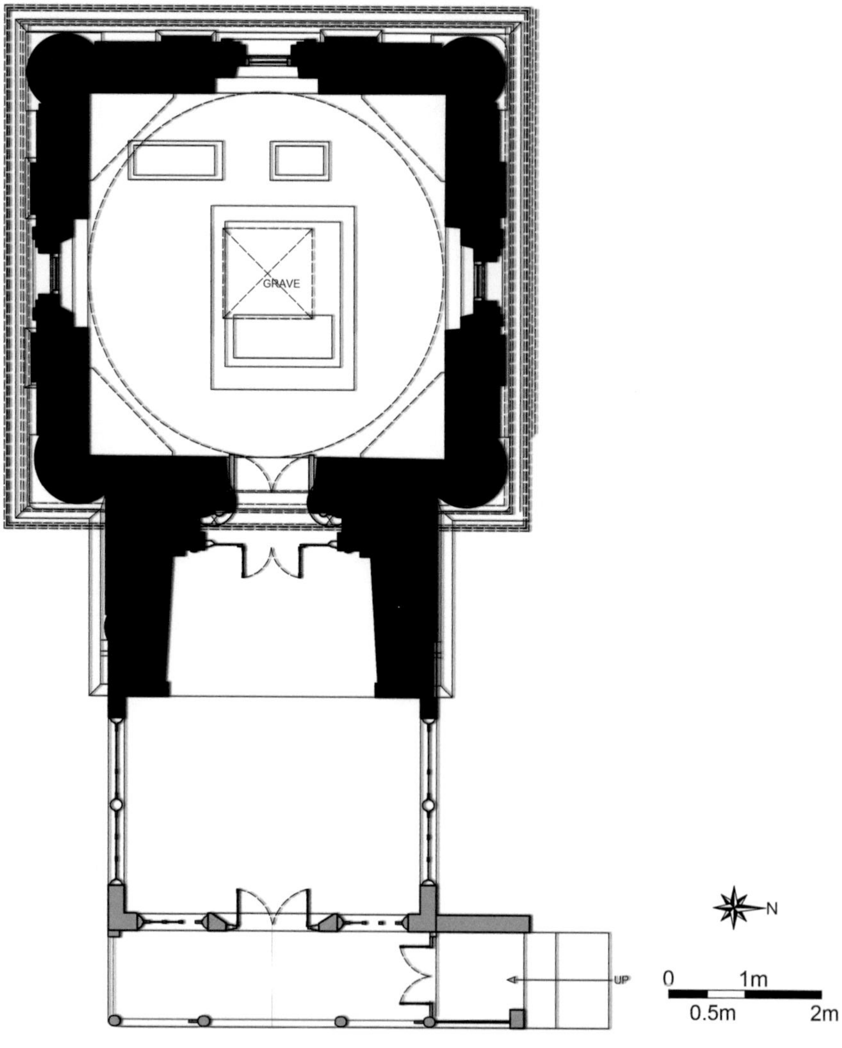

Figure 3.20 Rahim Sāhab,, plan, © INTACH, Kashmir.

with the original construction, with only the wooden superstructure being raised at a later date. A stone water spout used to drain water can also be seen in the plinth of the extension, though in the Muslim shrine it serves no functional purpose.

The shrine itself has been constructed on top of a temple base and retains the plan form of the older structure comprising three distinct chambers – the outermost chamber (*ardhamandapa*), the middle chamber (*antarala*) and the innermost sanctum (*garbhagriha*) – a traditional plan form associated with medieval stone temples and also seen at Martand[155]. Externally, the partially visible torus molding and massive stone blocks in the lower part of the plinth clearly indicate the older pre-Muslim origins of the site. During excavations that were undertaken in the late twentieth century CE, remnants of a stone pool[156] were found at the site, which I could not identity on the site during my study. This does indicate that the shrine, in its original form as a temple, was a part of a larger compound.

The conversion of the temple into a place of worship and then a shrine was accompanied by rebuilding the entire superstructure. The upper part of the plinth with its ill-fitting stone blocks is also a part of the reconstruction. Of the original architectural elements, only the stone gateway with its semi-circular opening leading into the main shrine chamber was retained.

The shrine itself comprises a single domed chamber measuring 4.65m × 4.6m internally. The grave of Malīk Rahim and an unknown disciple are located on a rectangular platform. The placement of the platform and the stone cenotaphs follows the usual Muslim practice of a north-south orientation. As an established practice, most Muslim shrines in Kashmir follow a north-south orientation with the entrance door to the shrine located on the southern side, facing the feet of the buried saint. At Soura, given the position of the door on the eastern façade, the graves are approached from the side. Two additional unknown cenotaphs are located to the west of the main burial platform.

Three pointed arched niches located centrally on the three sides facing the doorway are placed with small window openings. Internally the burial chamber is plain and without any adornment. The dome (5.9m) is supported on squinches which are also plain. A decorative band of V-shaped moldings defines the transition zone; the shape of the molding is derived from a similar trefoil band that is normally found on pediments in case of a temple.

Externally, the shrine has a symmetrical façade on the three sides, comprising a small window niche surrounded by brick pilasters. The window fenestrations which are shaped in the form of trefoil openings are set within a pointed arch and framed by square brick band. The brick pilasters which like the rest of the superstructure have been plastered during recent renovations follow the same detail as at Madnī's mosque. A significant feature of the building façade is the detailing of the building corners as circular brick columns – a feature that is generally associated with Samanid architecture (ninth-tenth century CE) of Central Asia.

The conversion of the temple into a Muslim place of worship in the sixteenth century also fits in with the ideological and theological foundations guiding the cultural and social vision of Malīk Rahim's spiritual preceptor, Shaykh Hamza. This strictly sharia-minded *Suharwardī* saint is said to have converted numerous revered Hindu sites into mosques, while also actively seeking to change the prevailing reverence that the Muslim society had for older established customs and beliefs[157]. As such, the conversion of a Hindu temple into a Muslim site should be seen as reflection of the socio-religious environment that Malīk Rahim was associated with.

Cave shrines associated with the *Reshī* order

Generally, the shrines of Kashmir can be broadly divided into two categories: the urban and the rural. Though some of the present-day urban shrines were invariably part of an urban fringe rather than the city proper even up till the mid part of the twentieth century CE, yet they depict a commonality of characteristic with their urban counterparts. These urban shrines were mostly located at the center of an immediate and expanding residential quarter: the *moḥala*. In fact, in many cases, they serve as pivots for further urban developments. This is a feature which was initially seen in the construction of *Khānaqāh-i Mʿaulā* in the early part of the Muslim rule. The proximity of all major Muslim shrines of Srinagar to the river Jhelum indicates both the need for easy line of communication as well as an abundant source of easily available water, a prerequisite for ablution. As the city of Srinagar was mostly organized around the river itself; therefore, the location of these prominent shrines along its bank also acted as visual indicators of a new order.

As opposed to this, most of the major rural shrines especially those associated with the indigenous *Reshī* order were located in isolated locations – the choice of a recluse. In the sacred geography of Muslim shrine culture of Kashmir, the shrines associated with the *Reshīs* show a marked predilection towards a silent communion with nature, a life of severe penance and worship. Aside from the principal shrine at Char-i Sharief (the burial place of Shaykh Nūr-al Dīn), most of the *Reshī* shrines still retain a spirit of physical detachment in spite of development and urbanization in the surroundings. While today many of the shrines survive as vast building complexes drawing a steady stream of devotees, yet at their core they remain small and secluded places of worship. Located away from main population centers, at the top of a mountain or the bank of a lake, these shrines are a symbol of the simplicity associated with the order.

Interestingly, within the wider genre of buildings and shrines associated with *Reshīs*, five sites predate Islam in the region. These are the cave shrines at Tapil, Loduv, Shree Gupwar, Aeshmuqam and Bamzu[158]. In oral traditions maintained amongst the community, the shrines at Tapil and Loduv are directly linked with Shaykh Nūr-al Dīn, while the shrine at Shree Gupwara and Aeshmuqam are linked to his disciple, Bābā Zain-al Dīn[159]. The shrine of Bābā Bām-al Dīn at Bamzu was originally a temple, which on the conversion and subsequent death of its Hindu administrator, Bām-al Dīn, served as his burial chamber.

Historically, Shaykh Nūr-al Dīn had embarked on his spiritual journey in a cave at Qaimoh, which he had dug out from a mound of earth, spending twelve years in it. The memory of the cave is preserved in a verse of the Shaykh. It is said that when the Shaykh was asked by his mother to dissociate from a life of discomfort in the cave, he replied:

> *Mauj ghoupi bi wandey handi ler*[160]
> (transl: O! mother I prefer this cave over a mansion).

The name used for the cave, *ghoup,* is a local derivative from the original Sanskrit *ghumpa*. In Kashmir, aside from the famous cave shrine of Amarnath, not many known recorded examples of caves used for religious practices are to be found from pre-Muslim period. Of the ones we know, are three rock cut cave temples at Bamzu and another rock cut cave at Satbaran, Lolab[161].

Interestingly, in the *Reshī* order of Kashmir, we find a revival of the tradition of caves. Not only the Shaykh but also his principal *khalīfas* spent a large part of their life in caves. This tradition continued with the future generation of *Reshī* saints in Kashmir till the mid-part of the Mughal rule, when the order seems to have lost its vitality as well as sway in the region, though it never ceased its existence. Two of the Shaykh's principal disciples, Bām-al Dīn and Zain-al Dīn, are buried in caves. Architecturally, the caves associated with the *Reshīs* of Kashmir are devoid of any decorative quality. The cramped space enclosed within these caves represents the severity of life associated with the founding fathers of the *Reshī* order. Unlike the *khānaqāhs* of the established Sufi orders, the *Reshīs* never desired an attendant community of disciples, requiring the need of large congregational spaces. The spatial quality of the cells and the caves associated with them preclude public or congregational worship or assembly. Rather, these chambers and cells served as monastic retreats, either carved from earth mounds or found naturally in the slopes of mountains and cliffs. Indeed, where they occur naturally, no effort was made to hollow out the chambers to provide more space, rather the limitation of the space was seen as a part of the severity associated with worship. It is worthwhile to note that most hagiographic accounts are replete with the severity of life that most *Reshīs* imposed on themselves.

Shaykh Nūr-al Dīn is said to have reduced his daily diet comprising a glass of milk to a glass of water during the latter part of his life. We also have accounts of at least one *Reshī* starving himself to death[162]. Similar is the case with many other *Reshīs*, who even stopped partaking of any vegetable, in the belief that it amounts to killing a living soul[163]. Such a belief system stands in sharp contrast to the practices that were being adopted in the *langars* (public kitchen) of major Sufi *khānaqāhs* of the time[164]. The *Reshīs* even came for severe criticism from Mīrzā Haidār during his rule. Regarding the Kashmiri *Reshīs*, he denounces them as having:

> [...] Legitimized so many heresies that they know nothing of what is lawful or unlawful. They consider that piety and purity consist in night vigil and abstinence of food[165].

The *ghār* (cave) of Tapil is located on the eastern bank of the Anchar lake on the outskirts of the historic Srinagar[166][Figure 3.21]. The shrine itself comprises a series of small manmade cells carved inside a tableland overlooking the surrounding lake. The approach to the cave is from the lake front, where

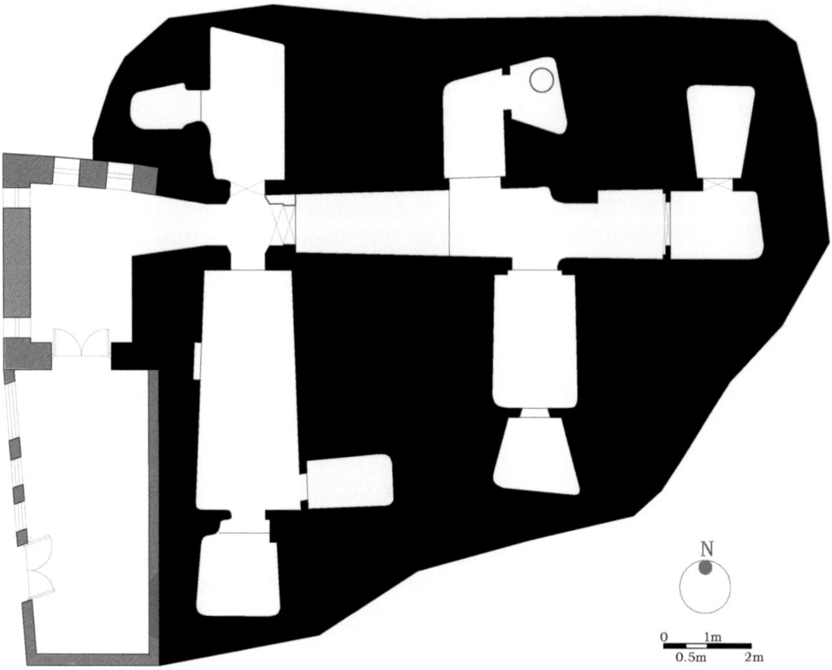

Figure 3.21 Ghār-i Sharīf at Tapil: plan, © Hakim Sameer Hamdani.

the natural fall of the table land provides easy access. Internally, a narrow 1.5m wide vaulted passage opens onto narrow cells on either side. In all, eleven small cells open out into the passage and have been excavated in the form of barrel vaults. A contemporary single-story structure has been recently constructed at the entrance to the cave on the western side (lake side) which serves as an entrance chamber. The entrance to the cave is on the extreme north-eastern corner of the chamber and leads into a passage with a ceiling shaped as a vault sloping toward the main part of the cave. Internally, the builders have followed a simple principal, that of a linear passage along which a series of cells are carved out. The passage and the various cells opening onto it have been created from a solid – an earthen mound – by hollowing it out. This is unlike what can be seen at Aeshmuqam, Shree Gupwara and Loduv, which basically comprise natural phenomenon.

The cells vary in size, but generally, all of them branch out into a smaller side chamber. While most of the door openings are rectangular, with some supported on wooden lintels, the main entrance opening has a carved-out arched mud pilaster framing the opening. Though most of the cells are at level with the adjacent passage, a couple of cells are located a step down. One of the cells also holds an open well.

A significant feature of the Tapil cave is the presence of an unusual bas-relief midway in the passage, which is easy to miss in the darkness of the interiors. The iconography and the style of this intriguing relief is totally devoid of an Islamic meaning or influence, giving rise to the question of its source, whether it is part of the *Reshī* culture, or predates their arrival and use of the cave?

An inspection of the relief indicates certain clumsiness in its making, which may very well indicate that the makers of the relief were not part of an established high artistic tradition. Most probably those who had carved the cave, and used it, were the ones who made the relief.

As far as the nature of the relief is concerned, it gives the impression of a Buddhist *chorten* that we also see impressed upon clay votive offerings linked to Kashmir's pre-Muslim medieval period. The arch-shaped opening that makes up for a major part of the relief also mimics the three-lobed arch which serves as the halo (flaming mandorla) for many of the Buddhist metal statutes of Kashmir dating to medieval period[167]. It gives us sufficient ground to advance the hypothesis that the construction of the caves at Tapil predates the arrival of Islam in Kashmir. The appropriation of the cave by the *Reshīs,* its symbolic association with Shaykh Nūr-al Dīn, marks the propensity of the *Reshī* order for overt syncretism that helped in continuing some of the older established native traditions in a society that were under increasing pressure from immigrant missionaries to mold into a totally different, more orthodox character.

The association of the caves with Shaykh Nūr-al Dīn is based on oral traditions maintained within the surrounding community, rather than any historical reference. Nevertheless, the spirit of the site resonates with the life and preachings of the saint.

Unlike the cave at Tapil, the *ghār* at Loduv is located on a hillock in close vicinity of a historic site: the stone temple of Loduv. The ruins of the temple, whose circular plan indicates its Buddhist origin before being converted into a temple, are located within a small water body fed by springs, at the foothills of the hill. The temple, spring as well as the cave, is part of an ensemble of natural and man-made features that constitute the memory of the site, revered in three belief systems: Buddhism, Hinduism and Islam[168]. The identification of the *ghār* at Loduv with Shaykh Nūr-al Dīn is another case of re-appropriation of an ancient venerated site in a new emerging socio-cultural environment, marking the continuity of that reverence, now as a sacred Muslim site. The small cave itself is a natural formation whose only distinct feature remains a mark of a hand on the wall, said to be of Shaykh Nūr-al Dīn. Over the years and centuries, this section of the cave has acquired a glossy texture, a result of constant rubbing by devotees at the shrine.

The cave at Shree Gupwara is associated with Bābā Zain-al Dīn (d. 857 AH/1453 CE), a Hindu who converted to Islam at the hands of Bābā Bām-al Dīn, the principal *khalīfa* of Shaykh Nūr-al Dīn[169].

Like most *Reshis,* a recluse from court life, Zain-al Dīn is said to have incurred the displeasure of the reigning sultan, Zain-al Ābidīn, who briefly banished him towards Ladakh, before repenting and recalling him back to Kashmir.

Most Muslim historians and *tazkira nigārs* of the region maintain that on the advice of his spiritual mentor, Zain-al Dīn left for Aishmuqam in South Kashmir, spending most of his life in the cave at Aishmuqam. Additionally, there are caves in South Kashmir, which legends maintain, are interconnected with the Aishmuqam cave. One of these is the cave at Shree Gupwara. A beautiful small, almost square, shrine measuring around 7.92m × 8.22m has been constructed over the cave in the nineteenth century CE [Figure 3.22].

The cave can be approached from small wooden portico, supported on wooden columns, on the southern side. A series of five steps lead down into the main cave which is almost oblong shaped measuring around 4.87m × 1.82m, aligned along the east-west axis. A small opening on the northern wall of the cave provides entry to a secondary cave, which according to local custodians, connects through tunnels to the cave at Aishmuqam. Access to this part of the shrine could not be gained. The main cave, which seems to be a natural phenomenon, has been plastered in parts, yet retains its original, natural ceiling form.

Also associated with Zain-al Dīn is the vast shrine complex at Aishmuqam. It was at Aishmuqam that Zain-al Dīn spent most of his life in solitary, severe religious penances. And it is at Aishmuqam that Zain-al Dīn along with a host of his disciples lies buried.

The larger shrine precinct presently comprises the main shrine, located over the cave were Zain-al Dīn prayed and lies buried, a mosque and a subsidiary shrine further uphill wherein many disciples of Zain-al Dīn are buried.

The various buildings within the precinct date from nineteenth century onwards, of which the double-story building serving as the mosque is the most interesting, architecturally. The cave, which is again a natural phenomenon, is aligned in a linear direction along an east-west axis, with a total length of 23.7m and an average width of 5.7m. At the far end of the cave, a small antechamber connects to a side grotto, serving as the final resting place of the saint. Marble dados, flooring and odd-shaped multi-lobed arches in the interior of the cave are twentieth century addition to the shrine, altogether adding to a kitschy feel that unfortunately has been the fate of many historic Muslim religious places in Kashmir.

The widespread prevalence of the culture of cave shrines amongst the *Reshī* order is indicative both of the unworldly outlook of the adherents of this order, as well a deeply felt desire to preserve revered spaces of past. In trying to do, the members of this order, while re-appropriating older sacred spaces, helped in preserving the cultural as well as a spatial link with Kashmir's pre-Islamic past and enshrining non-Muslim customs, practices and spaces within the emerging body of Muslim community and culture.

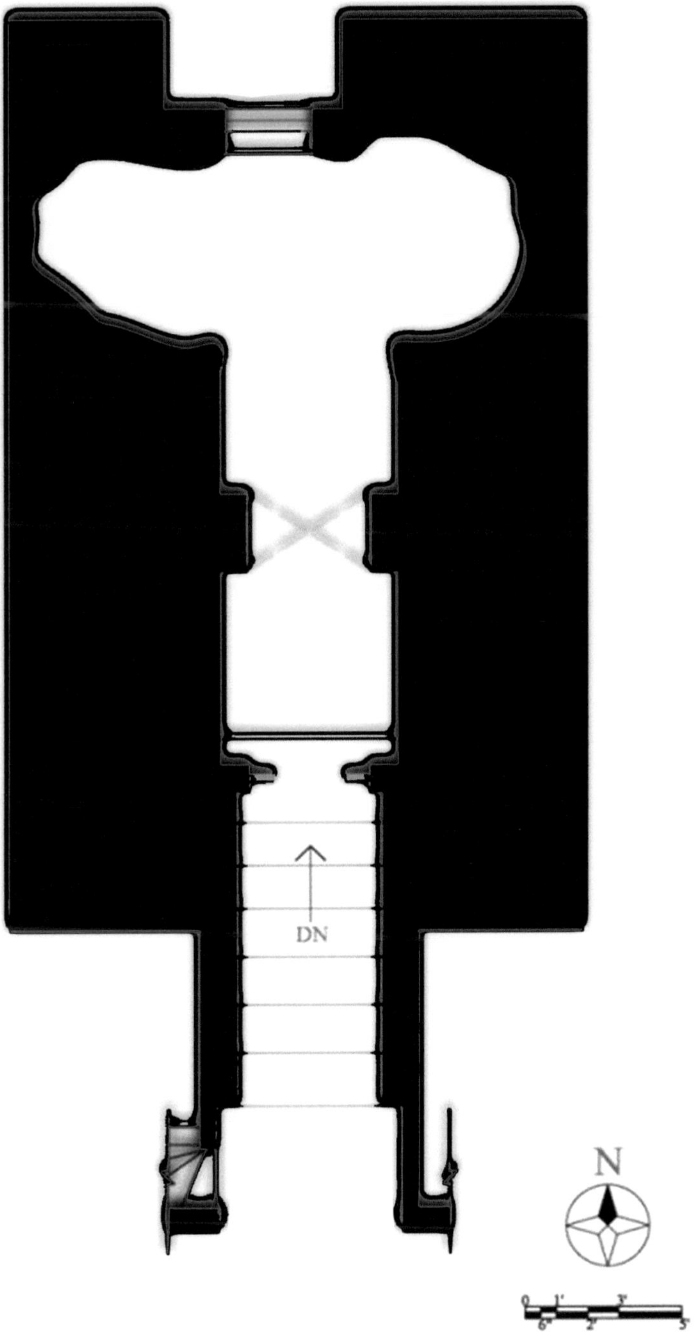

Figure 3.22 Ghār-i Sharīf at Shree Gupwara; plan, © INTACH, Kashmir.

The *Mʿārak* at Zadibal, Srinagar

It was during the reign of Sultan Muhammad Shāh (r. 1517-25 CE) that his powerful Shi'a *vazir,* Kājī Chak, built the *Mʿārak*, the first *imambāda* in Kashmir at Zadibal in the capital Srinagar[170]. Historically, the *imambāda* at Zadibal can be seen as one of the first such building that was constructed in the Indian subcontinent. The etymological origin of its more widespread name *Mʿārak* is said to be derived from the Persian word, "*muarika*" (lit. battlefield)[171].

While a nascent Shi'a community had existed in Kashmir since the beginning of the Muslim rule, it was only in the fifteenth century that the members of the community started acquiring political power. This new quest for power and conversion was mostly based on missionary activities of the *Nūrbakshiya* shaykh, Mīr Shams-al Dīn (d. 1525 CE) and the rising clout of the Chak clan, whose members had converted to the Shi'a creed by Mīr Shams-al Dīn. The building of *Mʿārak* marks the beginning of a transition in the history of the Shi'a community of Kashmir, from the periphery to the center of power and patronage.

The *imambāda* was constructed in an area which served as the nucleus of the *Nūrbakshiya* activities in Kashmir. Both the *khānaqāh* and the shrine of Mīr Shams-al Dīn are a part of this *moḥala* of Srinagar. Located on the banks of Khushalsar Lake, between Zain- al Ābidīn's capital of Naushahr and the more historic older parts of Srinagar city, Zadibal, with *Mʿārak* at its heart, has since then served as the focus of Shi'ite cultural and religious activities in the region.

Following its construction by Kājī Chak, *Mʿārak* was burnt down in 1545 CE by Mīrzā Haidar[172]. The fall of Dughlat at the hands of a Chak-led insurgency led to the reconstruction of the *imambāda* during the premiership of Dawlat Chak (1551-54 CE). Thereafter, the building was again burned down repeatedly due to prevailing political instability and sectarian tensions in the region.

Though the building had been rebuilt numerous times, it is evident from the construction as it stood prior to its demolition, as well as oral traditions preserved within the community, that each reconstruction[173] adhered strictly to the original plan dating back to the sixteenth century CE.

Forming the prototype for all major *imambādas* built in Kashmir, the building was based on a courtyard plan historically associated with the Iranian mosque. This was a form that had been adopted earlier in Kashmir for designing of the principal mosque of region, the Jamia at Srinagar. Given the impressive scale of the Jamia Masjid, one can assume that the courtyard plan weighed heavily on the builders while constructing Kashmir's first *imambāda* as a symbol of Shi'a faith [Figure 3.23].

Unlike a mosque with its requirement to accommodate linear rows of worshippers and the resulting rectangular shape, the square form associated with the courtyard plan was also functionally in tune with the main

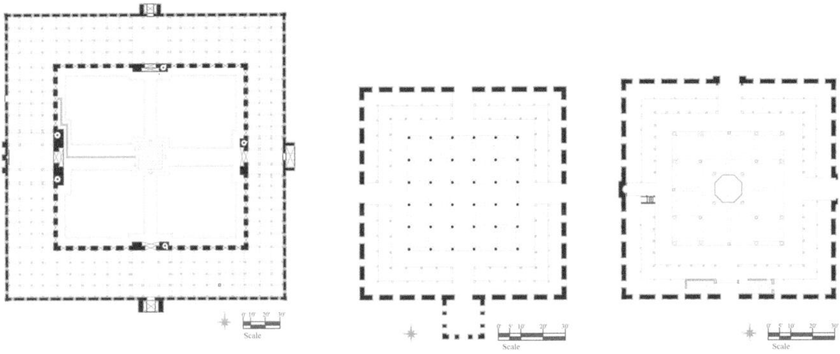

Figure 3.23 Courtyard plan in Kashmir, Jamia Masjid Srinagar (L) formed the inspiration for designing of *Mʿārak* (R), © Hakim Sameer Hamdani.

ritual enacted in an *imambāda* reciting the *marthiya* (elegy). In Kashmir, the *marthiya* is recited by a *z̲ākir (*the lead vocalist), his troupe of reciters along with the whole assembly of mourners which may be in thousands, comprising both men as well as women. In both private as well as public congregation, the mourners sit on the floor in concentric rings, with a central circle (*dʿiara*) of the *paskhawns* (primary group of chanters) acting as the focal point of the entire assembly. The *z̲ākir* himself remains standing, moving amongst the crowds of mourners from one end to another, theatrically invigorating the entire congregation with a deep feeling of sorrow and sadness.

The architectural form of the *imambāda* also suits the recital of *marthiya* amongst the mourners. A slightly raised and covered central square courtyard (*pūkhir*) easily accommodates the concentric rings of the main assembly. The *pūkhīr* is in turn demarcated by a parallel ambulatory space running on all four sides. This ambulatory space, known as *ghulām gardish,* is in turn surrounded by a two-storied block of galleries (*dalāns*). Traditionally, the *ghulām gardish* is never covered with a roof. The *dalān* on the ground floor serves as an open gallery overlooking onto the *pūkhīr*. Generally, it is raised on a slightly higher plinth as compared to the *pūkhīr* so as to provide a clear line of vision into the main assembly. The gallery on the upper floor overlooking the *pūkhīr* is reserved for women and is screened off from public view by wooden screens with *pinjrakārī* (lattice work). Overall, the effect of the interiors is that of a centrally planned square housing the *pūkhīr* with all other spaces opening into this very part of the building.

At the old *Mʿārak* which dated back to the reconstruction of 1872 CE, the outer dimensions of the building were 22.86m × 22.86m[174]. The roof of the *pūkhīr* (15.24m × 15.24m) was supported on 36 wooden columns 7.6m in height, a freestanding wooden structure, in itself an architectural marvel. The *ghulām gardish* was 2.1m wide while the most conspicuous feature of the surrounding gallery was an array of 113 ornamental wooden columns supporting a low-height ceiling. To provide for a better view towards the *pūkhīr*, the *dalān* with a width of 3.6m was designed in two steps.

The building had four principal gateways, centrally located along the four cardinal directions. Overall, the various entrance doorways to the building were as much associated with specific paths of rituals as with the surrounding urban morphology based on community and family linkages. Originally, the main entrance doorway to the building was from the rear, on the western side facing the *qiblā*, at a place which would traditionally in a mosque mark the *miḥrāb*. This unique location of the main entrance door was due to the fact that up till mid-twentieth century CE, public access to the building was from the western side along the Khushalsar Lake. Also, historically, unlike many other *imambādas*, the *Mʿārak* was generally never used for the purpose of congregational prayer.

The interiors of *Mʿārak,* like most other shrines and mosques of the region, were not permeated with natural light. In fact, in the interiors, there was a marked contrast between light and shade as sunlight filtered through the narrow small *pinjrakārī* wooden shutters with their intricately detailed geometric patterns. This interplay of light and shade was at times heightened by the contrast between the richly colored papier-mâché ceiling, the dark tone of the forest of wooden columns inside the building and the somber earthy color of the mud plastered walls. The feel of the building interiors also reflects a preference of the builders for the traditional Kashmiri color palette broadly comprising pastels with a predominance of green and blues, referred to as *ṣūfīyāna rang* (color of the Sufis) as opposed to the vibrant red and yellows which simply go by the name of *tayẓ rang*: the fast color.

Unlike Iranian mosques where the side halls *(liwans)* comprise arcade of masonry pillars supporting domed or vaulted ceiling, the Kashmiri builders adopted a trabeate system wherein a flat wooden ceiling is supported on wooden beams and columns. This feature is found uniformly in all religious buildings associated with Islam in Kashmir. At *Mʿārak*, the wooden columns supporting the ceiling depicted a multiplicity of form; octagonal plain columns were as much a part of the order as are the more ornate baluster columns which owed their origin to the Mughal period. The multi-cusped arches in the wooden *varusī* also traced their roots to the Mughals.

The ceiling of the double height *pūkhīr* was done in papier-mâché. Historically, the papier-mâché craft (*kār-i mūnaqash*) was exclusively associated with the Shi'a community of Srinagar. The papier-mâché at *Mʿārak* dating to nineteenth century CE was probably the finest representation of this art form used in the decoration of a building and prior to the demolition would have been the oldest extant example in Kashmir.

Externally, the building façade was based on a uniform arcade of two rows of small arches in brick masonry, an element that all *imambādas* share. Interestingly, this feature also traces its roots partly to the Jamia Masjid of Srinagar. The roof of the courtyard was in shape of a multi-tiered pyramidal roof surmounted by a square wooden pavilion. Overall, the outer appearance of the building was that of a self-contained, low-lying, earth-hugging horizontal composition screening, much like the *pinjrakārī* in the window openings – the architectural richness that was a part of the building interiors.

Traditionally, the building and the rituals enacted therein represents a synthesis of a universal pan-Islamic culture and folk traditions relating to the theme of death and remembrance prevalent in Kashmir. Architecturally, it represents a tradition where a non-native plan form, that of the Iranian courtyard mosque plan, was adapted and modified to cater to the needs how in Kashmir the ritual of remembrance of Muharram was performed and enacted. This phenomenon of homogenizing heterogeneous design schemes had been seen earlier also, most famously in the designing of Jamia Masjid at Srinagar.

Conclusion

The fifteenth century CE saw the revival of Kashmir as a major Himalayan kingdom, outward-looking, and with new territories acquired outside the natural physical barrier of the land. This new glory of the Sultans of Kashmir was also noticed by Muslim Sufis and preachers from countries to the west of Kashmir, who combined their missionary zeal with the quest for engaging the interests of powerful patrons and courts. Thus, in the aftermath of Sultan Qutub-al Din's conquest, we notice the arrival of a steady number of Sufis and preachers as well as men of letters from Persianate lands. These non-native Muslims with their strong links to established Sufi *silsilas* laid the foundation of Muslim exclusiveness as a force in the socio-political and cultural life of Kashmir. By their acts, they aimed at building a recognizable Muslim image – a Muslim-ness pervading through all sections of the community and the ruling system. The image they sought to introduce in the society mirrored the image of Islam that these Sufis and preachers had bought from their native land.

While the non-Kashmiri Muslim missionaries evolved a strategy of polemical debate and questioning of local traditions, the practice of the native *Reshis* was more based on sharing personal experiences and respect for the native way of life. As opposed to the argumentative debates of the non-natives, the *Reshis* were involved in a conversation of self-realization with contemporary seekers of other faith, at times leading to conversion.

It was in this cultural background that new building typologies were introduced in the region as were new ideological debates, resulting in iconoclastic activities as well as synthesis of a new art and craft forms. It was also a period of intense building activity involving construction of *khānaqāhs*, roza, mosques and the first Jamia of Kashmir at Srinagar. This period marks gradual shift from the earlier period of hesitant transition, to the development of native Kashmiri idiom for building Muslim places of worship reflecting a synthesis of diverse architectural traditions. An architectural outpouring that saw a marked predilection of Kashmiri builders to emphasize their buildings in a language of local distinctiveness and local aspirations; of which the ubiquitous soaring pyramidal brangh served as the most powerful, unifying visual tool.

Notes

1 ʿAli, *Tārīkh-i Kashmir*, 1; Sufi, *Kashīr*, 86. Also see, Beatrice Forbes Manz, *Power, Politics and Religion in Timurid Iran* (Cambridge: Cambridge University Press, 2007), 240.
2 Dedhmārī, *Waqāt-i Kashmir*, 87.
3 '[...] the said Sultan also had nothing Islamic about him except his name; his clothes and attire were also like those of the infidels', Malīk, *Tārīkh-i Kashmir,* 53.
4 *Bahāristān-i Shāhī*, 29.
5 See, Muhammad Qasim Shāh Farishtā, *Tārīkh –i Farishtā* (Lucknow: Munshi Nawal Kishore, 1823).
6 Jonāraja, *Rajatarangini*, 306.
7 Sayyid ʿAli's political thoughts are summarized in his treatise, *Zakhirat-al Mulūk*. About non-Muslims living in a Muslim state, while respecting their right of life and property, he stipulates they will not construct any new temple or be allowed to repair old ones, Hayat Aamir Husseni, *The Religious Thought of Mir Saiyid Ali Hamdani* (Srinagar: Jay Kay Bookshop, 1998), 155–56.
8 To account for their heroic account of Sayyed ʿAli's proselytizing zeal, later authors would account for three separate visits of the saint to Kashmir. Bhat in his notes on *Tārīkh-i Kashmir* has authoritatively established that Sayyid ʿAli Hamdanī visited Kashmir only once, ʿAli, *Tārīkh-i Kashmir*, 88–97. The outcome of Sayyid ʿAli's mission can also be analyzed from the author of *Bahāristān-i Shāhī,* who writes:

> [...] Quṭub-al Dīn failed to propagate Islam in accordance and wishes and aspiration of Amīr Sayyid ʿAli Hamdanī and as such the latter found himself reluctant to stay in the land. Consequently, after a short while, he left [...], *Bahāristān-i Shāhī*, 30.

9 Hillenbrand, *Islamic Art and Architecture,* 22.
10 Of the various Sufis who arrived in Kashmir from the reign of Quṭub-al Dīn till Zain-al Ābidīn, only one was from Arabia, one from Asia Minor (Bālād-i Rum) while the rest were from various parts of Iran and Persianized Khurasan including Balkh, Herat or Transoxina (Mawrah-ul Nahar).
11 '[...] so was Mahammada of Mera country among these Yavnas, and although he was a boy, he became their chief by learning. The king waited on him daily, humble as a servant and like a student, he daily took his lessons from him', Jonāraja, *Rajatarangini*, 308.
12 Hasan, *Kashmir Under the Sultans,* 241.
13 G N Gauhar, *Kashmir Mystic Thought* (Srinagar: Gulshan Books, 2009), 38.
14 The Shaykh (d. 1415 CE or 1438 CE) was second-generation convert to Islam, said to have been born in 1377 CE, though 1355 CE is also mentioned as his year of birth, see Bābā Nasīb al-Dīn Ghāzī, transl. Marghub Banhali, *Nūr Nāmā* (Srinagar: Markaz-i-Nur, 2013).
15 Gauhar's hypothesis is based on a verse of Nūr-al Dīn, where the saint describes himself as the fifth Kashmiri in the line of spiritual preceptors of the *Reshī* order, an order which then traces its spiritual genealogy to the Prophet Muhammad through one intermediatory.

In one of his verse, the Shaykh defines his perception of reality in these words:

He alone was and He alone will be Oh!

My soul keep reciting He alone He

Though these verses can be traced to Islamic mysticism, yet they also reflect native traditions that were popularized in the *Pratyabhijna* school of Kashmiri Shaivism, with its belief that everything is Shiva – the Absolute reality. This school originated in the ninth century CE, and was greatly expanded by Abhinavgupta (950-1016 CE), see, N Isaeva, *From Early Vedanta to Kashmir Shaivism: Gaudapada, Bhartrhari and Abhinavagupta* (New York: State University of New York Press, 1995).

16 Ranjit Hoskote, *I, Lalla, The Poems of Lal Ded* (Gurgaon: Penguin Random House India, 2013), xviii. Lʿalā, is seen as the spiritual preceptor of Shaykh Nūr-al Dīn, and one of the Shaykhs *shruks* is dedicated to the memory of the *yogni*.

17 See, Malīk, *Tārīkh-i Kashmir.* The first written account of the life of the Shaykh dates back to the sixteenth century CE and is found in a short poetical work, *Lamieh,* written by Bābā Dāwūd Khākī. This was followed by a detailed account of the life of Shaykh compiled by Bābā Nasīb al-Dīn Ghāzī (1569–1637 CE) in his *Nūr Nāmā*. Nasīb is the first author to write about a meeting between Sayyid ʿAli Hamdanī and the Shaykh and associating a relationship of *pīr-murīdī* between the two, Ghāzī, *Nūr Nāmā*, 222–25.

18 Like in the case of Lʿalā, doubts have been raised about the authenticity of some of the verses generally attributed to the Shaykh. The collection attributed to the Shaykh was composed by Bābā Kamāl in 1251 AH/ 1836 CE.

19 Muzaffar Ahmad Khan, *The Shaikh and His Shrukhs*, ʿAlamdār, Vol.V, 2011–12, 24.

20 Local traditions maintain that the Shaykh spent some time meditating in the caves of Tapil located on the banks of Anchar lake. He is also said to have visited Dal lake, once. Though both Anchar and Dal were not a part of medieval Srinagar, yet they are the only record we have of the Shaykh in the environs of the capital.

21 Based on ʿAli, Dedhmārī, Malīk and Khuihāmī's account.

22 'Attracted by gifts and honors, which the king bestowed and by his kindness, the mlechchhas entered Kashmira, [...]', Jonāraja, *Rajatarangini*, 308.

23 Ghāzī, *Nūr Nāmā*, 8.

24 See ʿAli, *Tarikh-i Kashmir,* 17.

25 Jonāraja, *Rajatarangini*, 309.

26 Ibid, 308–09.

27 Both Sufi and Hasan lay the blame on Suha Bhatta who converted to Islam at the hands of Sayyid Mohammed Hamdanī and was renamed as Malīk Ṣaif-al Dīn (Sword of Faith), Sufi, *Kashīr,* 148, 149. The evidence of iconoclastic activities associated with the Sultan is corroborated by Jonāraja as well as Muslim author's likeʿAli, Malīk, etc.

28 Sufi, *Kashīr*, 157.

29 This would also include Sultans from the Chak dynasty, some of whom adopted the title of *Padshah*.

30 *Bahāristān-i Shāhī*, 50–51.

31 'By and large, his courtiers and the men of learning of his times were of cheerful disposition, experts in the art of versification, and subtle in discourse', *Bahāristān-i Shāhī*, 59.

32 Sufi, *Kashīr*, 163.

33 Zain-al Ābidīn's successor, Haidar Shāh (r. 1470–72 CE), followed his father's liberal policies. During his rule, there was a riot around a *khānaqāh* in the city between Hindu and Muslims, which resulted in severe penalties being imposed by the Sultan on the Hindus. Shrivara, a contemporary of Haidar, recalls reading out passages from *Puranas*, *Dharamshastras* and *Samhitas* to the Sultan at night. Haidar's son, Hasan (r. 1472–84 CE) continued the liberal policies of his grandfather, constructing mosques, *khānaqāhs* and temples, see, Shrivara, *Rajatarangini*, 357, 360, 367, 368, 370.

34 Sufi, *Kashīr*, 178.

35 Shrivara, *Rajatarangini*, 383.

36 On assuming power, Sayyid Hasan proclaimed:

> [...] he would not outstrip the limits of *sharia*', and negligence 'in its observance would not be tolerated', *Bahāristān-i Shāhī*, 65.

37 Shrivara, *Rajatarangini*, 368.

38 *Tuḥfatūl Aḥbāb: A Muslim Missionary in Medieval Kashmir: Being English translation of Tuḥfatūl Aḥbāb,* transl. K N Pandita. (New Delhi: Eurasian Human Rights Forum, 2009), 118–119.

39 Sufi, *Kashīr* 195.

40 Ibid.

41 Hasan, *Kashmir Under the Sultans,* 121.

42 Ibid. 'Then the Kashmirian warriors [...] made peace among themselves and drove the Turshkas (Mughals) away, 'as the sun's rays drive away darkness', Shuka, *Rajatarangini*, 418.

43 Hasan, *Kashmir Under the Sultans,* 125–127.

44 '[...] these incendiaries conquered the town of Sekandhra in order to burn it [...] The Turushkas robbed the crops, killed the villagers in anger [...]', Shuka, *Rajatarangini*, 418.

45 'Let it not remain unknown that after Mughal troops quit Kashmir, her chiefs and nobles compromised to forge unity among themselves [...]', *Bahāristān-i Shāhī*, 106–107.

46 Hasan, *Kashmir Under the Sultans,* 129.

47 *Bahāristān-i Shāhī*, 102.

48 Hasan, *Kashmir Under the Sultans,* 134.

49 For an account of Mughal empire under Akbar, see Irfan Habib, *Akbar and His India* (New Delhi: Oxford University Press, 2010).

50 Mīrzā Haidar Dughlat, *Tārīkh-i Rashidī: A History of the Moghuls of Central Asia*, transl. E D Ross, (Srinagar,: Gulshan Books, 2012), p.691. Some of the crafts being practiced in Kashmir that are recorded by Haidar include stone-cutting, stone-polishing, bottle-making, window-cutting, gold-beating etc.

51 Kalhānā, *Rajatarangini,* 447.

52 Goetz, *Studies in the history and Art of Kashmir*, 92.

53 Tadgell, *Architecture in Context*, 492.

54 In Kashmir, the only surviving Mughal monument belonging to this genre is an unknown structure at Ilahi Bagh, Srinagar.

55 'Centralized plan, especially octagonal ones, can be found in funerary structures belonging to a number of architectural traditions, including those of the Abbasids, Timurids, Ottomans and Mughals', Muhammad al-Asad, 'Application of Geometry', in *The Mosque*, Frishman and Khan ed., 57.

56 Hillenbrand disccuses the Seljuk origin of the design and the indebtedness of the building to Iranian and Central Asian traditions, importantly to that of tomb of the Ilkhanid ruler, Uljaytu at Sultaniya, Iran, as well as Samanid monuments, see Robert Hillenbrand, 'Turco-Iranian Elements in the Medieval Architecture of Pakistan: The case of the Tomb of Rukn-i ʿAlam at Multan',

Muqarnas, (Leiden: Brill,1991). The tomb of Nasir al-Din at Delhi set within an octagonal cell can be seen earliest use of a octagon in India, see John Burton Page, *Indian Islamic Architecture* (Leiden: Brill, 2008), 5.

57 'The migration of architects or artisan helped to disseminate artistic ideas, regardless of whether they sought work in an economically more prosperous place, or had been invited by an artistically inclined ruler', Richard Ettinghausen, 'The Man-Made Settings', in *The World of Islam,* Bernard Lewis ed., (London: Thames & Hudson, 1976), 59.

58 Kak, *Ancient Monuments of Kashmir*, 6.

59 Ibid, 149.

60 Ibid, 83.

61 Archaeological Survey of India Report, (1906–07:162).

62 For Samarra, see, Sheila S Blair and Jonathan M Bloom, *The Grove encyclopedia of Islamic Art and Architecture* (New York: Oxford University Press, 2009).

63 See, *Tuḥfatūl Aḥbāb* and Malīk, *Tārīkh-i Kashmir*. As opposed to this, Sayyid ʿAli writes that Mir Sayyid ʿAli converted the priest of temple to Islam, and then undertook the first major iconoclastic act in the valley, by demolishing the temple. Khuihāmī repeats the narrative of temple destruction, and names the destroyed temple as Kaleshavar. The commemoration by Hindus of the western retaining wall of the *khānaqāh* overlook the *ghāt* as the temple of Maha Kali dates back to the nineteenth century CE, when during Sikh rule, the Hindu community could lay claim to a part of the precinct under a favorable political condition. Though not exactly a case for syncretism, the temple-*ghāt-khānaqāh* complex has since then continued to serve the two communities. Both continue to function with each community evoking their own spiritual and historic memory of the site. See, ʿAli, *Tārīkh-i Kashmir,* 6; also Khuihāmī, *Tārīkh-i Hasan* for account of temple destruction.

64 *Tuḥfatūl Aḥbāb*, 93.

65 ʿAli, *Tarikh-i Kashmir*, 15; Malīk, *Tārīkh-i Kashmir,* 56.

66 *Bahāristān-i Shāhī*, 46.

67 Ibid, 40.

68 Dedhmārī, *Waqāt-i Kashmir*, 177; Khuihāmī, *Tārīkh-i Hasan,* 418–419.

69 *Bahāristān-i Shāhī*, 40.

70 In mediaeval texts, the *khānaqāh* is alternatively also referred to as *Khānaqāh -i Amiriyah* and *Khānaqāh -i Hamdaniya.*

71 Dedhmārī, *Waqāt-i Kashmir*, 90.

72 When during the closing part of the fifteenth century CE, Ṣaif Dar assumed the office of primership; he held a meeting of ulema and state officials at the *khānaqāh*. During the reign of Sultan Habīb Shāh, the wooden column of the *khānaqāh* was broken by a musket shot fired on an assembly of nobles in the building, Malīk, *Tārīkh-i Kashmir*, 70; *Tuḥfatūl Aḥbāb*, 105, 121.

73 *Tuḥfatūl Aḥbāb*, 264.

74 *Tuḥfatūl Aḥbāb, 133.*

75 ʿIraki's intention to demolish the temple and cut down the old trees in its vicinity faced opposition from Khawājā Gharāmi, a local notable. Gharāmi was able to successfully resist ʿIraki's first attempt at demolition with the help of local inhabitants. Significantly, these muslim defenders of older native traditions retained attachment not only to temple but the entire 'place' comprising the building, the grove of trees and the adjoining spring, see *Tuḥfatūl Aḥbāb*, 225.

76 See, Abū'l Fażl, transl. H. Beveridge, *Akbar Nama*, 3 vols., (New Delhi: Low Price Publications, 2011) and Nūr-al Dīn Jahāngīr, transl. A Rogers, *The Tuzuk-i Jahāngirī* (Delhi: Low Price Publications, 1999).

77 Hakim G Safdar Hamdani, *Shiyan-i Kashmir*, (Srinagar: Ali Muhammed & Sons, 1974), 280.

78 Shahzad Bashir, *Messianic Hopes and Mystical Visions: The Nūrbakhshīya between Medieval and Modern Islam.* (Columbia: University of South Carolina Press, 2003), 227.
79 *Tuḥfatūl Aḥbāb* also provides us with the brief glimpse of the vernacular architectural traditions prevelants at that time. The author notes the use of deodar, *snober* (pine) and *nagoo* (fir) wood in the construction. He also notes the use of *pinjras* in windows, see *Tuḥfatūl Aḥbāb*, 58–59.
80 It seems that *sajjāda tāzemī* – protestations before the spiritual preceptor, a much debated and critiqued ritual, was also observed at the *khānaqāh*.
81 See, *Tuḥfatūl Aḥbāb.*
82 Literally, the new *khānaqāh*.
83 See, *Bahāristān-i Shāhī*, 138.
84 Ibid, 138–203; also see Hamdani, 161–162.
85 '[...] Ali Khan left the battle field and walked the distance from Idgah and arrived at the *khanqah* of Baba Khalilu'llah', *Bahāristān-i Shāhī*, 160.
86 Ibid, 159, 160. The *khānaqāh* was burnt down during Shi'a-Sunni riot after the fall of the Sultanate. Consequently, it came to be known as *Khānaqāh - i Sokhtā* (Burnt *Khānaqāh*).
87 The area, also known as Dedhmar, was settled by the Queen Diddā who also built a *matha* (monastery) here. Possibly, the stones used in the plinth are quarried from the *matha*.
88 The present flight of steps is a modern alteration and comprises a single flight parallel to the wall. Given that till recent time open land was located immediately in front of the *khānaqāh*, it is entirely probable that the original entrance was frontal.
89 Goetz, *Studies in the History and Art of Kashmir*, 73.
90 W M Thackston, 'The role of calligraphy', in *The Mosque*, 45.
91 The date was calculated by a contemporary Muslim scholar of Kashmir, Aga Sayyid Baqir.
92 Anthony Welch. 'The Emperor's Grief: Two Mughal Tombs', in *Frontiers of Islamic Art and Architecture*, in *Essays in Celebration of Oleg Gebbar*, ed. Gülru Necipoğlu and Julia Bailey, *Muqarnas* (Boston: Brill, 2008), 271.
93 Dedhmārī, *Waqāt-i Kashmir*, 110. The Kaaba measures 10.97m × 11.88m.
94 Geometrical design based on an arrangement of smaller pieces held together by a simple mechanism of tongue and groove joint.
95 W H Nicholls, 'Muhammadan Architecture in Kashmir', in *ASI Annual Report* (New Delhi: ASI, 1906–07), 87.
96 This mosque is constructed by the faqir, Muhammad al-Madnī, resident of Kashmir. The date (of construction) is the year 848 AH.
97 The building was considerably renovated during the 1920–1930s on the technical advice of the ASI. The lower part of the exposed brick façade was entirely reconstructed. For details on the conservation work, see ASI (1923–24:46, 1916–17:8); also see ASI (1906–07:162).
98 Malīk, *Tārīkh-i Kashmir*, 56; Kak, *Ancient Monuments of Kashmir*, 85.
99 The work on the mosque commenced in 796 AH/1394 CE.
100 'One of the most typical *iwan* arrangements is to have four *iwans* opening on to a central courtyard. The first occurrence of this plan is at the Assyrian site of Ashur in Iraq, although this later became a typical arrangement of mosques, *madrassas* and palaces', Andrew Petersen, *Dictionary of Islamic Architecture* (New York: Routledge, 1999), 130.
101 *Bahāristān-i Shāhī*, 39.
102 While some of the columns date from ninth century CE, the mosque which is located in present-day Uzbekistan was partially rebuilt in 1788-89 CE. I am thankful to Ebba Koch for drawing my attention to the mosque.

103 *Lank*, Sanskrit for island.
104 See Malīk, Jahangir and Dedhmārī.
105 May this edifice be as firm as the foundation of Heavens!
May it be the most renowned ornament of the Universe.
As long as the monarch *Zain-i Ibad* holds festivals therein
May it be like the date of his own reign – happy

Sufi, *Kashīr*, 160.

106 ʿAli, *Tārīkh-i Kashmir*, 20, 21. The Sultan was also well versed in Hindu philosophy and had undertaken a study of *Yoga Vasistha*. According to the court historian, Śrīvara, during his final days, the Sultan, he:

> [...] listened to the *Mokṣopāyasaṃhitā* from me as I commented upon it in order to pacify the sorrow of existence in the world (*saṃsāra*). [...] Through that, the king became instantly free from all sorrow, Luther Obrock, 'History at the End of History: Śrīvara's Jainataraginī', in *The Indian Economic and Social History Review*, 50, 2 (2013), 234.

107 See, ʿAli, *Tārīkh-i Kashmiri* and Malīk, *Tārīkh-i Kashmir*.
108 Jonāraja, *Rajatarangini*, 319–20.
109 Malīk, *Tārīkh-i Kashmir*, 57. Crossing the lake, especially in stormy weather was and is still considered a dangerous venture. It seems that the boats with sails helped in offsetting this danger.
110 ʿAli, *Tārīkh-i Kashmir*, 18, 19.
111 Ibid, 20, 21.
112 Jahāngīr, *The Tuzuk-i Jahāngirī*, 94, 95. It is safe to assume that Jahāngīr's description of buildings constructed by Chaks is based on local reports. Most probably, the Chaks repaired the buildings. The author of *Bahāristān-i Shāhī* commemorates the enduring legacy of the *lank* in these words:

> It has been seen that some of the rulers who attained power and authority ordered the pulling down of some ancient buildings. They raised new structures on these sites to be ascribed to them. But the palaces and the mosque of Sultan Zain-al Ābidīn cannot suffer such an alteration, *Bahāristān-i Shāhī*, 59.

113 Charles Ellison Bates, *A Gazetteer of Kashmir* (Srinagar: Gulshan Books, 2005), 255.
114 Ibid, 255.
115 Kak, *Ancient Monuments of Kashmir*, 163–65.
116 According to Haidar, the height of the island was 10*gaz* (8.38m) from the lake water.
117 Sufi, *Kashīr*, 160.
118 Bates, A *Gazetteer of Kashmir*, 255.
119 This is achieved by reducing the thickness of the wall.
120 Kak, *Ancient Monuments of Kashmir*, 164.
121 Ibid, 164-65.
122 For a description of the *Darwaza*, see M Allen, *Ornament in Indian Architecture*. (Newark: University of Delaware Press, 1991) and G S Khawja, *Islamic Architecture of Delhi* (Delhi: Bharatiya Kala Prakashan, 2012), 54.
123 During the fifteenth century CE, the prominent Muslim religious sites in the vicinity of the hillock were the *khānaqāh*s of Shaykh Ismāʿīl Kubrawī, Shams Chak and Mullā Pārsā.
124 See Bābā Dawud Khākī, transl. Qari Ṣaif al-Dīn, *Dastur-al Sīlikin* (Srinagar: Ashraf Book Center, 1971) and Mohammed Yosuf Teng, ed., *Kashir Encylopedia*, 3 vols. (Srinagar: Jammu & Kashmir Academy of Art, Culture and Languages, 1986).

125 The tomb of Shaykh Hamza is located to the southwest of the Zakir Masjid on a lower terrace. To the west of the tomb lies the Salar Beg Masjid originally constructed by a Mughal noble in Jahāngīr's court. Another Mughal-era mosque, Masjid-i ʿInayat Khan, is located to the east of Zakir masjid on a slightly higher level. While the Salar Beg Masjid was rebuilt entirely in the twentieth century CE, the ʿInayat Khan Masjid (Hammam Masjid) survives from its nineteenth century CE additions and alterations.
126 Ebba Koch, *Mughal Archtecture* (Delhi: Primus Books, 2014), 79–80.
127 Flood, *Before the Mughals: Material Culture of Sultanate of North India*, 4.
128 John Burton-Page, ed. George Michel, *Indian Islamic Architecture: Forms and Typologies, Sites and Monuments.* (Leiden: Brill, 2008), 54, 55.
129 The epigram containing date of construction, which has been deciphered by Bates, *A Gazetteer of Kashmir,* 361.
130 Khuihāmī, *Tārīkh-i Hasan*, 426–27.
131 This area was made livable during the times of Zain-al Ābidīn when he partly drained the vast marshy area of Brar-i Nambal by constructing the Nallah Mār canal.
132 Dedhmārī, *Waqāt-i Kashmir*, 109.
133 Ibid.
134 Traces of the original torus molding can still be seen in the lower part of the stone plinth, though partially hidden.
135 The top moulding is cyma recta, and the plinth moulding bears a resemblance to the temple at Narastan.
136 Today the water access has been transformed into a motorable road.
137 My first visit to the site was somewhere around 2004. At that time, traces of human sculpture (badly disfigured) could be still seen near the main entrance.
138 P A Khaliq Tahirī, *Awliyā-i Kashmir*, (Srinagar: Gulshan Publication, 2003), 59–60.
139 Both Dedhmārī and Khuihāmī speak of Lachma Khātūn as the daughter of Malīk Ṣaif-al Dīn.
140 She joins the list of other leading women who were responsible for patronage of Muslim places of worship. Apparently Lachma Khātūn is also buried in the same *mazar* as her husband.
141 The canal which was named *Lachma kul* (the stream of Lachma) was in use till early part of the twentieth century CE.
142 No date is available for the passing away of Malīk Jalāl. His tombstone is covered in *thuluth* script, but the same is not decipherable.
143 Of the original *khānaqāh* no trace survives, though it survived as a major center of learning till seventeenth century CE. Today, a modern structure serving as a mosque exists in its place, Khuihāmī, *Tārīkh-i Hasan*, 432.
144 Before its reconstruction in 2011, the *mazar* of Malīk Jalāl comprised a series of stone cenotaphs located on top of a stone plinth. Today, only parts of the compound wall and the segments of the stone entrance gateway to the compound survive.
145 Major medieval Kashmiri temples were designed as rectangular quadrangles with the temple at center, raising the possibility that the same design was repeated here too.
146 'All those temples and idol houses of the infidels, which had been destroyed totally in the reign of Sultan Sikander, may God bless his soul, were re-built and re-habilitated by him [Zain-al Ābidīn]', *Bahāristān-i Shāhī*, 52.
147 This is a pattern that continues even today, albeit on a limited scale.
148 In addition to hill and mountains, Srinagar's physical expansion was also limited by the various lakes and marshes.

149 *Bahāristān-i Shāhī*, 70–71; Dedhmārī, *Waqāt-i Kashmir*, 173.

150 The relation between *vazir* and the sultan is best described by Malīk in these words:

> Although the government was in the name of Fatah Shāh, all power was held by Ṣaif Dar who did not trust the word of Fatah Shāh, Malīk, *Tārīkh-i Kashmir*, 60.

151 Tahiri, *Awliya-i Kashmir*, 54–55.

152 The Jamia Masjid at Bijbehra was constructed by Sayyid Muhammad Qureshī on a site of an existing temple. Part of the site was later used as a burial place for Sayyid Muhammad Qureshī, Dedhmārī, *Waqāt-i Kashmir*, 94.

153 Teng, *Kashir Encylopedia*, 198.

154 This includes two works of Khākī covering the life of Shaykh Hamza, *Dastur-al Salikīn* and *Vird-al Muridīn*, both are silent on Malīk.

155 Kak, *Ancient Monuments of Kashmir*, 132.

156 The stone pool was excavated 20 *gaz* (18.2m) to the west of the shrine, Teng, *Kashir Encylopedia*, 184.

157 See, Dedhmārī, *Waqāt-i Kashmir*.

158 The earliest cave-shrine associated with the Shaykh is at Koimuh, South Kashmir. Some other caves associated with the *Reshīs* include those at Rahmu (Pulwama), Kanur (Budgam), Rangil (Ganderbal) and Mawar (Handwara).

159 Bābā Nasīb al-Dīn Ghāzī, transl. Marghub Banhali, *Nūr Nāmā* (Srinagar: Markaz-i-Nur, 2013).

160 Ibid, 60, 74.

161 Two cave temples exist at Bamzu, one near Mattan town and the other overlooking the Lidder River. The one overlooking the Lidder is a Shiv temple. The cave temple at Mattan comprises of two temples within individual small caves opening into another caved passage. The rock-cut cave at Lolab is characterized by seven door openings (Satbaran) imitating the design of the trefoil arch which became the standard of Kashmiri stone temple architecture. These rock-cut caves and cave temples have a crude and clumsy architectural quality as compared temples dating from seventh century CE, indicating an earlier origin.

162 Ghāzī, *Nūr Nāmā*.

163 Even today, the vegetarianism associated with the *Reshis*, persists in local folk culture, though such customs are increasingly being challenged and eroded.

164 A contemporary scholar views the *Reshis* as 'crude synchronized form' of Sufi ideas that were introduced into Kashmir by non-native missionaries, see Hamid Naseem, *Muslim Philosophy: Science and Mysticism* (Delhi: Sarup Publishers, 2001), 325.

165 Dughlat, *Tārīkh-i Rashhidi*, 695.

166 The caves were first documented by INTACH in 2003 and then again in 2005.

167 A similar representation of the deity within the trefoil arch can also be seen in the stone temples of medieval Kashmir.

168 Spring as source of water and life is also held in special esteem by the local Muslim community. In Kashmiri folklore, *Nāg* refers to a spring as well as snake, the presiding deity of the spring. In a mythical past, *Nāgs* are said to have been the first inhabitants of the land, and the people of Kashmir emerge from these legends as *Nāg* worshippers. On the other hand, in traditional Islamic cosmology, snake is generally identified with Satan, a connection missing in popular Muslim culture of Kashmir.

169 Dedhmārī, *Waqāt-i Kashmir*, 150.

170 Hamdani, *Shiyan-i Kashmir*, 288.

171 In South Asia, the event of Karbala is also referred to as *marikā-i Karbala* (the battlefield of Karbala) or simply as *marikā*. Badaunī in his history mentions that during the reign of Emperor Hemayun, Moharram ceremonies known as *marikā* used to be enacted in Delhi, Hamdani, *Shiyan-i Kashmir*, 290.

172 Ibid, 288.

173 The current ongoing reconstruction started in 2001 is moulded on Safavid model.

174 Teing, *Kashir Encylopedia*, 35–36.

PLATES

Plate 1: Kashmir: The image of a Himalayan Paradise, Kishansar-Vishansar lake, Kashmir: 2019, © Niraj Kumar.

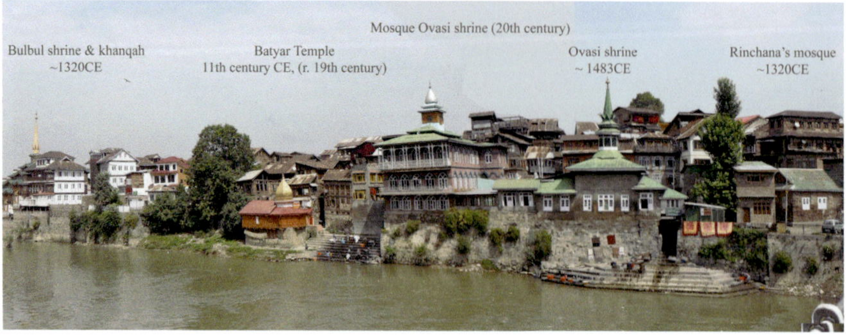

Plate 2: Jhelum river front: The riverfront as a maker of the city's cultural ethos, the mosque of Rīnchanā is in the foreground, Srinagar: 2018, © Hakim Sameer Hamdani.

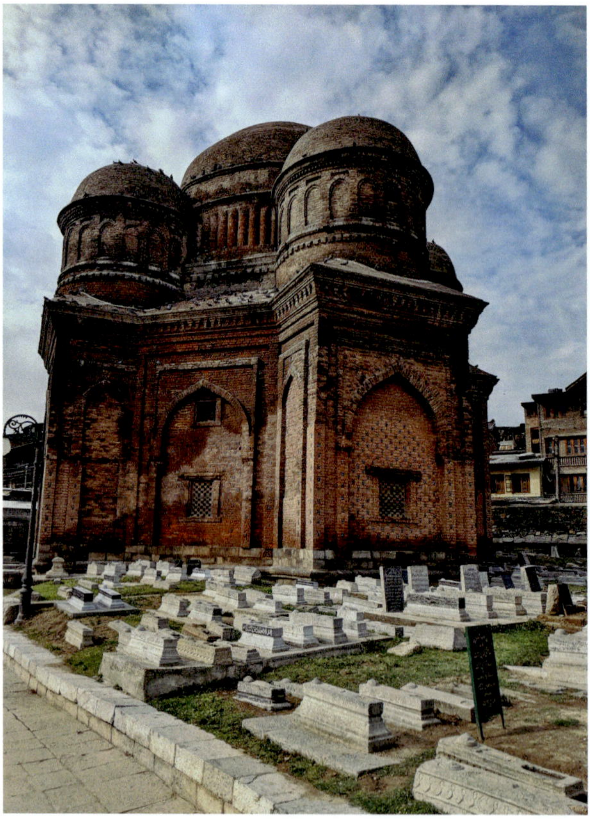

Plate 3: *Dumath*: Mausoleum of Zain-al Ābidīn's mother, based on a centralized octagonal plan, showing deep influences of Timurid architecture, Srinagar: 2019, © Niraj Kumar.

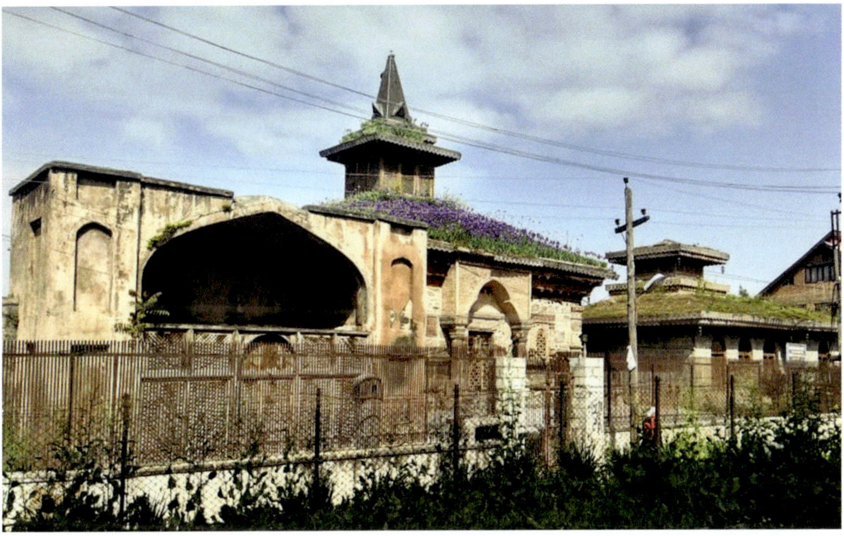

Plate 4: Mosque of Madnī, main eastern façade, the Mughal gateway to the tomb of Madnī is located on the right of the main mosque, Srinagar, 2019, © Zubair Ahmed.

Plate 5: Jamia Masjid: Northern *iwan* from across the central courtyard, Srinagar: 2007, © Hakim Sameer Hamdani.

Plate 6: ʿAālī Masjid: Hypostyle hall with Deodar wooden columns, Srinagar: 2010, © Ram Rehman.

Plate 7: Achabal bāgh: The *bāgh* owes its development to two women: the Empress Nūr Jahān and Princess Jahān Ārā, a reminder of Kashmir's fascination for the imperial household, Achbal: 2011, © Hakim Sameer Hamdani.

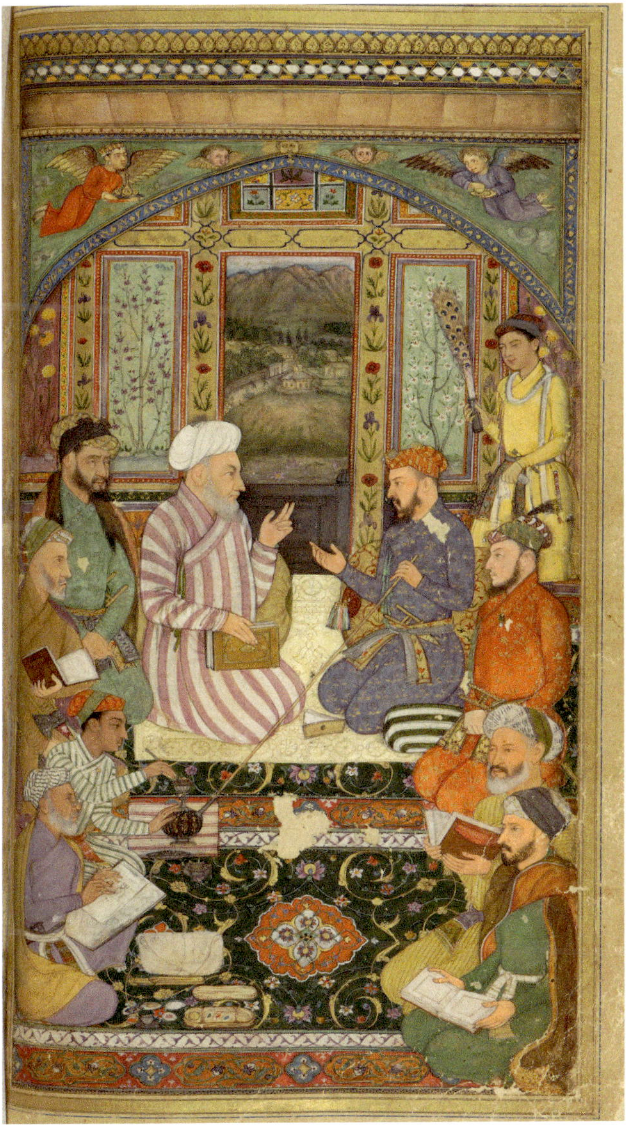

Plate 8: Zafar Khān Aḥsan (blue dress) holding a majlis at his *ḥavelī* at Srinagar. The rich Mughal decorations of *ṣubedars ḥavelī* contrast with the rustic appearance of a Kashmiri shrine which can be seen in the background (from the window), manuscript: c. 1073 AH/ 1662 CE, © Royal Asiatic Society.

Plate 9: *Khānaqāh* of Bābā Nasib: The *Khānaqāh* from the south-east with the modern masonry pillars replacing wooden columns in the entrance porch, Bijbehara: 2017, © Hakim Sameer Hamdani.

Plate 10: *Khānaqāh-i Mʿaulā*, Main eastern façade with painted naqāshī work on the walls and door frame. Most of the colours have undergone through a gradual change during successive repair works in the post-1945 period, Srinagar: 2018, © Niraj Kumar.

Plate 11: Interiors of the *Khānaqāh-i Ghusīyah,* Srinagar, 2019, © Niraj Kumar.

Plate 12: *Asār-i Sharīf*, Hazratbal, the new building at Hazratbal was inspired by Mughal architecture, especially Taj Mahal, Srinagar: 2018, © Mukhtar Ahmad.

Chapter 4

THE MUGHAL INTERLUDE: 1586–1752CE

bi-khūbītāshavad Kashmīr mazkūr
bi-'ālamnām-i nīkashbādmanshur
kunaddaryūzakūh-i PīrPanjāl
zichatr-i daulatashrif'athamasāl

As long as Kashmir is mentioned with good words, may it be renowned in the world

The Pir Panjal mountain seeks elevation from the parasol of his fortune, all year.

Kalim Kashani, **Mughal Arcadia**, Sunil Sharma, 192

Looking at the diverse range of Muslim places of worship described in Chapter 3, it becomes clear that by mid sixteenth century CE, Kashmir had evolved a standard narrative of Islamic religious architecture. Though experiments based on Timurid architecture had been introduced in the region during Zain-al Ābidīn's reign, yet the appeal of the native architectural idiom remained well established, and largely unchallenged. By the time Mughal rule was established in Kashmir, the precedents for what constituted both the image as well as the form of Muslim religious buildings had acquired wide legitimacy both in urban as well as rural settings.

The Mughal rule in Kashmir, would establish a new set of architectural aesthetics- a new *ṭaraḥ* (style) in Kashmir. This chapter explores the transformation that Kashmir underwent through under Mughal rule and interprets the changes that took place in the socio-cultural landscape of Kashmir in the aftermath of Mughal conquest. The chapter examines how in their building proclivities in Kashmir, Mughals introduced an architectural language that was at odds with the native building traditions both in terms of material preference as well as the overall architectural vocabulary. The chapter also discusses the Kashmiri reception of this new architecture and through it, Mughal projection of their imperial power and unlimited munificence.

The empire and the Royal *bāgh*

It was on 14th October of the year 994 AH/1586 CE, Kashmir was finally annexed by the Mughals and *khuṭba* was read in the name of Emperor Akbar (r.1556–1605CE) in Srinagar's principal mosque, the Jamia Masjid. From henceforth, Kashmir would no longer function as a *mūlk* (country), but exist as *ṣubah* (province) of the Mughal Empire. The advance of Mughal rule in Kashmir was visited in the annals of Mughal historians as a natural process of replacing chaos with order and progress[1]. In these accounts there is no perennial tension between the center represented by the imperial court in Delhi (or Agra) and the periphery, in this case the former Sultanate of Kashmir. The official Mughal narrative of how the annexation was received by native Kashmiris is best exemplified by the historian and confidante of Akbar, Shaykh Abū' la Fażl:

> The conquest of this country was a new instance. [...] no thought of strange conquest troubled the mind of the inhabitants of Kashmir[2].

For Akbar the new acquisition was to serve as his *bāgh-i khās*–his own special garden[3]. The image of Kashmir as *bāgh* [Plate 7] was reinforced during the period of Mughal rule in Kashmir by not only EmperorJahāngīr (r.1605–27CE) but also those in attendance at the royal court serving as creators and promoters of the cultural values of the empire. This was especially true of Mughal *sh'ura*(poets) and *mūnaqash nigār*(miniature artists), many of who were linked with Kashmir, either through their work or by birth[4].

The establishment of Mughal rule in Kashmir coincides with the widespread prevalence of *sabaq-i hindī* (the Indian school), a genre of Persian poetry that found favor with Indian poets[5], especially at the Mughal court during the sixteenth and seventeenth century. Many of the poets associated with this genre, whether Persian émigré at the Mughal court or native Indian poets writing in Persian, celebrated the narrative of Kashmir as *bāgh*. In their imagery of Kashmir these poets helped in reinforcing the Mughal representation of Kashmir, as an idealized picturesque *bāgh* – imagery devoid of any sense of reality, depicting the socio-political landscape of Kashmir [Plate 8].

The absence of any reference to a political reaction or regional antagonism towards the newly established Mughal control of Kashmir, the absence of any celebration of Kashmir's past pre-dating the advent of Mughal rule, makes the entire corpus of Persian poetry from this period read as a poetical ode to Mughal enterprise in Kashmir. Yet there are instances, a few solitary verses, where Kashmiri poets otherwise engaged in weaving of elaborate and rhythmical *mathnawis*, *qasidas* and *ghazals* do seem to engage with the idea of Kashmir as a homeland[6].

Mughal architectural traditions in Kashmir

The Mughal rule would help in bringing much sought about peace and stability in Kashmir, but it would also result in erosion of Kashmiri identity, politically as well as culturally, of which the Mughal architecture in the land would stand as the most visible manifestation.

The various buildings that were commissioned by Akbar and succeeding generations of Mughal emperors and their courtiers in Kashmir revolve along established Mughal architectural principles. The overall uniformity of the Mughal style within specific imperial epochs underlies the great degree of standardization of basic forms and the architectural elements involved, while also providing leverage for the individual idiosyncrasies of the emperor. To a large extent such individual preferences, whether it be Akbar's appreciation for red stone or Shāh Jāhān's predilection for white marble, provided an added impetus for the overall evolution of the Mughal *tarah*. In such a scheme of things, regional (cultural) aspirations, if not found worthy or compatible of being incorporated, were simply ignored[7]. Thus in Kashmir local architecture was simply sidelined by the Mughals as being incompatible with their own tradition and preferences. Additionally, as an example of public iconography aimed at promoting the aesthetic idioms of the empire, Mughal architecture in Kashmir emerges as an important visual tool to promote the munificence as well as the power of the empire. The most distinct example of this power projection is to be found in the mosques commissioned by Mughals in Kashmir. Mughal architecture in Kashmir is also testament to the highly efficient and centralized nature of the court, with experiments, designs and motifs generated in the imperial atelier being rapidly transferred and executed in this remote part of the empire.

In his rule of the newly acquired land, the first major building activity undertaken by Akbar aside was the construction of the walled city of Nāgar Nagar (c.1597CE). Physically Nāgar Nagar was separated from the more historical and populated parts of Srinagar by Malkah, the vast open ground, which since fifteenth century served the Muslim population of the city as their principal cemetery. In the urban morphology of seventeenth century CE, Srinagar, the environs of the Mughal city emerge as depopulated of the people of Kashmir, as the narratives of the court poets celebrating the land. Historically, we find that the Mughals modified the older Timurid practice of locating their palaces on the outskirt of city, by setting their residences, 'on the edge of a river or lake, and at the same time in the heart of the city'[8]. Yet, in Kashmir, the palace magnified into a city opening out on to a Nigin lake, and physically removed from the Kashmiri city, though visually towering over it from the summits of Koh-i Maran hillock.

As a city within a city, Nāgar Nagar served as the nucleus of the Mughal administration in Kashmir, incorporating the *ḥavelīs* of the Mughal princes and their *ṣubedars*, ateliers, pavilions, mosque, *khānaqāh*, gardens as well a host of ancillary buildings housing the Mughal garrison. Unfortunately aside from its religious buildings, nothing of the city remains barring the rampart wall (*kalāye*) and two gateways; Sangin Darwaza [Figure 4.1] and Kathi Darwaza. Contemporary sources are mostly reticent in their

Figure 4.1 Sangin Darwaza: Akbar's symbolic entrance gateway to the nāgar Nagar, Srinagar: 2018, © Hakim Sameer Hamdani.

description of the city aside from a singular record of Jahāngīrabout one of the palaces and an atelier. The construction of the city gateway brings to fore the Mughal preference for their own building traditions developed in the plains of the Indian subcontinent. Most historians record that Akbar was forced to draw masons from the plains, as these were no longer available in Kashmir. Given the political disturbances for past quarter of a century and the preference of Kashmiri builders for wood based construction, it is quite possible that the sufficient skilled manpower was found wanting for the scale of project undertaken, not that it was totally unavailable. The inscription on the Kathi Darwaza[9], the more public gate of the city, states that two hundred Indian master builders (*du ṣad üstād-i hindī*) were employed in the construction. Again, the epigraphy of the gate reads as a public commemoration of the benevolence associated with the Mughal Empire and its unlimited resources.

It was also at Srinagar, that Akbar constructed a shrine over the grave of Shaykh Hamaza Makhdūm. The Shaykh had been a severe critic of the Chak Sultans; and his disciples[10] were part of a small delegation of Kashmiri Sunni elites who invited Akbar for the conquest of Kashmir. In the construction of the *rūżā*, we see an instance of Mughal patronage of a revered site, associated with a section of Kashmiri audience seen as sympathetic to the imperial cause.

Akbar was succeeded by his son Jahāngīr (r.1605–27 CE), whose memoir is a living testament of the emperor's love for the land of Kashmir. In his reign of nearly two decades, Jahāngīr visited Kashmir on seven different occasions undertaking multiple constructions, as did his son and the future emperor, Shāh Jāhān (r.1628–58 CE).

The only major building activity undertaken during Aurangzeb's (r. 1658–1707 CE) long reign was the reconstruction of Jamia Masjid at Srinagar after it was burnt down in 1674 CE[11].

Following Aurangzeb,[12] no Mughal emperor visited Kashmir and as political dissensions and troubles grew in the capital, Kashmir relapsed into distant memory, as a frontier *ṣubah* bordering onto the more central province of Punjab. Increasingly, Kashmir came to be administrated by *ṣubedars* residing in Lahore, who in turn transferred the responsibility of administrating the land on their *naībs*(deputy). A majority of the *ṣubedars* no longer bothered to visit the land, whose arduous mountainous roads would only have taken them away from the affairs of the empire at Delhi.

The gradual loss of imperial prestige in the wake of Bahādur Shāh I (r.1707–12CE) death was followed by revolts in the border areas[13] of Kashmir province as well as worsening inter-community relations in the main urban center, Srinagar.

In these changing times, with dwindling imperial authority, the court at Delhi was neither capable of effectively governing the frontier province of Kashmir nor could it provide relief to the Kashmiris in face of political disturbances or natural hardships. Due to continuing political disturbances in the *ṣubah*, organized by rival claimants to the office of *naīb-ṣubedar*, the economic activity of the province was deeply affected disturbing both traders in the city as well as those engaged in agricultural practices in the rural areas[14].

Additionally, Kashmir also witnessed natural calamities in this period in the form of flood, earthquake, fire, famine and cholera. These repeated natural and man-made disasters sapped the remaining strength of Mughal power in Kashmir. During the famine of 1745 CE the *naīb-ṣubedar* found no help from the court in Delhi, and we find reports of impoverished Kashmiris selling their children and resorting to cannibalism of dead bodies[15].

In the aftermath of Nādir Shāh's(r. 1736–47 CE) invasion and despoliation of Delhi in 1739 CE, the *ṣubedar* of Kashmir declared his allegiance to the Persian king. But the bid proved unsuccessful and the *ṣubedar* was forced out of Kashmir by local population, who assisted his replacement form the imperial court in this endeavor[16]. The gradual emergence of local Kashmiri elites in making their presence felt on the contours of local politics was seen in full after Nādir Shāh's invasion. A presence that also manifested itself in architecture in the reconstruction of the *Khānaqāh-i Mʿaulā*. And as power devolved on to local actors, the court at Delhi also distanced itself from the troubles and intrigues brewing up in the distant Himalayan province. It was in these circumstances that two disaffected Kashmiri nobles, Mīr Muqīm and Khawājā Zāhir Dedhmārī, proceeded to Lahore and invited the Afghan king, Aḥmad Shāh Abdalī (1747–72 CE) to annex Kashmir, which he readily did in 1166 AH/1752 CE marking the end of Mughal rule in Kashmir.

Masjid-i Naū at Srinagar

According to Kashmiri vernacular sources, the oldest extant Islamic religious building from the Mughal period in Kashmir is the *Masjid-i Naū* at Srinagar. The mosque also known as *Shāhī masjid* (Royal mosque) and *Pather Masjid* (Stone mosque), is said to have been constructed in 1032 AH/1622 CE[17]. As an architectural enterprise, it is the most significant Mughal intervention in the heart of the historic Srinagar city. Constructed along the left bank of the river Jhelum, the building stands in stark and dramatic contrast to the local wooden architecture, represented in this case by the *Khānaqāh-i Mʿaulā* on the opposite bank. The positioning of the first Mughal congregational mosque in Srinagar, the architectural idiom employed and the choice of the materials used in the construction are strong indicators of the political message that the construction was deemed to convey [Figure 4.1].

Given what we understand of the period, *Khānaqāh-i Mʿaulā* was the dominating religious monument that existed in the heart of the Srinagar city on the river front. The construction of a new mosque on the opposite bank of deeply revered established religious site is indicative of an architectural experiment based on projection of Mughal authority rather than a benevolent concern of the empire for meeting the needs of local population. Historically the need to cater to larger congregation, the need for more covered space could, and had been met by expansion or even reconstruction of existing structures. The expansion and reconstruction of *Khānaqāh-i Mʿaulā* in the preceding century are indicative of these historical precedents, where existing buildings were enlarged to accommodate larger congregations[18]. The construction of *Masjid-i Naū* not only ignores the local architectural traditions, it also raises an interesting question, why? What was the need of building the mosque, especially given where it was built? If 'creators or patrons of a work or an edifice always aspire to fix its meaning and direct its reading, use, and interpretation'[19], what was the political and social locus behind the construction of the *Masjid-i Naū*, that its patron sought to propagate? Unlike the royal *bāghs* constructed by them in Kashmir, which were out of bounds for ordinary Kashmiris[20], the construction of a mosque was an example of public iconography, set right opposite the most visited religious site of Kashmiri Muslims. In building the mosque, the Mughals redefined the image of what a mosque would look like. In building it in stone, they marked the permanence of their construction as well as their empire.

The 'New Mosque' establishes not only a new language of architecture in Kashmir, but also marks a stark break with the past artistic traditions

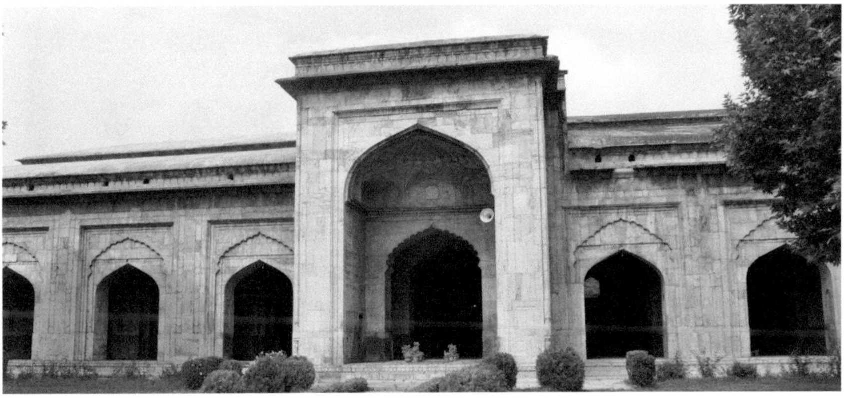

Figure 4.2 Masjid-i Naū, eastern façade: notice the cusped arches set within the rectangular recessed panels, Srinagar: 2018, © Hakim Sameer Hamdani.

of Kashmir. Yet, the mosque was and is a public building. While the construction of the mosque and the meaning behind its creation was governed by imperial authority, its approval as a place of communal worship was governed by public reception and acceptance. Local folk traditions maintain that the mosque was never used by Kashmiri Muslims. On the other hand repairs undertaken to the mosque during the Mughal[21] and Afghan period would indicate that the building was in use, even if intermittently way down till the advent of Sikh rule in the valley, when the building was officially closed down. Nevertheless, the mosque never found favor with the Kashmriri audience; neither did it help in promoting architectural ideas associated with the Mughal style.

Unfortunately and intriguingly, Mughal sources are silent on the patronage of the mosque[22]. Contemporary Kashmiri historians of the Jahāngīri era like Malīk,[23] also do not write about the construction of the mosque. It is only in Kashmiri vernacular histories of later generations that we find the association of the mosque with Nūr Jahān in an anecdote that is used to belittle the empress for her conceit. Art historians while not exactly mentioning the patron do attribute the construction to Jahāngīr's reign[24]. But based on stylistic grounds, I would argue for a later date for the mosque, given the close parallels we find in the decoration of the building and architectural features introduced under Shāh Jahān.

According to Ebba Koch, the design of the mosque is based on the 'arched hypostyle hall plan comprising of domed bays demarcated by pillars or piers arranged in grid pattern'[25] which was initially associated with a new style of mausoleums introduced by Jahāngīr. The mosque was a part of a walled compound with apparently blind arcade on three sides, traces of which can still be observed at the site, and also established from archival images dating back to the early twentieth century CE. The building itself is preceded by an open *ṣaḥn*(courtyard).

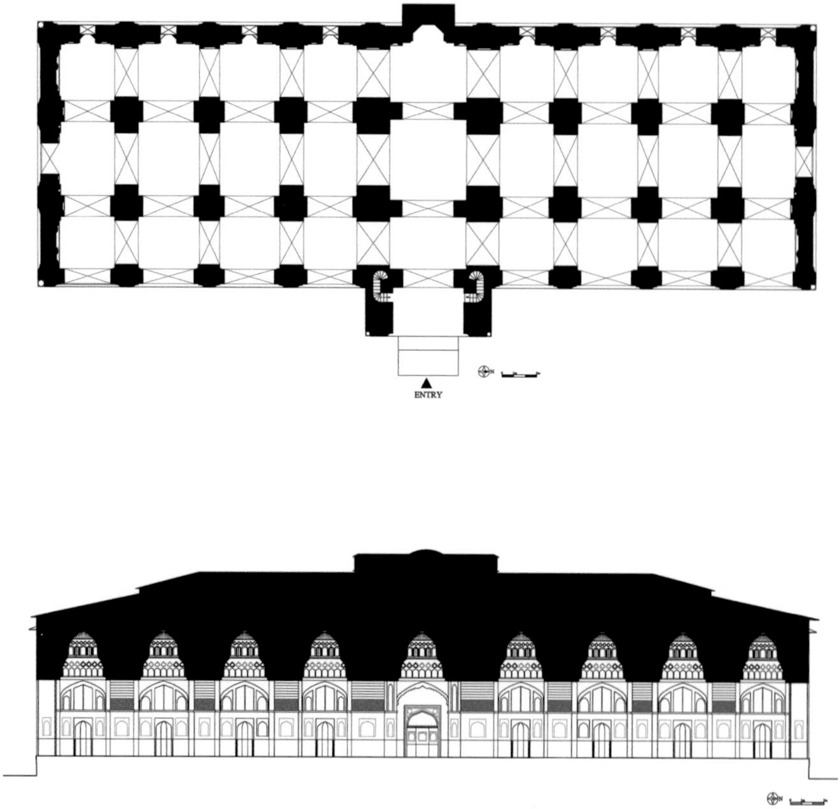

Figure 4.3 Masjid-i Naū, plan and longitudinal section, © INTACH, Kashmir.

The mosque is based on a rectangular plan measuring 62.7m × 20.8m [Figure 4.3]. The main entrance to the building is from the eastern façade which comprises a series of well proportioned double arches. An interesting feature of the façade is the placement of well proportioned arches within decorative cusped arches which in turn are set within rectangular panels. The central arch projects out from the building in the shape of a high *pīshtāq*. Internally, the mosques comprises a single large hall measuring 59.7m × 17.6m with the hall divided into three aisles parallel to the *qiblā* wall, comprising of nine bays each[26]. The central bay, which includes both the *miḥrāb* as well as the *pīshtāq*, is slightly larger than the rest of the bays. Significantly all the nine bays end with individual *miḥrābs*, though the central *miḥrāb* is more ornate and detailed out. In Kashmir, this feature is unique to Mughal mosques alone. While the entire eastern façade open outs in the shape of an arcade [Figure 4.2], only one opening can be found on the southern and western façade, located on the central bay.

Like most Mughal buildings in Kashmir, the coping stone of the plinth is carved with large lotus leaves in relief. Other decorative features used in the building include the corner bedpost (*gūldasta*) as well as the as the arch netting in the plaster covering the half dome of the entrance *pīshtāq*. The building like most Mughal structures in Kashmir is covered with a two tiered pyramidal roof, and is conspicuous for the absence of an outer dome.

The well polished limestone cladding used in the building facade follows the set precedent of Mughal projects in the region, while also highlighting a strong point of departure from local wooden architecture and the visual image they portrayed.

The surface decoration of Pather Masjid bears a marked similarity to similar decorative features found in the Mullā Shāh Masjid at Nāgar Nagar. The extremely well executed corner *guldastas*, and the carved floral band at plinth level, are similar in detail and executions in both the mosques. Similarly, the band in the rectangular panel surrounding the arcade in the main building façade at Pather Masjid, defined by the presence of a star, is to be found only at Mullā Shāh Masjid. No Jahāngīri era building in Kashmir depicts a similar detailing. The most conclusive evidence to posit a new reading for dating the building is the presence of well proportioned, multi cusped arches in the building façade [Figure 4.4]. These so called Shāh Jahāni arches are associated with architectural innovations undertaken under Shāh Jahān, and are conspicuously absent in any Jahāngīri era building, in or outside Kashmir. The association of the mosque patronage with Nūr Jahān, is a local Kashmiri legend, that was recorded centuries later by native historians of the nineteenth century CE.

Figure 4.4 Stylistic resemblance: the setting of a cusped arch within a recessed rectangular frame, a surrounding star motif and carved plinth stone at Masjid-i Naū (L) and Mullā Shāh mosque (R), Srinagar: 2018, © Hakim Sameer Hamdani.

Within the city of Nāgar Nagar, two Mughal mosques survive, both collectively forming a part of a large precinct known as Mullā Shāh Masjid. These mosques are located on the southern foothills of the Koh-i Maran hillock which lies at the center of Nāgar Nagar. Of the two, the larger one located on a higher terrace with is the Mullā Shāh mosque-*khānaqāh* complex, while a smaller building one on the lower level is the mosque-hammam of Dārā Shīkoh [Figure 4.5].

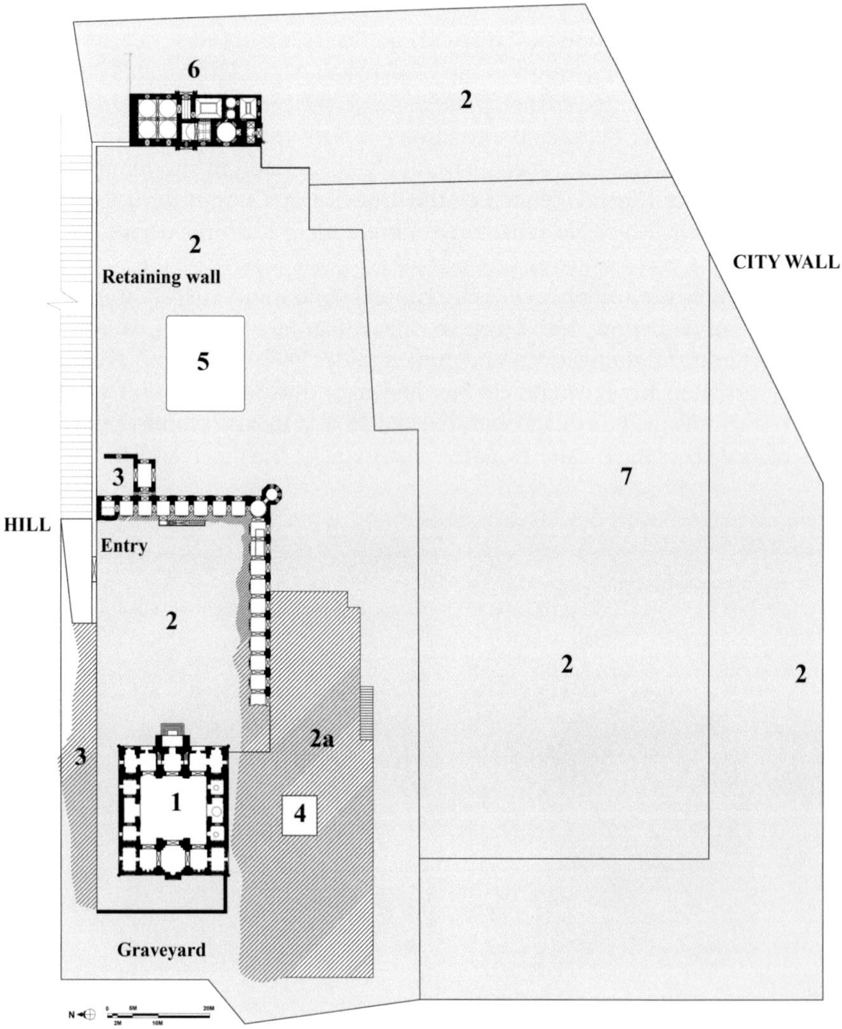

Figure 4.5 Mullā Shāh complex: Mullā Shāh mosque (1), terraces (2), terrace with cells below (2a), cells (3), pavilion (4), pool (5), Dārā Shukoh hammam mosque(6), open well (7), © Hakim Sameer Hamdani.

A stone inscription found on the main entrance gateway of the hammam-mosque, gives the date of construction of the building as 1059 AH/1649 CE, ascribing the construction to Dārā. The inscription also defines the building as a hammam-o *masjid* (hammam and mosque), serving both as a space for prayers as well as ablution, an innovative architectural experiment undertaken for the first time in Kashmir. The designing of a mosque with an attached hammam would emerge as a prominent architectural feature of many new mosques to be constructed in latter times, especially in the nineteenth century.

Given the arrangement of various building and structures in this vast precinct, most writers have assumed that the date 1649 CE refers to the construction of the entire ensemble of buildings, including the Mullā Shāh mosque. Koch is the first art historian who based on Mughal sources links the vast architectural outpouring associated with Dārā to a collaborative workshop of the prince, his sister Jahān Ārā Begam, and their pīr, Mullā Shāh[27].

Mullā Shāh was originally from Badakshan, who immigrated to India during the reign of Shāh Jahān, before settling down in Kashmir[28]. At Srinagar some of his ideas enraged the local religious elite, who got a death decree issued in his name from the *ṣubedar*[29]. The relationship between Mullā Shāh and Dārā dates from this period, when the prince not only intervened with his father, Shāh Jahān, on behalf of Mulla Shah, but also became a dedicated disciple. Along with Jahān Ārā, Dārā in collaboration with Mullā Shāh, left Kashmir with numerous architectural landmarks, including mosques, *sarāʿīs*, *khānaqāh*s, gardens and at least one tomb.

The mosque-hammam of Dārā predates the construction of the larger mosque-*khānaqāh* complex of Mullā Shāh by two years, and is an early example of single compact structure which includes a hammam as well as a mosque. The designing of the prayer hall as one of the main rooms of the building, rather than forming the entirety of the structure gives the mosque its unique characteristic, while also misleading writers, who have seen it as a hammam.

The building consists of a single storey linear structure aligned along the north-south axis, measuring 25.4m × 9.8m with a series of interconnected chambers of varying sizes[30]. Given the need to accommodate a hall for offering prayers as well the highly elaborate Mughal hammam, the building design assumes a complex arrangement of room form. The main entrance door to the building is on its eastern façade, comprising an arched *iwān*, replicated on the western wall by another similar gateway linking the building visually with the adjacent mosque of Mullā Shāh. Unlike usual Mughal practice, the gateway is not located at the middle; consequently the building does not possess a symmetrical façade. The main hall, serving as the mosque comprises a square room measuring 7.5m × 7.5m, located along the north-east, and occupies the entirety of the building on this side. A stone column lies at the centre of the hall supporting the ceiling, comprising of four shallow domes. On the opposite side lies a cove vaulted chamber (5m × 3.85m) on the opposite side which is in turn connected to a secondary room (5.4m × 3.25m) of almost similar dimensions, though visually divided into two parts. This room in turn leads into domed octagonal room (4m dia.), devoid of any opening. This seems to indicate that this self enclosed room might have been used as the hammam proper.

Though the building has lost all traces of its original decoration, yet its planning is in itself indicative of the unique set of architectural experimentation that Dārā would be involved in Kashmir. Two years after the construction of the mosque, Jahān Ārā would sponsor an even larger mosque complex next to her brother's mosque, for Mullā Shāh. Together these two mosques, located as they were within a shared *bāgh*, would represent an architectural undertaking that in sheer size would remain unsurpassed in Kashmir's medieval history while also serve a testament to the extensive canvas that defines Mughal style.

Constructed in 1061 AH/1651 CE, at a cost of 40,000 rupees[31], the mosque of Mullā Shāh has been ascribed by most art historians to Dārā, rather than its actual patron, Jahān Ārā.

The vast complex of Mullā Shāh mosques comprises a courtyard mosque located on the southern foothills of the Koh-i Maran hillock with *ḥujras* (cells) on three different levels constructed at an additional cost of 20,000 rupees, which has led to its interpretation as a mosque-*khānaqāh -sarāʿī* complex. Further down to the east lies the hammam-mosque of Dārā. Both the mosques are located on the same east-west axis which would indicate a close degree of cooperation in the execution of the project, between the royal siblings and their spiritual preceptor. As the two mosques were completed within a gap of two years, it is quite possible that the design and execution of both the buildings started simultaneously, with the smaller hammam mosque completed earlier.

The location of the Mullā Shāh mosque follows the pattern of Mughal *bāghs* in Kashmir, especially those carved out of mountain slopes like Nishat and Pari Mehal, with artificially created terraces retained with masonry walls. The mosque situated on top of a retaining wall, is designed as the central architectural marvel of a *bāgh* which terraces down to the city walls. Though the approach to the mosque-complex is defined by the north-south axis, the terraces in turn generate a secondary, east-west axis, with both culminating at the Mullā Shāh mosque.

A series of cells, *ḥujras* located to the south of the mosque serve both as the retaining wall as well as providing a sense of enclosure to the mosque compound. Entrance to the precinct is from this level, beneath an arched opening located on the north-eastern corner of the retaining wall.

In plan the outer mosque quadrangle measures 24.3m × 21.4m, with a series of domed and vaulted chambers; one bay deep opening out into a small *ṣaḥn* measuring 12.98m × 12.1m.The entrance to the mosque is from a *pīshtāq* located centrally in the eastern wing of the mosque. An interesting feature of the entrance *pīshtāq* is the presence of highly polished stone door frame which is also inscribed with two calligraphic panels. The panels bear two Quranic verse 'O Allah, who opens doors!' and 'whoever enters it shall be secure' (Quran: 3:97). While the supplication 'O opener of doors' is widely found over the entrance door in many especially Arab homes, the combination of the two verses would indicate a deeper symbolic meaning. The second verse 'and whoever enters it shall be secure' is part of a larger Koranic verse signifying the sanctity of *ḥaram*: the Kaaba at Mecca. In Kashmir we have numerous instances where religious places associated with certain Sufis are referred to as *Kaaba-i Sānī*: the lesser Kaaba. The verses inscribed on the doorway of the Mullā Shāh Mosque makes a similar assertion though in a more subtle manner. Both the inscriptions are rendered in extremely fine *naskh* script.

The entrance *pīshtāq* is repeated in the main bay of the prayer hall facing the *qiblā*. Interestingly, like the Pather Masjid, all the three bays of the mosque possess individual mehrabs. Spatially, the mosque of Mullā Shāh belongs to the tradition of imperial mosques built for private use, such as the Nagīnā mosque built by Shāh Jahān at Agra Fort juxtaposed onto a courtyard plan with a central *ṣaḥn*. Yet, the stone paved courtyard with its surrounding arcade, rising to a height of 7.62m from the floor till the roof top gives the impression of 'cramped proportions'[32].

Furthermore in spite of its overall size, the arrangement of the building makes it unsuited for larger congregational prayers. The dominant impression one gets in the mosques is of a series of interconnected chambers opening out into the courtyard more suited for the purpose of solitary rather than congregation prayers.

The roof of the building comprises domed ceiling is externally rendered in the shape of sloping roof, though with a pronounced curve at the end. This is opposed to other Mughal mosques of Kashmir where the roof forms with their pent roofs are closer in shape to Kashmiri sloping roof. Within the *ṣaḥn* of the mosque are located fragments of the lotus shaped stone finial, part of which still survives over the main prayer chamber. The mosque also poses a finely rendered *miḥrāb* projecting out from the *qiblā* wall.

The main eastern entrance façade of the mosque comprises two rectangular openings set within the arches. Of the two arches, the one next to the entrance *pīshtāq* is wider and recessed. The overall composition being that of ABCBA with a deep and shallower openings make the façade design interesting experiment of balance and harmony as opposed to the rigid symmetry that can be observed at *Masjid-i Naū*.

The nature of the experimentation can also be seen in the rest of the outer building facades none of which are similar. While the east, west and northern façade comprise plain arches set within rectangular panels, the arches on the southern façade are designed in the shape of typical Shāh Jahāni arch with its series of multi foliated cusps. As the southern façade overlooked the rest of the terrace garden that were part of the larger mosque precinct (while providing an overview of the city), it is possible that this part of the building was consequently more detailed and embellished. This decorative nature of the façade can also be seen in the broad calligraphic bands that were designed on the façade but never completed, some of which include verses of Shah Jahān's poet laureate, Abū Ṭālib Kalīm[33].

Overall the building gives more than enough indications to the fact that it was never completed, the work apparently being interrupted by Aurangzeb's seizure of throne and Dārā's execution. Aside from the unrealized calligraphy bands, the entire site is still littered with unfinished architectural elements indicating the interrupted nature of work. Also in the arcade opening out into the*ṣaḥn*, regularly spaced and shaped holes can be seen. For what purpose remains a mystery and is open to conjecture.

The Mullā Shāh mosque at Nāgar Nagar represents a unique coming together of three individuals in establishing a new language of mosque architecture in Kashmir [Fig.3.13]. Inspired by local geography, the mosques that Dārā, Mullā Shāh and Jahān Ārā patronized were uniquely situated within a setting of terraced gardens, for which Kashmir was famed at the imperial court. Under the influence of their spiritual masters, Mullā Shāh, the royal siblings helped in expanding the scope of this terrestrial paradise from a royal retreat of sensual pleasure into a setting for spiritual retreat. The change in the political climate at the imperial court, with Dārā's execution, resulted in abandonment of this architectural experiment as well as the mosque of Mullā Shāh. Soon after, the saint would be recalled to Lahore and the numerous buildings associated with him in Kashmir would stand abandoned, forgotten and forlorn.

Amongst these forgotten buildings is the mosque at Ganderbal set in a garden, known as Mullā Shāh bāgh. In the entirety of mosque architecture in the Indian sub-continent, this building because of its setting stands as an historical exception. Confirming to the idealized Mughal image of Kashmir as a *bāgh*, the building in its entirety is conceived as pavilion of spiritual contemplation within a garden. Located on the spur of a Behama hill, overlooking what in the past was the wide expanse of Anchar lake, the situation of the mosque is more reminiscent of Mughal *bāghs* of Kashmir, than of a religious structure. In the solitary, isolated setting with an overview of the adjoining lake, the mosque of Mullā Shāh at Ganderbal shares a sense of surrounding similar to some of the royal Mughal *bāghs* of the period, especially Chashma Shāhī (c. 1632CE) and Pari Mahal (c. mid 1600's).

The mosque is designed as *bārādarī* within the terraced garden[34]. Historically, it is the second Mughal mosque in Kashmir associated with Mullā Shāh. Given the architectural proclivity of Mullā Shāh-Dārā-Jahān Ārā in Kashmir[35], it is safe to presume that the mosque is also part of the same genre of Mughal buildings overseen and associated with the trio.

The Mullā Shāh bāgh comprises a series of terraces leading down from the hillock towards the Anchar lake, along a longitudinal north-south axis defined by a central water channel (*nahr*). Traces of the *nahr* can still be seen on the first, as well as the second terrace which also serves as the location for a *ḥauz*(water tank), the mosque and a small hammam. While most of the terraces along with parts of the buildings within it have been lost, it is still possible to form a basic idea of the site. Traces of three terraces can be discerned before a steep descent into what today serves as the surroundings, comprising individual residences, road and cultivated land.

The water in the channel flowing through the garden is sourced from the top most part of the garden from a natural stream (*Pādshāhī kul*[36]) and flows through a linear *nahar* on the first terrace, before cascading from a masonry retaining wall into a *ḥauz*. The retaining wall as well as the *ḥauz* is coeval with the construction of the *bāgh*, though the tank has been repaired in recent time. Two chinars are located on either side of the *hāuz* on the second terrace, which is the widest (and the biggest terrace) in the *bāgh*. A number of old trees chinars and fruit trees can still be seen at the site on this terrace. Traces of brick masonry retaining wall can be seen on the western as well as southern side of the terrace at this level, defining the linear shape of the terrace. A cross axial division of the garden (between the water channel and the path) is in keeping with the *chār bāgh* typology which was modified by the Mughals in their terraced gardens of Kashmir[37].

The water from the *ḥauz* is channeled through a narrow *nahar*, which though retaining its alignment has been entirely rebuilt. The *nahar* forms the central defining landscape element of both the *bāgh* as well as the mosque, flowing right through the middle of the later which is essentially designed as a low height large pavilion.

The mosque itself is located at the edge of the retaining wall on the second terrace. The placement of pavilions (*bārādarīs*) on the top of the retaining wall, overlooking the next terrace is a design scheme that was employed by the Mughals both at Shalimar as well as Nishat[38]. The building comprises a relatively large size mosque (15.90m × 15.78m), too big for the use of solitary worship, yet its square shape makes it's an exception to the linear plan of Mughal mosques, reinforcing the idea of the building as a pavilion [Figure 4.6]. The building comprises three bays on either side, with a larger central bay, serving as the principal axis, coinciding with the water channel. Based on the nine fold plan (*hasht bihisht*)[39], the building plan is derived from a Mughal typology that is traditionally associated with designing of pavilions, gateway buildings and tombs with a central room surrounded by eight chambers. The water channel enters the building from the northern side and cascades down the retaining wall from a stone *chādhar* on the opposite side.

This principal axis is bisected at the centre by a secondary east-west axis, which defines the *qiblā* wall, marking the building as a mosque. A small, 4.45m × 2.62m porch on this axis, on the eastern façade, helps in defining this *qiblā* axis of the building, while also opening out to the small hammam building which is also located on this side towards the eastern most corner of the terrace.

The principal spaces within the building are located on the cruciform shaped axis; this includes the central domed chamber as well as the small

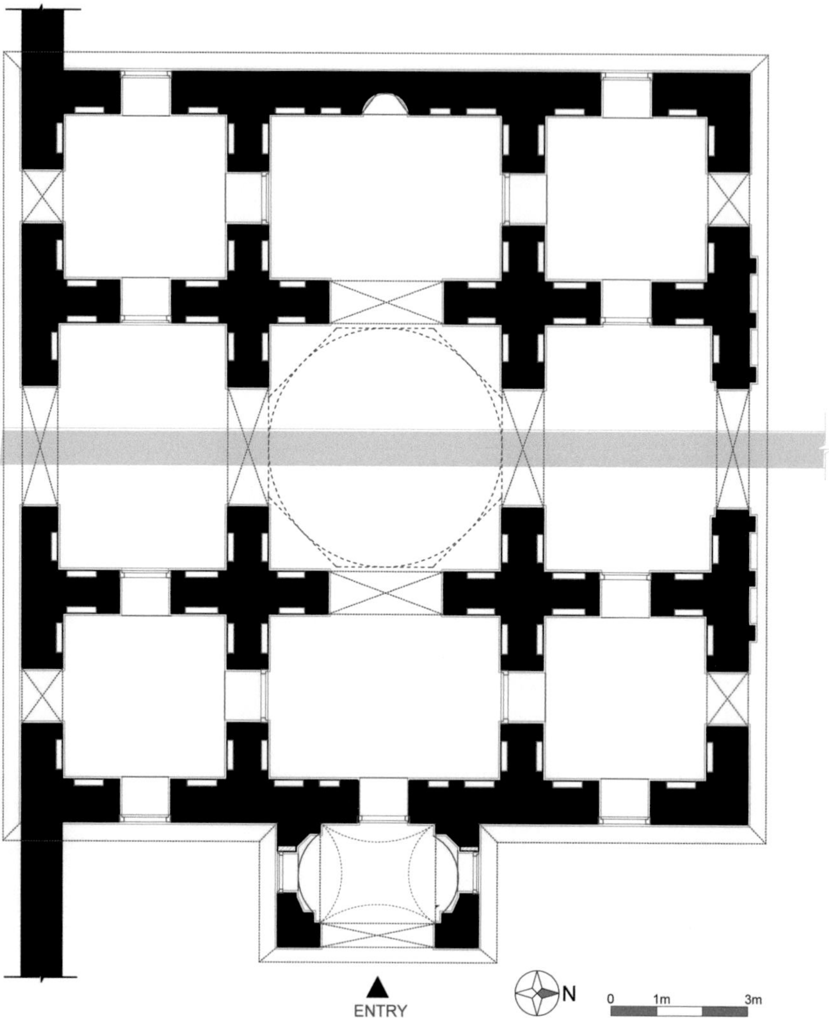

Figure 4.6 Mullā Shāh Bāgh masjid, plan, © INTACH, Kashmir.

side room located on the west. It is possible given the organization of the spaces and their interconnection, that the entire building was not conceived as a mosque, rather only the extreme western chamber on the east-west axis alone served this purpose. Unlike the rest of the chambers in the building, it alone is devoid of any window opening. Measuring 3.41m × 4.94m this room does indicate a space oriented for solitary worship.

The central domed room (5.23m × 4.94m × 7.22m) can be approached from both directions through well proportioned lofty arched openings, while the rest of the connections between the rooms have been designed as low height rectangular doorways. Many of the original stone door frames can still be seen at the site, though some have been lost. The central chamber provides a series of framed views towards the hillock and the Anchar lake. In fact, given the architectural arrangements of the spaces and the need to bridge the water channel bisecting the building, it would be the obvious location for placement of a platform to bridge the channel. In the Mughal *bāghs* of Kashmir, such arrangements are invariably designed as stone platforms (*takhtā*)[40], symbolic of throne.

In the hierarchy of spaces within the building, the actual prayer chamber recedes in comparison to both the central room as well as the other side chambers which command a fine view of the picturesque surroundings. The room of prayers and worship remains just another chamber in the building, not the principal chamber. This arrangement, where the main prayer hall or chamber is designed as a part of a larger space can also be seen in the Mullā Shāh mosque at Nāgar Nagar.

The building façade comprises three arched opening on the principal north and southern façade. The eastern façade also favors a similar arrangement of arched openings, but is differentiated from the rest by the rectangular arched extension serving as the porch. The western façade comprising the *qiblā* wall, on the other hand, is marked by arched openings which have been walled clearly differentiating the mosque from a pavilion.

Given the design of the building, with a water channel passing through it, we do not find any trace of a platform or high plinth on which the building would rest. The entire building is covered with a sloping roof that was characteristic of Mughal buildings in Kashmir. Presently the roof is in an advanced state of decay and is overgrown with vegetation, lending a pleasing vision, especially in spring when it is overgrown with various wild flowers.

The building which has been much vandalized in modern times still retains traces of original fine plaster work in lime. Also, traces of original paint work in the dado comprising rectangular bands in red, green and ochre can also be seen in the building interiors.

Aside from the mosque, a small hammam (5.8 m × 5m) also stands in the *bāgh*. The hammam comprises a single room with a water tank, preceded by a narrow passage which opens out towards the mosque on the western facade. Part of the structure has collapsed. The hammam which like the mosque is constructed on the stone retaining wall (6.48m~4.48m) also houses rooms on the lower level which are closed.

The mosque of Mullā Shāh is a part of the tradition of terraced gardens that the Mughals constructed all over Kashmir. The setting and the design of the mosque-garden helps us in determining how deeply ingrained the image of Kashmir as a terrestrial paradise was within the Mughal court culture. For the Mughals, the physical celebration of Kashmir as *bāgh* commenced in the laying of numerous gardens, it continued in their residences, was celebrated in their poetry before being replicated in the construction of the mosque at Ganderbal. Though conceived as a place of worship, the location of the mosque places it outside the use of the local community. By constructing a personalized space of worship in a heavenly *bāgh,* the Mughals sought to advance their esthetics of a terraced garden into that of another, and till now unrealized typology –that of a mosque. The symbolism of a communal space of worship being converted into a private, detached yet heavenly spiritual retreat nevertheless does contrasts vividly with how distant the Mughal court remained from the reality of Kashmir.

Gateway at Madnī's shrine

One of the significant structures dating from the Mughal period is the entrance gateway to the shrine of Madnī at Naushera. Most historians, specifically art historians, assume the gateway to be coeval with the actual shrine and mosque of Madnī[41]. Unfortunately, in-spite of being one the most documented Muslim shrines of Kashmir, few writers who visited the site, has noticed the clearly visible verse on the inner wall of the gateway, dating the construction to the reign of the Mughal emperor, Shāh Jahān.

Constructed during Shāh Jahāns rule, the gateway is designed as a low height *pīshtāq,* which hides the original stone gateway to the shrine resting on fluted stone columns constructed by Zain-al Ābidīn [Plate 4]. In local vernacular sources this Mughal extension of a shrine, which is claimed by the Kashmiri Shi'a community, is associated with the Shi'a ṣubedar, Zafar Khān. The gateway has attracted wide attention primarily for the tile work that was used in its surface decoration rather than any architectural pretensions of the structure.

The structure of the gateway measures 8.1m × 3.2m, 2.6m deep; and like traditional Mughal portal gateways, consists of an arched niche covered with a half dome [Fig. 3.8]. The side masonry panels enclosing the gateway are accentuated by two niches, an arched one at top and a rectangular at bottom. Unlike the monumental *pīshtāqs* traditionally employed in Mughal architecture, the gateway at Madnīs shrine assumes a modest height with the total rise from the ground till the top of the *pīshtāq* standing at 5m. Given the relatively modest scale of the adjoining mosque of Madnī, it is possible that the Mughal builders decided to not over emphasize the height of their structure, which nevertheless, given its architecture, looks highly incongruous with the rest of the ensemble of buildings at site. Additionally, the Mughal builders have bridged the gap in between their *pīshtāq* and the stone gateway of Zain-al Ābidīn, by constructing an odd looking vault sandwiched between the two structures.

The glazed tiles that were used in the surface decoration of the *pīshtāq* have been studied by Susan Stronge[42]. The square tiles used at the gateway were sufficiently in place for Nicholls to provide us with a brief description and a sketch of the tilework. Of particular note is the presence of human figures in the spandrel of the arch depicting which he describes as:

> […] beast with the body of a leopard, changing at the neck into the trunk of a human being, shooting apparently with a bow and arrow at its own tail, while a fox is quietly looking among flowers and cloud-forms[43].

This highly unorthodox depiction on a site associated with Muslim faith, portrays the zodiac sign of Sagittarius *(Qaus)*[44], widely depicted in Persian art of the Safavid period. The Persian origin of the zodiac motif is further collaborated by the headgear of the archer, which resembles a Safavid rather than a Mughal turban. The employment of tile revetments in surface decoration of a simple and modest structure is a tradition that is found in Persian architecture of the Safavid period, where such a technique often concealed 'structural banality'[45]. Regarding the use of such an unorthodox motif in a religious setting, we have no plausible explanation beyond the reference to such motifs in contemporary Safavid art, which also serves as the point of origin for its use in Kashmir. Significantly, the presence of the Sagittarius on the *iwān* of the *bazzar* at Isfahan, is linked to the establishment of the city under this astrological sign rather than any symbolic meaning[46]. It is possible that a similar occurrence happened during the construction of the gateway but in the absence of any textual or archaeological reference this remains an untested prospect.

Barring the human-animal mythical figure, most of the tiles depict floral or vegetal motifs on a background of cobalt blue, yellow, deep orange and green[47]. Combined with the tile work the builders had also painted murals and calligraphic bands on the walls of which a few isolated traces can still be seen.

The construction of the gateway was realized due to the sectarian need of its patron to beautify a revered shrine in an architecture style that was rooted in Mughal idiom. The iconography of figural[48] depiction on the spandrel of the entrance gateway to a prominent shrine of the city, the use of tile revetments in surface decoration of an otherwise modest structure, the Shi'a origins of the shrine[49] and the commission of the enterprise by a Shia *ṣubedar* make the extension an interesting example of Mughal munificence employed for sectarian benefit.

At Madnīs shrine-mosque complex, the Mughal entrance gateway, today shorn of all of its glazed tiles, offers a sharp visual contrast to native Kashmiri architecture of the mosque and shrine, be it the shape of the arch or the difference between the brick masonry of the gateway with the composite stone and wood style of construction employed in the Sultanate period mosque [Figure 4.7]. Historically Kashmiri architecture is a synthesis of diverse architectural traditions, in the Mughal gateway this synthesis is missing. Though both form a part of architectural language used in designing of Islamic religious buildings, yet the Mughal *ṭarah* stands in stark contrast

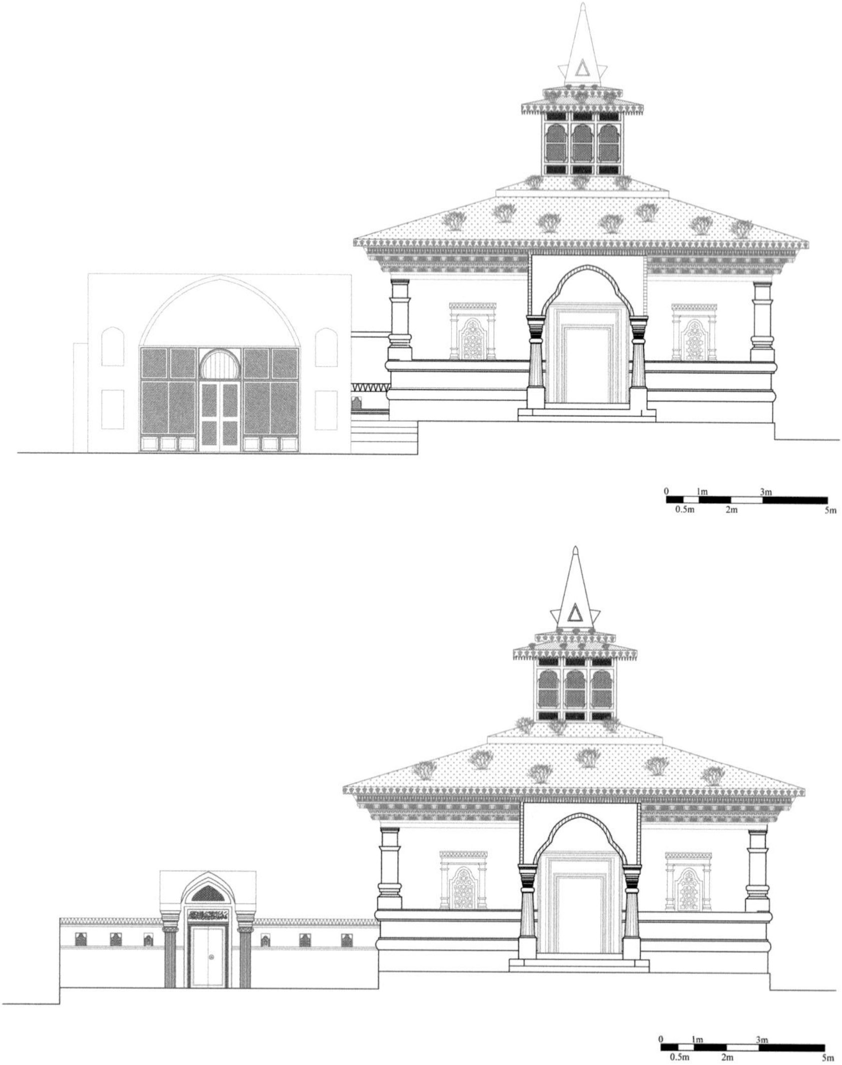

Figure 4.7 Tomb of Madnī, eastern elevation: comparison between the mughal entrance gateway to the tomb (top) and sultanate period entrance gateway to the tomb (bottom), © Hakim Sameer Hamdani.

to the Kashmiri shrine-mosque complex, the incongruity between the two unresolved.

Thag Bābā shrine

Located on the left bank of the Jhelum, the *rūżā* of Thag Bābā is the only tomb constructed by the Mughals extant in the valley of Kashmir.

Stylistically, like all Mughal constructions in Kashmir, the shrine of Thag Bābā forms a major departure with the indigenous tradition of building in wood. The saint, Shaykh İbrāhīm popularly known as Thag Bābā, is said to have flourished in the seventeenth century during the reign of Aurangzeb (r.1658-07CE), though neither the saints name or his time period is firmly established.

Regarding the construction of the shrine, Khuihāmī says that it was undertaken by Aurangzeb and then rebuilt in the nineteenth century CE, by Shaykh Ghūlām Muhyi-al Dīn, the governor of the region during Sikh rule. Given his puritanical outlook building, it seems highly improbable that Aurangzeb would have been interested in the idea of such a richly decorated structure for a saint who in his eyes could at best have been considered rather unorthodox.

The absence of any mention of the building in imperial histories of Aurangzeb's reigns seems to be indicative of a patron other than the emperor himself. Given the time and the style of building as well as its association with a highly unorthodox saint, it predisposes us to Dārā, who lost the throne to Aurangzeb. Dārā who was given to an ecumenical spirit much to the distaste of his brother and the more orthodox section of the Muslim polity in the imperial court, was also well versed in the mystical Sufi traditions. The spirit of the Thag Bābā shrine fits in with the architectural experimentation associated with the Dārā and his sister in Kashmir as seen in the mosque at Ganderbal. As a patron, the shrine of Thag Bābā points more in the direction of Dārā the unfortunate prince rather than Aurangzeb the successful king.

The shrine of is approached from a narrow paved bylane (*kūchā*) with residences on either side in one of the poorer rundown *moḥala* of Srinagar city. The entrance to the shrine compound from the *kūchā* is framed by low arched gateway on the south-eastern corner. The main entrance to the shrine itself is from a small stone verandah on its southern side. The entrance doorway to the building is articulated by stone band in polished grey limestone. A beautiful circular medallion with *pietre dure* work on white marble framed by a decorative stone foliate arch defines the entrance from the surrounding brick masonry. Two small marble medallions on either side of the spandrel are inscribed with the divine name 'Allah' in the *naskh* script.

The building is based on a rectangular plan measuring around 7.3m × 6.5m, and a three *tāq* masonry structure. As with most buildings in the region, the masonry superstructure is raised on a low rubble stone plinth plastered in lime. The richly carved plinth stone shows a marked resemblance to the plinth stone at Shalimar bāgh, constructed in phases during Jahāngīr and Shāh Jahān's reign. The structural system adopted here, as in all Mughal constructions in Kashmir is the arcuate.

Internally, the shrine comprises a single domed chamber (5.3mx4.8m), with each façade comprising three arched openings. A number of graves, including those of the saint and his followers, are located inside this spacious,

Figure 4.8 Thag Bābā shrine: view of the marble cenotaphs over the grave, Srinagar: 2010, © Hakim Sameer Hamdani.

airy chamber [Figure 4.8]. A raised decorative marble platform (*takhtā)* with four *gūldastas* (bed impost) on the corners forms the base for three beautiful prismatic (*qalamdan*) cenotaphs. Of the three, the larger one with white inlay work on black marble is generally presumed to be of the saint. It was originally decorated with semi-precious stone inlay work as were the decorative *gūldastas*. The base of the platform itself is decorated with a realistic floral depiction carved in marble, a feature that was introduced in Mughal architecture by Shāh Jahān and finds its greatest representation at the Taj Mahal. The limited use of *pietre dure* is reminiscent of a technique which was first employed in the surface decoration of I'timād-al Daula's tomb (c.1628 CE) at Agra during Jahāngīr's reign. Thereafter this technique was employed more elaborately by Shāh Jahān. The mural work (*naqāshī*) on the inner walls of the shrine also bears a close resemblance to that seen in the interiors of I'timād-al Daula's tomb; in fact here, it achieves a poise in the detailing of flowers and vases that represents the pre-eminence of Kashmiri *naqāsh*. A row of brick and lime cenotaphs presumably those of the saint's intimate circle are located further down near the entrance door in a linear row.

The ceiling of the building was decorated with mirror work embedded in moulded plaster work which Koch has described as a, 'system of stars or partial stars arranged in concentric circles, linked by a network forming kite-shaped compartments'[50]. The structural transition from a square into an octagon to support the dome is undertaken using squinches which had been decorated with *naqāshī* work. Interestingly the zone of transition actually starts at the window level, with the corner taking the shape of a half dome. Rendered in extremely fine gypsum plaster with a varying thickness (100mm to 200mm), it is decorated as a pseudo-*muqarnas*, a purely non-structural decorative scheme. Even the plain arched window openings by use of plaster work are transformed into well proportioned multi lobed foliate arches, the so called Shāh Jahāni arch. This plan form gets repeated in the main shrine of Shaykh Amin Mantāqī at Aālī Kadal, which was reconstructed during the nineteenth century CE.

The building façade used to be of glazed *bādshāhī* brick cladding which was plastered with a thin layer of lime plaster at a later date during the repair works carried out by Shaykh Ghulām-al Dīn. The roof soffit (*chajja*) is of lime stone and is supported on carved monolithic stone brackets.

Overall, the building appearance is that of a self contained single composition, which unlike the more traditional architecture of the region, makes no attempt to open out onto the river. The absence of any projections welcoming the river- a porch, balcony (*dub*) or a roofed verandah (*dalān*) is what sets it apart from local architecture, isolating it from the surroundings. Yet because of the smallness of its size, this dissociation of the building from the surroundings does not act as a brutal intrusion but rather as a curios exception, achieving a level of congruity with the surrounding landscape that would otherwise have been inconceivable.

Asār-i Sharīf at Hazratbal

Probably the greatest addition to the socio-religious landscape of Kashmir, especially of the Muslim community of Kashmir during 165years of Mughal rule was the setting up of *Asār-i Sharīf* at Hazratbal, Srinagar in the seventeenth century CE [Plate 12]. While the establishment of the *Asār-i Sharīf* does not represent a paradigm shift in the life of the community, as Kashmiri Muslims were well adapted to the custom of holding relics in great veneration, it nevertheless marks a novelty- a new addition both socially as well as architecturally. Again it is significant that the setting up of the shrine at Hazratbal was entirely a Kashmiri venture, overseen by community elites who in the end also managed to co-opt the local Mughal court into the enterprise.

The holy relic, comprising a hair of the Prophet Muhammad, was acquired by a Kashmiri trader Khawājā Nūr-al Dīn Ishbarī, from a family of Sayyids who had migrated to India during Shāh Jahān's rule, and are said to have been *mutwalī*(custodians) of the Prophets shrine at Medina[51]. The dispatch of the relic (*asār*) to Kashmir was initially obstructed by Emperor Aurangzeb, it reached Srinagar and was publicly displayed for the first time in 1111 AH/1699 CE at *khānaqāh* of Khawājā Muʿīn-al Dīn Naqshbandī[52]. The arrival of the relic in Kashmir and its association with the Prophet, seems to have caught the imagination of the common people, and soon it was found that the space in and around the *khānaqāh* was not enough to accommodate the large congregations. Consequently the local notables approached the Mughal *ṣubedar* Fāẓil Khān and it was decided to remove the relic to a *bārādarī* at *Bāgh-i Ṣadiq Abād*[53] on the western banks of the Dal lake. The *bāgh* was a part of the large genre of gardens that had been constructed in Kashmir by the Mughals in and around the Dal lake. Consequently the relic was deposited in the *bāgh* which became famous as Hazratbal (The Revered Hill), *Asār-i Sharīf* Hazratbal or simply as *Dargāh* Hazratbal.

The Hazratbal shrine (e.1699CE) is the first instance of setting up of an *Asār-i Sharīf* in Kashmir. This building typology primarily served as a shrine for holding and displaying of holy relic (*asār*) specifically associated with the Prophet. While Hazratbal would be the first *Asār-i Sharīf* in the city of Srinagar, it would be followed by establishment of three more such institutions in the city, the *Asār-i Sharīf* at Kalashpora, Soura and Narwara. Another such shrine in the city was located in Lal Bazar but for some mysterious reasons the shrine did not achieve a deep spiritual connection with the city or the Muslim community of Kashmir at large. Though these *Asār-i Sharīfs* would serve as sanctums for a varied assortment of relics related to different revered Muslim figures, yet the principal relic and source of sanctity remained the *asār* of the Prophet, the *mūi-i pāk* (holy hair). In addition to these *Asār-i Sharīfs*, many shrines and *khānaqāh*s across Kashmir dedicated to memory of different Muslim saints and Sufi orders also lay a claim to possessing relics of the Prophet in the shape of footprint, *khūlā*(skull cap), *ʿalm* (flag standard) etc.

An interesting link between the *Asār-i Sharīf* at Hazratbal and Kalashpora is that both the shrines are linked with Kashmiri traders, who in traditional Kashmiri accounts are said to have been associated with the court of the Mughal Emperor Aurangzeb[54]. Additionally, the claim to sanctity of both the shrines lies in possession of the *mūi-i pāk* of the Prophet, which was either acquired from the royal family (Kalashpora) or whose acquisition involved a member of the royal family (Hazratbal)[55]. Though the relics at Kalashpora are said to have been bought to Kashmir in 1080 AH/1669 CE, the actual public display of the relic commenced at a much later date in 1139 AH/1726 CE[56]. Was the establishment of an *Asār-i Sharīf* at Kalashpora in the heart of Srinagar city, in the face of a recognized shrine at Hazratbal an attempt to offset the appeal of the older established shrine? Or an attempt to set up a similar if not rival institution in the heart of the city given that till nineteenth century CE, Hazratbal remained a village on the outskirts of the city? While the relationship between the different *Asār-i Sharīfs*, their functioning and the relationship between their patrons needs to be explored in detail, one can not dismiss such a possibility especially given the manner in which the phenomenon was repeated. This can also be seen in the manner a third *Asār-i Sharīf* at Soura on the outskirt of the city was established in 1225 AH/1810 CE.

The setting up of the *Asār-i Sharīf* at Soura came about due to differences between the hereditary caretakers of the Hazratbal shrine (the Bandey family) and a leading trader of the city Khawājā Munwar Shāh Dīwanī. Khawājā Munwar also co-opted other city elite in the project and the first public display of the *mūi-i pāk* took place in 1225 AH/1810 CE during Afghan rule, amidst much fanfare. The *Asār-i Sharīf* at Lal bazar evolved from a *khānaqāh* that was established by the *Naqshbandhī* shaykh, Khawājā Abdul Rasul Dehbadī, a native of Bukhara who arrived in Kashmir in 1062 AH/1651 CE during the reign of Shāh Jahān. The arrival of Khawājā Rasul took place in the aftermath of Shāh Jahān's campaign in the Central Asia(1645-47 CE) and the Mughal attempt at conquest of Bukhara. Though Khawājā Rasul returned back to his native Bukhara, he later on dispatched his son Khawājā Aftab to Kashmir. It seems that the display of the relics at the *khānaqāh* commenced during the time of Khawājā Aftab. The *khānaqāh* was also richly endowed by the Mughal court and housed a separate *langar*[57].The *Asār-i Sharīf* is said to have been ransacked by the Sikhs in the nineteenth century CE, though no historical reference to the event seems to exist[58].

In the aftermath of the establishment of Hazratbal shrine, we see that aside from the principal *Asār-i Sharīfs* that came up in Srinagar, a number of instances outside the city where relics associated with the Prophet were transferred to the valley by Kashmiri traders. This includes a *mūi-i pāk* at Anderwarah that is reported to have been bought to Kashmir by a Kashmiri trader in 1083 AH/1672 CE, though the actual public display like at Kalashpora took place at a much later date in 1145 AH/1732 CE[59]. Similarly, the *mūi-i pāk* at *Khānaqāh* Dangerpora is said to have been bought by another Kashmiri trader from Agra during the reign of Aurangzeb, though like in the previous instances the *khānaqāh* was established at a much later date during the Afghan rule, when public display of the relic was undertaken[60]. Curiously, we find that in all most all the instances, the transfer of the relic to Kashmir is reported to have taken place at a date predating the establishment of Hazratbal shrine; yet, in all the cases the actual revelation and display of the relics takes place at a much later date. Also, almost all the instances of transferring the relic to Srinagar are said to have taken place during Aurangzeb's reign. Additionally, as previously mentioned, these newly set up shrines were on the whole richly endowed by the Mughal court. Nevertheless, the prominence of Hazratbal shrine as the premier Muslim shrine of Kashmir remained unaffected by setting up of new *Asār-i Sharīfs* in the city. Almost two centuries after its establishment towards the end of nineteenth century CE, the *Asār-i Sharīf* at Hazratbal was seen as the principal Muslim shrine of Kashmir.

The establishment of four *Asār-i Sharīfs* in the city (or in close proximity of the city) within a passage of fifty-seven years cannot be seen as a simple case of coincidence[61]. Also, it is worthwhile to note that the *Asār-i Sharīfs* were also endowed by the Mughal court in Kashmir with substantial revenue as has been recorded by native historians, highlighting how wealth and social prestige was linked with the phenomenon of *Asār-i Sharīfs*.

Nevertheless, we find that the sanctity and authenticity of these relics or the institutions that they came up because of them, was widely accepted and respected amongst the Muslim community.

From written sources, we know that the *Asār-i Sharīf* at Hazratbal was established within a Mughal *bāgh*. Located on the banks of the Dal Lake, the *bāgh* would have been inspired by the traditions of the imperial Mughal gardens of Kashmir, one of which, Nasim bāgh was located within walking distance of *Bāgh-i Ṣadiq Abād*. Laid out in ascending terraces the Mughal *bāghs* of Kashmir, while conforming to the overall geometrical layout of a traditional *chār bāgh,* took on an entirely different character that was governed by the local setting.

What were the contours of *Bāgh-i Ṣadiq Abād*, is something we cannot be sure about, given the vast changes that have taken place at the site, including reconstruction and expansion of both the building as well the *bāgh* itself[62]. Nevertheless it is certain that the *bagh* comprised arrangements of chinar either along avenues of walkway *(khaiyaban),* or along the corners of the garden quadrants. Traces of both arrangements can still be found at the site, though some of the chinartrees date from nineteenth and twentieth century. Presently, the entire site comprises two terraces overlooking the lake, with the shrine itself located on the upper terrace. Archival pictures from the late nineteenth and mid twentieth century also indicate that the shrine-*bāgh* compound comprised two terraces, with the shrine building located centrally near the retaining wall. Given the plan of the present structure and comparing it with some of the archival images, it is possible to posit that the main sanctum of the shrine today has been designed on the footprints of the older building. The positioning of a *bārādarī* on top of a retaining wall is a common architectural element that we find in many Mughal gardens of Kashmir. A similar location of pavilions could be seen at Nishat on the second and twelfth terrace[63], aṣ well as Shalimar in the *Bāgh-i Farāh Baksh*. Regarding the building which was converted into the shrine in the seventeenth century, we can only opinion based on what we know of other Mughal gardens of Kashmir. In all surviving Mughal gardens of Kashmir, the garden pavilion was designed as an open pavilion supported on wooden, masonry or stone columns. The rectangular plan of these pavilions (Nishat, Achibal, Shalimar) essentially comprises a central hall with smaller side rooms, following the form of residential pavilions designed by Mughals. According to Koch, this is a plan form that found favor with the Mughals in their designing of garden pavilions during the seventeenth century CE the date from which the *bāgh* at Hazratbal also dates[64]. In virtually all the Mughal gardens of Kashmir, the pavilion stands on the central water channel. Was there a water channel in *Bāgh-i Ṣadiq Abād* before its conversion into a shrine? Probably, but of this we have no evidence baring our understanding of the layout of Mughal gardens in Kashmir and the description of a European visitor to the shrine in 1913, which seems to indicate the same[65]. Regarding the pavilion known as *'Ishrat Mahal,* which was converted into the shrine, it is evident that the structure would have followed traditional features of Mughal architecture both in its form and decoration. Possibly a rectangular, single storey pavilion, the building was expanded by the Kashmiris once the pavilion was converted into a shrine. When this change happened, we don't know. The images of the shrine from late nineteenth century CE onwards showing a double height square building with side *dalāns;* and traditional Kashmiri *chār bām* roof represent this later addition, undertaken by Kashmiris themselves.

Khānaqāh of Bābā Nasīb -al Dīn Ghazī at Bijbehara

The town of Bijbehara occupies a prominent position in the history of medieval Kashmir, a prominence that continued well into the *Shahmīrī* rule in Kashmir. During the iconoclastic days of Sultan Sikander, a Jamia masjid was constructed in the town which would indicate that the town was a flourishing urban centre even in the fifteenth century, catering to the needs of a significant Muslim community[66].

While the establishment of a Jamia at Bijbehara in the fifteenth century CE would indicate the importance of the town, yet during subsequent period of Sultanate rule in Kashmir, the town remains mostly untouched by native historians. It was only in the seventeenth century that the town re-emerged on the sacred map of Kashmir when a leading *Suharwardī* saint, Bābā Nasīb -al Dīn Ghazī (d. 1047 AH/1638 CE) was buried in the town.

In local hagiographical accounts Bābā Nasīb emerges as a tireless missionary who spent a major part of his life in conversion of non-Muslims and building of mosques[67], madrasa and also engaging in civic activities related to community welfare such as constructing of bridges, community washrooms and sarā'īs[68].

In spite of his proselytizing activities, the life of Nasīb marks the continuation of the syncretic traditions that were exemplified by the practices of native Reshīs. Though non-vegetarian food was cooked at *langars* operated by his disciples, Baba Nasīb remained a vegetarian through his entire life[69]. Like the *Reshīs,* he remained a celibate though he never encouraged or forbade such practice amongst his disciples. Interestingly Nasīb would pray for deceased irrespective of their faith[70].

On his death, Bijbehara emerged as permanent seat from which his disciples started operating. Consequently, one of his leading disciples, Shāh 'Abdül Raḥmān constructed a small shrine and a single storey *khānaqāh* at the site in 1076 AH/1665 CE. In 1127 AH/1715 CE, 'Abdūl Raḥmān's son reconstructed and expanded the shrine, completing the process of establishing the shrine and its attendant shrine culture.

The *khānaqāh* of Nasīb is part of a larger precinct, which in addition to his *rūżā* includes a hammam mosque and public cemetery [Plate 9]. The entire precinct is located within the older part of the Bijbehara town, known as Bābā *moḥala* and surrounded by residential houses that used to belong to the families of shrine attendants.

While the *rūżā* dates to the early eighteenth century CE, and was the subject of major renovations in the late twentieth century CE, the ground floor of the *khānaqāh* retains its original character dating back to the seventeenth century CE.

The *khānaqāh* comprises a two storey building, with the upper floor dating to nineteenth century CE. The original ground floor of the *khānaqāh* measures 13.25m × 11.87m with the entrance from a rectangular doorway centrally placed on the main eastern façade. Following the tradition of Sultanate buildings, the *khānaqāh* is built is stone masonry, comprising large blocks of stones. The irregular arrangement of the stones indicates that these were sourced from an existing site and reused in the construction of the *khānaqāh* -probably from the ruins of a stone temple. Externally, the ground floor of the building is devoid of any significant architectural feature, barring the presence of clearstory windows. While the main lower windows are rectangular in shape, those used in the clearstory are arched and are recessed within rectangular masonry panels.

Internally, the building comprises a single hall measuring 11.9m × 10.2m with the double height ceiling supported on four centrally located multi-faceted wooden columns, dividing the entire area into three bays. The placement of the columns has been done in a manner which has resulted in irregular bays, with the central bay being wider than the end bays. Where the *khānaqāh* at Bijbehara differs from traditional *khānaqāh* of Kashmir, is in the absence of cells on the sides which are used for solitary worship. Historically, the practice of solitary worship is what has differentiated the form of a *khānaqāh* from that of a mosque. The wooden base and capitals of the columns are modeled on Mughal design, especially *muqarna* capital, which found widespread use in Mughal architecture, showing how individual motifs and design features linked to the Mughal style were getting incorporated in local architectural traditions. The windows which are fitted with glass panels would originally have been fitted with *pinjrakārī* work, for which the town of Bijbehara was renowned till recent times.

The first floor of the *khānaqāh* follows the native vocabulary of wooden architecture that was widely used in the construction of *khānaqāh* and mosques in the eighteenth and nineteenth century CE. In this system of construction, alternative layers of wooden beams and brick are used to construct the wall, with the brick serving as a filler material. At the *khānaqāh* of Bābā Nasīb, the builders have additionally added three wooden balconies centrally on the north, south and eastern façade. Unlike the practice in local vernacular, where a *dub* usually projects out from the wall, the dubs in the *khānaqāh* are supported on wooden columns resting on stone pedestals.

Thus the *dub* on the main eastern façade also serves as a porch. The wooden *dubs* are in-filled with foliated arched wooden screens filled with *pinjrakārī* work, features that dominate the building façade. The patterns of wooden beams and runners alternating with brick masonry and the rich detailing of the dubs in the first floor offers a stark contrast to the plain and somber appearance of the ground floor. The entire structure is covered with a *chār-bām* roof. Unlike most Muslim religious places of significance, the khanqah is devoid of a spire, the ubiquitous design feature associated with all prominent *khānaqāh* and *rūżā* of Kashmir.

Though the *khānaqāh* of Bijbehara retains the eye of the viewer with its interesting façade detail, it's the *rūżā* of Bābā Nasīb, with its soaring spire that commands the view of the observer.

The shrine of Nasīb is a single-storey, five *tāq* structure measuring 17.5m × 14.5m with a 1.5m wide *dalān* surrounding it. The *dalān* is supported on a colonnade composed of a single row of wooden baluster columns and cusped arches. While an essential feature of Kashmiri architecture, *dalān* is not uniformly found in all shrines, especially smaller ones dedicated to lesser-known saints.

The building's façade is dominated by a multi-tiered *chār bām* roof surmounted by an octagonal pavilion with arched openings. The use of an octagonal pavilion in such a position is usually seen at shrines associated with the indigenous *Reshī* order of mendicants, while square-shaped pavilions are more prevalent, especially for mosques and *khānaqāh*s. At Nasīb's shrine, the octagonal pavilion is itself surmounted by a spire with projecting gables at the base, and topped with a moulded brass finial. The octagonal pavilion acts as the transitional zone between the solid cubic base of the shrine and the soaring, slender *brangh*, thus achieving a harmony of horizontal and vertical elements.

The umbrella-shape of the finial at the apex of the *brangh* probably owes its origin to the *dūr*, the traditional Kashmiri earring. The same shape is repeated in the wooden pendants suspended from the corners of the roof. A series of wooden brackets decorated with carved floral patterns support the eaves and, in certain cases, like the shrine of Sayyid Husayn Simnānī at Kulgam, reconstructed in the early twentieth century CE, the brackets are shaped in the form of peacocks. Given the religious nature of the building, this is an architectural novelty serving as an exception rather than the rule.

The entrance to the shrine of Bābā Nasīb is through a centrally-located wooden doorway facing the porch. Inside, the graves of the saint and his principal disciples are separated by a wooden screen from the rest of the chamber.

This square chamber, known as the *ḥujrā* is centrally placed, and is highly reminiscent of the spatial layout of a traditional Kashmiri temple. In traditional Kashmiri architecture, a *varusī* (wooden screen) with intricate latticework, arranged between ornamental wooden columns, would define the *ḥujrā*, demarcating it from the surrounding *ghulām gardish*.

A number of cenotaphs marking the graves of Bābā Nasīb's disciples are located on the eastern side of the room, a feature found in many prominent shrines of the region. The saint's cenotaph, aligned on a north–south axis as required by Muslim burial custom, is sheltered by a raised wooden casket that is invariably covered with a heavy cloth, screening it from public view. Unfortunately, recent alterations have resulted in the loss beyond recognition of the building's original interior features, bringing to the fore the challenges faced in preserving Kashmir's built heritage.

Reconstruction of the *Khānaqāh-i Mʿaulā* at Srinagar

The reconstruction of the *Khānaqāh-i Mʿaulā* in the eighteenth century CE marks the high point of monumental wooden architecture of Kashmir [Plate 10]. Of all the Islamic religious buildings of Kashmir, barring the Jamia masjid at Srinagar, *Khānaqāh-i Mʿaulā* is the best preserved and the most impressive and monumental in scale. Though in the post-independence period, the larger shrine precinct lost a number of ancillary features such as the side *dalāns* over the *ṣufa* and the original wooden entrance gateway to the precinct, it still offers an authentic representation of the eighteenth century reconstruction. And with its wide gamut of *papier mache*, *khatamband, pinjrakārī,* calligraphy, stone work, wood carving etc, it also represents all the essential features that denote Kashmiri architecture as well crafts incorporated within architecture.

The reconstruction of the *khānaqāh* was undertaken in native Kashmiri idiom at a time when central Mughal authority had collapsed in Kashmir. The construction was overseen by the *naib-ṣubedar* Abū Barkat Khān and was completed in 1146 AH/1733 CE. Barkat Khān owed his position as much to the *ṣubedar* Amīr Khān as to the local citizenry, especially the *mujāvirs* (custodians) of *Khānaqāh-i Mʿaulā* who had helped him in ousting his predecessor. In these tiring times when his rule was dependant on local support, the *naib* would have been sensitive to the fact that the citizens would not look favorably on any attempt to tamper with the historic image of this highly revered shrine. This dependence helps in establishing the actual architecture of the building: its native-ness, within the socio-cultural realities of its construction. Thus the *khānaqāh* survives this Mughal rebuilding as one of the best examples of traditional Kashmiri monumental wooden architecture.

Given its monumental scale and central location on the main historic transportation spine of the capital city Srinagar, the building has also drawn a regular attention of visitors to the region in the eighteenth and nineteenth century CE. The reconstruction and decorative works undertaken at the *khānaqāh* have also been recorded by native historians of whom the description of Khuihāmī is particularly valuable.

The *khānaqāh* building is based on a square plan with the main structure measuring 22 m × 22 m [Figure 4.9]. Over the centuries a number of side *dalāns* have been added to the building, but the main eighteenth century

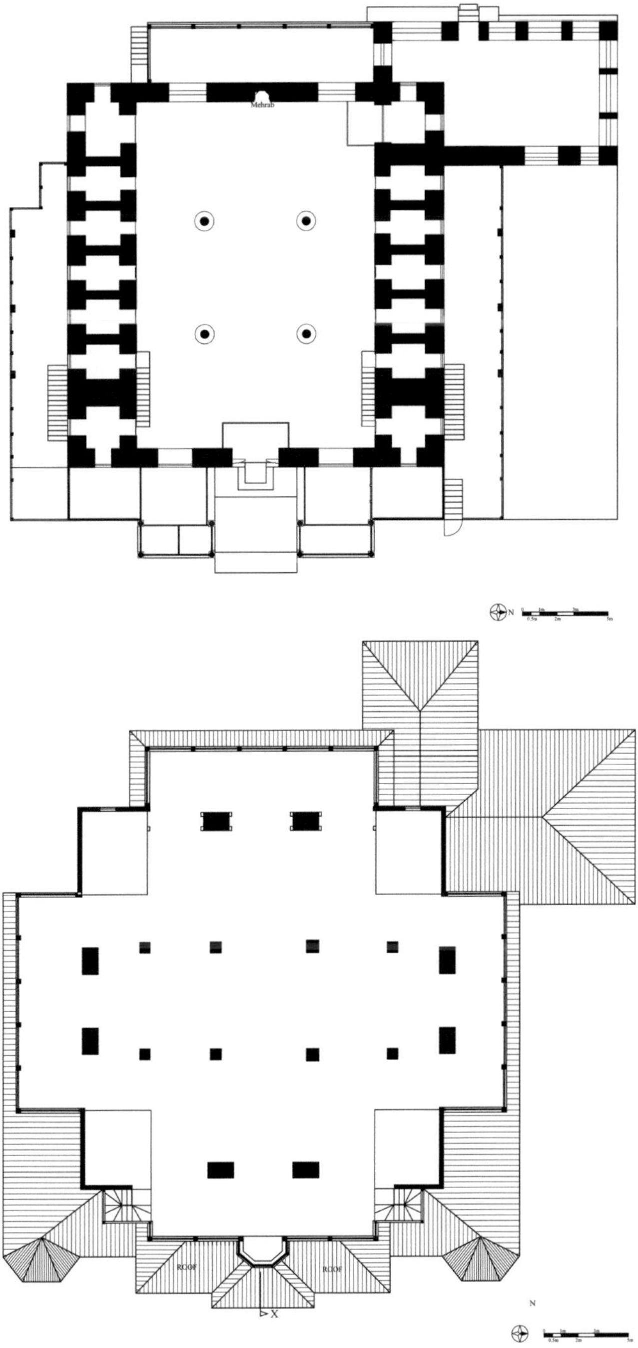

Figure 4.9 Khānaqāh-i M'aulā, ground floor and upper floor plan, © INTACH, Kashmir.

fabric of the building comprising a basic cuboidal massing surmounted by a pyramidal roof and spire has remained unchanged. The building which opens onto the Jhelum River from a *ghāt* on its western side has a traditional eastern approach. A series of steps lead down from the surrounding *moḥala* into the forecourt of the *khānaqāh*. Two stone *ṣufas* slightly elevated are located on either side of the stone path leading to the building entrance. The main entrance to the *khānaqāh* is from a high *dalān* supported on wooden columns that lead up to the main building. The *dalān* has gone through a series of changes and modifications, the most recent dating back to the twentieth century.

A low height doorway set in a wall covered with *papier mache* decoration leads into the main hall measuring 19.8m × 14.1m. This lofty double height hall serves as the main assembly and prayer space in the building. A series of small cells (seven on each side) serving as *chillā kuth* are located on either side of the hall, on the north and southern side, and open out into the central hall. The ceiling of the hall is supported on four wooden multi faceted columns. The entire wall surface of the double height hall, including the ceiling, are decorated with *khatamband* patterns and painted with *naqāshī* work.

The *ḥujrā*located on the extreme north-western corner is said to mark the spot where Mir Sayyid ʿAli Hamdanī used to preach. A small single storey building measuring 10m × 8.2m has been appended to this corner, and is reserved for women. Known as *Nūr Khāna*, this room has a separate entrance located on the west. The external façade of this building has *naqāshī* work dating from the mid part of the nineteenth century CE.

The double height hall at *Khānaqāh-i Mʿaulā*, with a ceiling height of 6.1m, includes two *dalans* on either side over the *chillā khuths* looking down into the main hall. Wooden staircases with intricate *naqāshī*work lead to this level from the main hall.

The upper floor of the *khānaqāh* comprises a large hall which takes the shape of a cruciform plan as it includes four centrally located *dubs* within the hall. From William Carpenter's painting of the *khānaqāh* in 1854 CE, it emerges that these rectangular *dubs* (balconies) projected from the second floor level. The linear double storey *dalāns* that are presently located beneath these *dubs* on the north and western façade are later additions. While this floor opens out in shape of arched screens filled within the supporting system of wooden columns, the corners of the building have been designed as rooms. This has been apparently done to add to the structural stability of the building, while also effectively helping in transferring the heavy dead load from the roof.

The entire building is surmounted by a traditional *chār bām* comprising four tiers till the opening of the square pavilion. The pavilion in turn, supports the wooden steeple with four gables at base and crowned with a brass finial. The prism shaped steeple has been constructed around a single deodar wooden pole 13.7m high, which is fixed within the forest of wood that forms the roof structure. The entire height of the building from ground till the roof spire stands at 36.8m. The roof, which like most pre-modern buildings is devoid of a truss, rises to a height of 6.4m from the ceiling till the square pavilion.

The original building façade comprised a simple cubodial massing with rectangular projecting bays at the second floor level. Given the roof form, it finds a clear parallel in the stone temple architecture of the region. Though the projecting *dubs* would have made the building significantly lighter, yet the overall appearance of the *khānaqāh* with its heavy wooden structure and limited small rectangular window openings would have weighed heavily on the viewer giving the entire building a massive appearance. The structural system adopted in the construction comprising alternative arrangement of wooden logs with brick infill between the gaps, also weighs on the heaviness of the structure. The addition of open *dalāns* and porches to the building with their arched frames, has helped in permeating the entire building with a sense of airiness that is found missing in the original square structure of the *khānaqāh*

While the building was constructed during Mughal period, the decoration of the interiors including the *khatamband* on the walls and ceiling was undertaken during Afghan rule. Though the *naqāshī* work, especially in the calligraphic bands and the ceiling dates from nineteenth century CE, that on the interior walls is a post twentieth century addition. This can be established from Kak's description of the interiors:

> [...] beautiful paneled wood-work on the walls, to which age has imparted a rich brown colour'[71].

Given that Kak's work was published in 1933, it is certain that the rich *naqāshī* of the interiors, barring that of the ceiling, is of a later dates. The building also possesses the best surviving example of carved wooden and stone cornice band at the plinth level. Additionally, the *pinjrakārī* work in the window openings is also of great interest and the oldest surviving example of this nature in the region.

The *Khānaqāh-i Mʿaulā* served as the prototype for construction of Muslim *khānaqāhs* in the eighteenth and nineteenth century given its religious and architectural image. The architecture and the detailing of its interiors found a resonance in the designing of number of Muslim religious buildings including the *khānaqāh* at Pampore, Naqshband Ṣāhab and the Dastgīr Ṣāhab. Though representing, the essence of a Kashmir tradition of building, it also incorporates significant Mughal motifs and decorative elements, especially the baluster column and the multi cusped arches, rendered in wood.

Mughal mosque at Hasanabad

The precinct of the *imāmbāda* of Hasanabad includes representation of Sultanate, Mughal, Sikh and Dogra period architectural activities. While today the precinct serves as one of the prominent cultural sites of Shi'a

Kashmir, due to the presence of an *imāmbāda* (r. mid twentieth century CE), the site still retains archaeological remnants of previous periods representative of diverse building typologies. Dispersed throughout the site are tombstones, some of which beside their historical relevance are also representative of elaborate works of calligraphic arts. Of particular interest are a series of limestone tombstones located to the north-east of the *imāmbāda*. These tombstones are located on a slightly elevated piece of land demarcated by large blocks of stone retaining wall. Comprising a series of vertical and horizontal tombstones, they are covered with prayers, supplications and elegies in *thuluth, naskh, rehan* and significantly *tughra* script. Mostly dating from the seventeenth century, the use of *tughra* in the tombstone indicates the royal origin of some of the deceased. It is worthwhile to note that the use of *tughra* was seen as a royal prerogative in many of ruling Muslim dynasties in medieval period.

Also located in the vicinity of the *mazar* are remnants of single multi cusped stone arch. These remnants belong to the erstwhile Mughal masjid whose remains could be seen at the site till nineteenth century CE. Locally remembered as the masjid of Nūr Jahān, the mosque is believed to have been constructed by the Empress who like the inhabitants of the *moḥala* of Hasanabad was of Shi's affiliation. Though there are no significant archaeological remains of the mosque left standing at the site, we do possess have archival images of the ruins of the building from early twentieth century CE [Figure 4.10].

Figure 4.10 Mughal mosque at Hasanabad, ruins of the mosque. Note the heavy brick masonry of the walls, Srinagar: early 20th century, © ASI.

From the visuals, it emerges that the building was a single storey square domed structure with heavy masonry walls, probably comprising three bays with the entrance from a high *pīshtāq*. What is interesting in the images, and can be correlated with Bates description, is the presence of well executed limestone cladding both in the interiors well as on the façade of the mosque. Traces of molded plaster work can also be observed in the images in squinches as well as ceiling. Given the detailing of the limestone cladding in the interiors, the use of Shāh Jahāni arch in stone niches, I would place the building during the reign of Shāh Jahān. Additionally, from local vernacular sources, we know that one of Shāh Jahāns *ṣubedar,* Zafar Khān constructed a *bāgh* at Hasanabad, where Muharram ceremonies used to be observed. Stylistically, the building fits in with architectural outpourings of the period, though it is possible that the mosque may be of an even later date.

The decay of the building fabric cannot be seen as a result of natural aging process or disasters, such as structural failure due to seismic activity. Most probably the destruction of the mosque was a result of sectarian strife that engulfed the region, with the collapse of Mughal authority, in the eighteenth and nineteenth centuries. The total disappearance of elements linked with the buildings can also be traced to vandalism, when stones from the mosque were employed in the construction of a *ghāt* at Basant bāgh in the nineteenth century CE.

Unfortunately nothing in the available archival images is conclusive enough to help us in recreating on how the building looked, beyond establishing the Mughal vocabulary of the mosque. A vocabulary which is also representative of the substantial resources that the empire could utilize in enshrining its image of a powerful, omnipresent and munificent benefactor. Constructed as a pace of worship for the Shi'a Muslim community of Kashmir, the building is also representative of how the Mughal Empire had moved from its initial adverse relation with the community to one of accommodation and patronage. Nevertheless, the building like all most all major public religious projects of the Mughals in Kashmir, failed to gain legitimacy or acceptance among the native community. Abandoned, and then pillaged at latter date, the memory of the building is also representative of how social acceptance is integral to architecture as it is to politics, today as it was yesterday.

Conclusion

Given its ubiquitous form, Mughal Architecture in Kashmir serves as the most remarkable manifestation of a process where Imperial architectural traditions remained socially disengaged with the intended native users. Built in stone, the architectural outpourings of the Mughals in Kashmir marked the projection of an image of permanence of Mughal power and hold over Kashmir as well as their munificence in creating new spaces of worship for the locals. Yet these activities also represent the Mughal disdain for local history or conditions, especially in the language of their buildings. The construction of the first grand Mughal mosque in Kashmir, *Masjid-i Naū*, sets the precedence for future Mughal architectural proclivity in Kashmir, involving the erasure of royal patronage for native architectural traditions, traditions that were emblematic of the entirety of Kashmir's experience of Islam. Nevertheless, given the physical and cultural distance between the two traditions, Muslim religious buildings commissioned by successive courts at Agra and Delhi remained mostly unutilized by the local community. During the last decades of Mughal rule in Kashmir, in the absence of a strong central authority, native building traditions re-shaped the architectural canvas of the region, drawing increasingly upon local resources and patronage, thus outliving both the empire and its architectural traditions.

Notes

1 'The ignorant wild people (of Kashmir) were pacified by the administration of justice and by increase of love', Abū'l Fażl, transl. H Beveridge, *Akbar Nama*, 3 vols., (New Delhi: Low Price Publications, 2011),770.
2 Ibid, 762.
3 Khawājā Nizam-al Dīn Aḥamd, transl. B De, *Tabaqāt-i Akbarī* (Calcutta: Asiatic Society of India, 1927), 645.
4 For an account of Persian poets of Kashmir, see Islah(1967), Sadiq(2009).
5 The earliest proponent of *sabaq-i hindī* is Amīr Khusrou Dehalvī (d.1325CE).
6 This includes Mullā Muḥsin Fanī remembering the homeland of Kashmir while presiding as judge in Allahabad. A verse of Mullā Tāhir Ghanī can be interpreted as a rejection of the Mughal rule:

Oh Ghanī! I wish such a revolution in the world

That the globe turns into dust in the skies.

Akhtar Mohi-ud-Din, 'Social Ideals and Patriotism in Kashmiri Literature (1900-1930)', *Indian Literature*, vol. 20, May-June 1977, 83.
7 'Mughal architectural tastes and idioms evolve from the centre outwards. It is triggered by imperial predilection, rarely arbitrary but embedded in political and cultural ideology [...]', Catherine B Asher, Architecture of Mughal India (Cambridge: Cambridge University Press, 1990), 17–18.
8 Catherine B Asher, 'Sub-Imperial Palaces: Power and Authority in Mughal India', *Ars Orientalis*, vol. 23. 282.
9 The verses written in a fine *nastaliq* script are the work of a native Kashmiri *khushnavis* (calligrapher), Muhammad Husayn Kashmirī(d.1621–22CE) who was rewarded with the title of *shireen kalam* (sweet pen) by Akbar.
10 Some historians include the name of Bābā Dāwūd Khākī, a prominent disciple of the Shaykh in the list of Kashmiri elite who approached Akbar for conquest of Kashmir, see Annemarie Schimmel, *Islam in the Indian subcontinent* (Leiden: EJ Brills, 1987), 47.
11 Vernacular sources also mention the construction of Jamia Shopian. The present building dating to a twentieth century reconstruction follows the courtyard plan of Jamia at Srinagar.
12 In 1665, Aurangzeb was accompanied in his travel to Kashmir by the European traveler François Bernier, who has left his impression of the valley in his writings. Amongst the Mughals emperors, Akbar visited Kashmir thrice, Jahāngīr seven times, Shāh Jahān three times and Aurangzeb once.

13 This included not only trouble in the frontiers bordering Ladakh but also the insurrection of Bombas in Muzzefrabad as well as revolts of the Gujjars in Poonch and Rajouri, see Dedhmārī, *Waqāt-i Kashmir*.
14 Ibid.
15 'In these circumstances one third of the population died. One third fled and one third remained safe', Dedhmārī, *Waqāt-i Kashmir*, 566.
16 Ibid, 557.
17 Khuihāmī, *Tārīkh-i Hasan*, 429.
18 This is a trend that has continued into our own times, giving rise to concerns about how integrity of historical sites can be maintained with ever increasing and changing requirements.
19 Juneja, *Architecture in Medieval India*, 66.
20 The Mughal bāghs of Kashmir were situated in areas removed from human habitation.
21 Mughal *ṣubedar* Fāẓil Khān repaired the mosque and constructed a hammam next to it. During 1203AH/1793CE the mosque was again repaired, Hamdani, *Shiyan-i Kashmir*286.
22 According to Koch (2018), Mughal texts are silent on the construction and patronage of the mosque.
23 Malīk's, *Tārīkh-i Kashmir* (c. 1620–21 CE) is one of the earliest and most detailed accounts of Kashmir in Persian, though it predates the date that is given for the construction of the mosque.
24 See, Nicholls, *Muhammadan Architecture in Kashmir.*
25 Ebba Koch, *Mughal Architecture* (New Delhi: Oxford University Press, 2002), 82.
26 Ibid, 84.
27 Ibid, 96.
28 It was a highly contentious verse of Mulla Shah which resulted in the wrath of Kashmiri ulema: I have given my hand in the hand of God What care do I then have for Mustafa. See, Abdul Majid Mir, *Al Qasaid-ul al- Arabia: A critical study* (PhD. Thesis: Centre of Central Asian Studies, University of Kashmir, 1995), 35–36. Kashmiri historians and hagiographers are silent on the issue of confrontation between Mullā Shāh and native Kashmiri *ulema*.
29 Interestingly even the local branch of Qadrī order does not seem to have embraced Mullā Shāh, who as the leading *khalifah* of Miān Mīr(1550–1635 CE), could be seen as the principal saint of the order in north India.
30 The building has gone through a series of inappropriate alterations and additions which mar its historical character and makes an understanding of the original functioning of the hammam difficult.
31 'Inayat Khan, transl. by A R Fuller, rev. and ed. by W E Begley and Z A Desai, *The Shah Jahan Nama of `Inayat Khan* (New Delhi: Oxford University Press), 458.
32 ASI, *Annual Report,1907–07*, 169–70.
33 Afshan Bokhari, 'Bewteen patron and piety: Jahan Ara Begam's Sufi affiliations and articulation in seventeenth century Mughal India' in *Sufism and Society,* ed. John J Curry and Erik S.Ohlander, (New York: Routledge, 2012), 142.
34 The association between Mullā Shāh and the mosque is based primarily on oral traditions, and a legal documents relating to the ownership of Muslim places of worship dating back to the 1930's. See, Hamdani, *Shiyan-i Kashmir*, 280.
35 'Jahanara and the emperor's favorite son, Dara Shukoh, started a small architectural workshop at Kashmir under the guidance of their spiritual teacher, the Sufi mystic Mulla Shah Badakshani', Ebba, *Mughal Architecture*, 96.

36 The *Padshāh kul* (also referred to as *Ara kul*)feeds one of the main water plant supplying drinking water to the city, at Alasteng.
37 This would require garden archaeology which would help in unearthing the original contours of the site that is increasingly being changed with new plantation patterns, constructions at site and leveling and filling of terraces.
38 Given the relatively flat terrain at Shalimar, the difference between the two terraces is insignificant. At Nishat two *bārādarī's* on the twelfth and third terrace were located on top of the retaining wall. A similar feature can also be seen at Pari Maḥal.
39 The nine fold plan was inherited by the Mughals form the repertoire of Timurid architecture, for details see Lisa Golombek and Ebba Koch, 'The Mughuls, Uzbeks and the Timurid Legacy', in *A Companion to Islamic Art and Architecture*, ed., Finbarr Barry Flood and Gülru Necipoğlu (John Wiley & Sons, 2017), 821. The use of a nine bay plan can be seen in earlier mosques, an early example from across the Islamic world would be *masjid-i Bāb-al Mardūm* (Cristo de la Luz) at Toledo, constructed in 390 AH/ 999 CE, on the mosque see Gregory S Hutcheson, 'Contesting the Mezqita Del Cristo De La Luz', in *La Corónica*, 43.1, 2014. For a general discussion on the plan form, see R A Jairazbhoy, 'The Taj Mahal in the Context of East and West: A Study in the Comparative Method', in *Journal of the Warburg and Courtauld Institutes*, vol. 24, no. 1/2 (Jan. – Jun, 1961).
40 This arrangement can be seen at Nishat as well as Achabal bāgh.
41 Goetz in a paper wrongly dates the tiles to Afghan rule; see H Gotez, 'Two Illustrated Persian Manuscripts from Kashmir', *Asia Asiatiques*, vol.9, no.1/2, 1962–63, 64.
42 Susan Stronge, 'The Tomb of Madani at Srinagar, Kashmir: A Case Study of Tile Revetments in the Reign of Shah Jahan' in *The Mughal Empire Between Jahangir and Shah Jahan*, ed. Ebba Koch and Ali Anooshahr (Mumbai: Marg, 2019), 220–45.
43 Nicholls, *Muhammadan Architecture in Kashmir*, 79–80.
44 In Persian the sign is known as *Kaman* (arrow). The sign also finds representation in gold *mohurs* of Jahangir and is referred to as *Azar*. According to Amanat the sign is also associated with, 'victorious rule in Perso-Islamic astrological culture, Abbas Amanat, *Iran: A Modern History* (New Haven: Yale university Press, 2017), 86.
45 Sheila S. Blair and Jonathan M. Bloom, *The Art and Architecture of Islam, 1250–1800* (Ahmedabad: Mapin, 1995), 183.
46 Ibid, 185.
47 Writing in 1975, Hamdani mentions that locals had dismantled the tiles from the gateway and sold it to dealers based in Calcutta, Hamdani, *Shiyan-i Kashmir*, 67.
48 Though Shi'a religious authorities have historically been more open to figural human depictions, yet we know of no instance predating Madnī's gateway where such a decorative technique was employed at a religious site in Kashmir.
49 The central stone panel over the entrance gateway of the mosque includes epigraphy, which in addition to commemorating Zain-al Ābidīn's patronage of the shrine also include a verse which is of Shia origin and indicates the Shi'a nature of the site.
50 Koch, *Mughal Architecture*, 70.
51 Tahiri, *Awliya-i Kashmir*, 686–688.
52 Dedhmārī, *Waqāt-i Kashmir*, 423–424.
53 The *bagh* was laid in 1623CE.
54 See, Dedhmārī, *Waqāt-i Kashmir.*

55 The interference in the case of Hazratbal is said to have been from Aurangzeb himself who is said to have initially obstructed the passage of the relic to Kashmir.
56 Tahiri, *Awliya-i Kashmir*, 695, 696.
57 The *Asar-i Sharif* is said to have been endowed with the revenue of forty one villages by the Mughal. This *jagir* was confiscated by Sikh governor of Kashmir during the nineteenth century CE, *Maulana Showkat Keng*, Islamic scholar, author's interview, Srinagar, September 2018.
58 The only armed attempt to counter Sikh hold over Kashmir was that of Sayyid Ahmad Barelvi (1786–1831CE). Sayyid Ahmad was also initiated in the Nakshbandhī order and it is possible that the Dehbadī family might have been in touch with him, and consequently invoked the wrath of the Sikh rulers.
59 Tahiri, *Awliya-i Kashmir*, 700, 701.
60 Ibid, 704.
61 Outside the city, the Asār-i Sharīf that came up in the nineteenth and early twentieth century CE, include those at Khiram, Panjirah, Yorinahama, Kaba Marg, Khawja Ṣāhab (Baramulla) and Berwah.
62 This includes acquisition of houses both on the northern as well as south-eastern side of the shrine.
63 Based on Koch's reading of the garden, this would be the tenth terrace, for details see Koch, *Mughal Architecture.*
64 Ebba Koch, 'Mughal Agra: A Riverfront Garden City' in *The City in the Islamic World*, vol.ii. ed. K Salma Jayyusi (Boston: Brill, 2008), 559.
65 About Hazratbal, Stuart writes:

> [...] The large mosque, where the hair of the Prophet is preserved, and specially venerated once a year at a great mela, is built round the principal garden-house. The narrow stone water- course runs beneath it [...], C M VStuart, *Gardens of the Great Mughals.* (London : A. and C. Black, 1913), 76.

66 Dedhmārī, *Waqāt-i Kashmir*, 94,103)
67 Based on Bābā Dāwūd Miskatī's *Żad-al Fuqra*, Muqbil asserts that during his journey in distant villages, Nasīb (and his disciples) would start and finish the construction of mosque within a day, M Maqbool Muqbil, *Abu'l Fuqra.* (Jammu: Qasmi Kutub Khana, undated), 16. This would indicate that the mosques so built would be small in size and very basic in their outlook. We can also infer from the statement that even during the seventeenth century CE; Kashmir retained a significant non-Muslim population.
68 Dedhmārī, *Waqāt-i Kashmir*, 312–14.
69 Again this stands in sharp contrast to the practices of the saint who can be seen as the tradition enabling figure within the *Suharwardī* order in Kashmir, Shaykh Hamza Makhdūm. Nasīb is connected to the Shaykh Hamza through one intermediary link, that of Dāwūd Khākī.
70 Muqbil, *Abu'l Fuqva*, 19.
71 Kak, *Ancient Monuments of Kashmir,*79.

5

RESURGENCE OF THE LOCAL IDIOM: 1752–1847 CE

> We passed through dirty streets, interminable *bazaars* and over two canals, to the fort on the Harni Parvat. We observed several large buildings on our route, tenanted in ancient times by the courtiers of the Moghul Emperors, and Kabul Sovereigns, but, with some few solitary exceptions, where these have been replaced by shawl manufactories, the dwellings are deserted, lonely ruins.
>
> Baron Charles Hugel, **Kashmir and the Punjab**, 119

In Chapter 4, we saw the emergence of a new style of building mosques and shrines in Kashmir, under the patronage of Mughal court. The esthetics of the Mughal monuments was at variance with how Kashmiri Muslims had traditionally built their place of worship. Nevertheless, the monumental scale of many of the buildings constructed by the Mughals in Kashmir is a material testament to the vast resources available to them. It is also representative of the use of set pattern of motifs, designs and architectural elements, standardized under the direct guidance of the emperor himself.

The collapse of Mughal rule in Kashmir and the establishment of Afghan (1752–1820 CE), and following them Sikh rule (1819–1847 CE) in the region, marks a period of great political and social upheaval in the land. With the end of the Mughal rule, resources required for undertaking public building activities on a monumental scale were no longer available with the Dūranī kings of Kabul. Under these adverse circumstances, patronage and upkeep of religious buildings shifted from state to the local Muslim community.

This chapter explores the wider consequences of the collapse of Mughal rule on Islamic religious architecture of Kashmir, resulting in the resurgence of native Kashmiri architectural traditions under local patronage. We will study the dynamics of this revival and explore how isolated elements associated with Mughal architecture were gradually incorporated in the local repertoire of traditional wooden construction.

From Delhi to Kabul and Lahore

The history of Afghan rule in Kashmir reads as a grim interweaving of mis-governance and official apathy verging onto brutality, economic degradation, chaos resulting from opportunism of court officials competing for power coupled with worsening intercommunity relations, especially in the capital city of Srinagar[1]. The depravation of the people was further compounded by natural calamities in the form of fire, flood, earthquake, famine and cholera.

Unlike the Mughal emperors, the Dūranī kings[2] never visited the land, their interest in Kashmir being sustained by steady arrival of revenue from the province[3]. Additionally, the political turmoil in the land resulting from armed conflict between contending Afghan nobles also had an adverse effect on the trade activities of non-native traders. During the six month rule of the first Afghan *ṣubedar* of Kashmir, ʿAbdullah Khān (r. 1166 AH/1753 CE), 80 foreign (non-Indian) traders stationed in Kashmir left, never to return back. The political uncertainty of the times can be understood in the way the rule of the province was decided, not by the authority of the court at Kabul, but by local intrigue, opportunism and shifting alliances amongst nobles.

Thus, ʿAbdullah Khāns replacement, Khawājā ʿAbdullah Khān (1753 CE) was killed by his own *naib,* Raja Sūkh Jewan Mal (1753–62 CE), who during his eight long years of rule, defied the Afghan king, temporally shifted his allegiance to the Mughal emperor[4] and also made a brief attempt at gaining sovereign power[5]. In his rule, Sūkh Jewan constantly kept on shifting the post of *naib-subedari* between two rival native claimants, Abū'l Hasan Bāndey and Mīr Muqim Kanth[6].

To a large extent, the locus of power during Afghan rule remained in Kashmir, in local Afghan and Kashmiri nobles, rather than in Kabul. The Kashmiri composition, in addition to prominent officials, included the tribes from the surrounding border areas, especially the Bombas and Khakas of Muzzafarbad and the Gujjars of Poonch-Rajouri. The urban elite, especially those in Srinagar, also emerged as important power players with their ability to organize mobs and riots in the city.

And it was this new dynamic of powerplay, with its measurable role of local actors, which successive Afghan officials operated in while resisting the Afghan court. And when a *ṣubedar* was served with dismissal, he more than often refused to quit. It was in 1783 CE, during A̲zad Khān's (1783–85 CE) rule, that a European, George Forster, visited Kashmir and left us with his impressions of difficulties of life under Afghan rule. In his account, he provides us with information on foreign merchants (including Georgians) visiting Kashmir, where in spite of the oppressive nature of the court, they 'were respected and even indulged'[7].

During the rule of Mīr Dād Khān (1786–88 CE), the Kashmiri Sunni religious elite locked the gates of Jamia Masjid and *Khānaqāh-i Mʿaulā* at Srinagar in protest against a prominent Hindu official of the revenue department, Dula Ram Qulī[8]. This episode brings to fore the powers of city elite and how they could force the hands of the *ṣubedars*, by raising religious passions within the masses. Amongst the later *ṣubedars*, who in their bid for power defied the Kabul court, we have the longest serving Afghan *ṣubedar* of Kashmir, ʿAtā Muhammad Khān (1795-1806 CE). In his bid for power, ʿAtā Muhammad built strongholds for himself in the valley, including the main fort of Srinagar at Hari Parbat. Significantly, the *ṣubedar* stuck coins in the name of Shaykh Nūr-al Dīn Reshī, the patron saint of Kashmir, in an attempt at rallying the local population with his cause[9].

In his bid to bring Kashmir back under Afghan control, the *vazir* of the Afghan king, Shāh Mahmūd (r. 1801-06 CE), made an uneasy alliance with Maharaja Ranjit Singh (1780-1839 CE) of Lahore. The combined Afghan and Sikh army proceeded towards Kashmir where they eventually managed to capture ʿAtā Muḥammad and his royal captive, Shah Shuja (r.1806-1809 CE), the former Afghan king and Shāh Maḥmūd's brother, who had escaped to Kashmir. The incursion of Sikh army into Kashmir and the gradual unraveling of Afghan power gave Ranjit Singh reason for annexing Kashmir. Aided by Raja Birbal Dhar, the Kashmiri *dīvān* at the local Afghan court, Maharaja Ranjit Singh advanced on Kashmir for a second time with the Sikh army, arriving in Srinagar in 1819 CE, bringing to end the Afghan rule. Thus ended the tenuous link between Kabul and Kashmir and with it ended almost five centuries of Muslim rule in Kashmir.

The Sikh rule of Kashmir lasting from 1819 to 1847 CE marks the end of the Muslim rule in Kashmir. It also serves as the harbinger of, if not colonial influences, but at least colonial interest in the region. This resulted in the visit of numerous Europeans and also officers linked with the East India Company to Kashmir who have left us with a vivid description of Kashmir and the socio-political conditions of the land in mid parts of the nineteenth century CE. The overall impression we obtain from their writings is of gloom, yet this breakdown of the land and its people was a progressive infliction, that had commenced with the breakdown of imperial Mughal authority. For the Kashmiri Muslims, the Sikh rule marked a political and religious upheaval in their community life. Not only did Kashmiri Muslims lose their place of power and patronage at the court, but symbols of Muslim-ness of the land were also curtailed. This included stopping the call to *aẕan* from mosques and *khānaqāhs*, and closing the gates of the principal congregational mosque of Kashmir, the Jamia Masjid at Srinagar[10]. At the commencement of the Sikh rule in Kashmir, an order was given to destroy the highly revered *Khānaqāh-i Mʿaulā*, but on the intervention of Pandit Birbal Dar, the order was rescinded[11]. A mosque at Hasanabad, dating from the Mughal period on the other hand, was dismantled and its limestone slabs used for the construction of ghāt at Basant bāgh opposite to the royal palace, Sherghari[12]. Like the Afghan rule before them, the Lahore *durbār* proved ineffectual in restoring a sense of governance in the land that had last been witnessed in the days of the Mughals. *Ṣubedars* were removed from their post with great frequency to ensure that they did not gain a foothold in the valley and entertain ideas of independence from the Lahore *durbār*[13].

Travelogues of European visitors to Kashmir from this period are replete with accounts of general decay in both urban and in rural areas, accompanied by exploitations of the *subedars* seeking to raise the required amount of revenue to be deposited with the court at Lahore. Like in the preceding Afghan rule, the economic ruin of the land was coupled with natural calamities in the form of earthquake (1827 CE), cholera (1827 CE, 1845 CE) and famine (1831 CE, 1833 CE)[14]. A Shi'a-Sunni riot (1832 CE) in the city of Srinagar and mutiny amongst the Sikh army (1841 CE) coupled with the revolt of the Bambas (around 1852 CE) further aggravated the already precarious political and social conditions of the land. Yet, the Sikh rule did offer relief to the Pandit community from the oppression they had witnessed during Afghan rule. This was though counterbalanced by the hardships and persecution that the Muslims had to face.

With limited influence at the court of the local *ṣubedar* or at the *durbār* in Lahore, the affairs of Kashmiri Muslim community dwelled with the community elite. While the maintenance of local mosques and shrines was undertaken by the community at large, in case of major shrines such activities involved considerable patronage form the merchant class, especially those involved in the shawl business. During the closing part of Sikh rule in Kashmir, two Punjabi Muslims, Shaykh Muḥyi-al Dīn (d. 1846 CE) and his son, Shaykh Imām-al Dīn (d.1859 CE), served successively as *ṣubedars* of Kashmir. They were not only responsible for repairs to some of the major Muslim religious places of Kashmir, but also bestowed *jāgīrs* widely amongst their Kashmiri loyalists. The elder Shaykh[15] was also responsible for opening the gates of the Jamia Masjid in 1843 CE after a gap of 25 years[16]. Still, patronage and maintenance of these places of worship remained with the members of Muslim community.

The rule of Imām-al Dīn saw the first Sikh war of 1845–46 CE, in which the Sikhs were defeated by the British. During the war, Gulāb Singh, the Raja of Jammu, and the Prime Minister at the Lahore court made his own terms with the British, independent of the Lahore *durbār* and consequently was conferred with the title of Maharaja by the British. The treaty by which Kashmir was transferred to the newly created Maharaja became famous by the name of *bi-nāma-i Amritsar* (The Treaty of Amritsar). The signing of the treaty marks the end of Sikh rule in Kashmir, and the creation of the state of Jammu and Kashmir. The Dogra rule would in turn last for a century from 1847–1947 CE, marking Kashmir's transition to modern times.

Cultural and architectural traditions

The Afghan rule in Kashmir was grafted on the cultural traditions that the Mughal had left in Kashmir and which the Afghans had themselves also inherited as a former province of the Mughal Empire. Yet, in their architectural ventures in Kashmir, limited as they were, the Afghan court adopted the local Kashmiri idiom rather than the legacy of Mughal architecture. Part of the reason lies with limited financial resources of the local *durbār*, which effectively curtailed any costly enterprise involving time consuming construction in masonry based on arcuate system. Also, the comparative ease of building in readily accessible and easily workable wood not only reduced the project cost but also the time of construction. While these practical considerations can be seen as an explanation for why local Kashmiri building traditions made a comeback with the establishment of Afghan rule, these are not the only reasons.

Afghan rule in Kashmir lasted for a period of more than 70 turbulent years resulting in the despoliation of the land and widespread socio-political stagnation. One of the few bright spots being the six-year governorship of Amīr Khān Javan Sher (1770–76 CE), who from all accounts was framed in the mold of his Mughal predecessors. Most of the Afghan *ṣubedars* were too interested in filling their coffers to undertake any major construction activity. Unlike the Mughals, the Afghans did not possess an established architectural style. Having been ruled by the Mughals, they imbibed a narrow provincial outlook.

Afghan construction in Kashmir, on detailed examination, depicts a certain sense of temporariness[17]. This can be seen at Nāgar Nagar on examining the construction and workmanship of Akbar's rampart wall and comparing it with that of the fort built within the same city by the Afghans more than two centuries later. Though both are a part of same building tradition and construction system – rubble stone masonry, yet the strength and durability which is seen in Mughal construction is found wanting in the Afghan structure. Same is true of the ʿAālī Masjid which was last rebuilt by the Afghans. During the conservation of the mosque in 2006, removal of damaged plaster from the walls revealed wavy out of plumb masonry walls of poor binding material, displaying both the haste with which the building was constructed and the poor workmanship employed in the construction.

The limited architectural proclivity of Afghan rulers was extended to repairs or reconstruction of major Muslim shrines in Kashmir which had either burnt down or needed repairs. This involved the reconstruction of the shrines at Chār-i Sharīf and repairs and extension at Makhdūm Saheb shrine undertaken by Ata Muhammad, and embellishment of the interiors of *Khānaqāh-i Mʿaulā* under Mīr Hazār Khān. Repair works were also undertaken at the Jamia of Srinagar during the rule of Karīm Dād and Azad Khān[18]. The Shi'a community also attempted to reconstruct the *imāmbādas* at Zadibal and Hasanabad, but seen as landmarks of Shi'a identity, the construction was contested by members of the local Sunni community, consequently both the structures were promptly demolished by the *ṣubedars*.

It was also during this period that the main Qadrī center in Kashmir, *Khānaqāh-i Ghusīyah*, came up at Srinagar. The construction of the *khānaqāh* was undertaken by elders of the Qadrī order; and like many similar projects undertaken during this period, the patronage devolved on members of the native Kashmiri Muslim community. Similar is the case with the *khānaqāh* of Sayyid Shāh Niyāẕ Naqshbandī (c. 1797 CE) and the *rūżā* of Sayyid ʿAli Akbar at Srinagar, which was constructed in 1801 CE[19]. Continuing with the Sultanate era practice of accommodating guests in *khānaqāh*s, we find in rural Kashmir mosques were used for lodging travelers[20].

The trend of local patronage in spite of limited and constrained socio-economic condition of the people continued under the Sikh rule. It was only during the ending part of the Sikh rule that the government was involved in repair works of some Muslim places of worship, most noticeably the shrine of Makhdūm Sāhab [Figure 3.13]. Repairs were also carried out in the Jamia at Srinagar after it was reopened. Interestingly, while the *ṣubedar* was officially involved, the expenses were met through financial contribution of the local citizens and supervised by Mīr Husayn Shāh Qadrī[21].

It is to the rule of Shaykh Muhyi-al Dīn that we owe the oldest extant example of *naqāshī* used in external surface decoration, on the walls of *Nūr Khāna*[22] at *Khānaqāh-i Mʿaulā*. The art work in the wall frescos of *Nūr Khāna* displays the same 'Punjabi exuberance [...] married to the Kashmiri instinct for color and proportion'[23] that was seen in the designing of Kashmiri shawls of this period. The *naqāshī* work undertaken in the façade of old shrine building at Hazratbal also dates from this period. The *naqāshī at Khānaqāh-i Mʿaulā* is undertaken on dry gypsum plaster, with the rendering of building façade in regular rectangular panels. Both the *naqāshī* of *Nūr Khāna* and Hazratbal shrine can be seen as derivative of Mughal practices, as seen in the huge wall mural of Lahore fort undertaken by Jahāngir. The emergence of this art form, at a period when Kashmir was ruled directly from Lahore, functioning from the same fort, must have served as a dissimulator of this decorative technique to a Kashmiri audience[24]. Both at Hazratbal and at *Nūr Khāna*, the detailing of the *darshan dīr* (viewing window), which is used for displaying of relics on the occasion of the *ʿurs*, is rendered in stucco plaster to give the shape of a *bangala* roof, highly reminiscent of the *jarokha* windows and balconies that were widely used in Mughal architecture, both in monumental and vernacular form. There is always a possibility that these artistic features were directly inherited by Kashmiris from the Mughals, but their widespread use during Sikh rule would indicate that the route of transmission was through Lahore.

It is this richness as seen in the wall *naqāshī* that differentiates the architecture of Sikh period[25] from that of preceding Afghan rule, though both draw upon the available architectural traditions of the land, both native as well as Mughal. Overall, the architecture of Afghan and Sikh period marks a continuing shift towards native building traditions and decorative features, though some aspects of Mughal architecture which had been incorporated in the local vernacular were also employed. This included the ever-increasing use of baluster columns and multi-foliated Shāh Jahānī arch with a significant departure, both the features were reproduced in wood rather in brick and stone.

Unfortunately, hardly any significant architectural remnants from the Sikh period survive in Kashmir, especially of secular genre, to help us form an overview of architecture commissioned under Sikh rulers. Aside from the buildings mentioned above, what we are left with are few sketchy reports of European travelers – a retainer of Maharaja Ranjit Singh constructed a garden in the valley which was named after him as Surij Bāgh. Baron Hugel's description of the *bāgh* provides an idea of the opulence of architecture from Sikh period:

> The pavilion where we slept consists of several little rooms, all of marble. The windows are most tastefully ornamented with the glass of Bengal; in the midst of the large square forming the garden, is an airy edifice of wood, with beautiful columns and lattice-work [...].[26]

The vernacularization of architecture was also seen in one other key cultural expressions of the period – poetry. Though Persian remained the official court language and Kashmir retained a fine tradition of Persian poetry way down till the end of nineteenth century CE, but with the onset of Afghan and Sikh rule, we find native poets increasingly resorting to Kashmiri language as a medium of artistic expression.

The leading poets from the period who wrote in Kashmiri include Arnimal, Parmanand (b. 1794 CE), Rasūl Mīr (d. 1870 CE) and Maḥmūd Ghami (d. 1855 CE)[27]. The development of Kashmiri as the language of literary expression was carried well into the post-Sikh period by poets such Maqbūl Shāh (1820–76 CE)[28], Vali-ul Lah Matū (d. 1870 CE) and followed widely by later poets. While most of the above-mentioned poets were involved in writing of romantic *ghazals* and *mathnawis*, devotional poetry also received due notice, especially in the works of Parmanad[29] (b. 1794 CE) and ʿAbdul Aḥad Nādim (d. 1865 CE) whose *nʿat* poetry gained wide popularity. Similar was the case of elegy writing, where the structure of Kashmiri *marthiya* was entirely transformed under Qāżī Aḥmed ʿAli and Khawājā Hasan Mīr. An overview of Kashmiri literature of the period reads similar to that of Kashmiri architecture, which was a blend of local traditions and externally introduced influences. In Kashmiri literature, we see the traditions of *sabaq-i hindī* which had reached its greatest height in Kashmir under the patronage of Mughal court, being grafted on local folk traditions. Similar was the experience of local architecture, where the soul and the form of architectural expression remained rooted in the land, though the phenomenon in its entirety continued imbibing external influences in making of an architectural canvas which though not pure was nevertheless harmonious.

Building in the native idiom: The khānaqāhs and mosques

Khānaqāh-i Ghusīyah at Khanyar

One of the major *khānaqāh* that was constructed in Kashmir during the late eighteenth century CE is the *Khānaqāh-i Ghusīyah* at Srinagar, popularly known as Dastgīr Ṣāhab. The *Khānaqāh-i Ghusīyah* would emerge as the principal seat of the Qadrī Sufi order in Kashmir and one of the most revered Muslim shrines of Srinagar city. The origin of the Qadrī order in Kashmir are lost in a series of conflicting accounts, though it seems that the order gained a foothold in the region during sixteenth century CE, under the leadership of Mīr Nāzuk Nazkī (d. 1022 AH/1613 CE). After Nazkī's death, the Qadrī *silsila* was eclipsed by older established orders both in the city and in the region. Even when Mullā Shāh arrived in Kashmir, neither his presence nor his *khānaqāh* advanced the cause of the order in Kashmir.

The order was revived during the latter part of the seventeenth century CE,[30] when two members of the Qadrī's *silsala*, the brothers Sayyid Muhammad Fażil and Sayyid Abu'l Hasan, arrived in Kashmir. The brothers settled down in Khanyar area of the city. On his death, Sayyid Fażil was buried in a small room that he had constructed for meditation in vicinity of his house at Khanyar.

More than half a century after Fażil's arrival in Kashmir, his grandson Sayyid Ghulām-al Dīn Azad constructed a *khānaqāh* at Khanyar. The Afghan *ṣubedar*, Sardar ʿAbdullah also deposited relics associated with the Qadrī *silsala* with Sayyid Azad and these were displayed in the *khānaqāh* on major *ʿurs*. The construction of the *khānaqāh* and the acquisition of holy relics from the Afghan *ṣubedar* assured wide spread popularity for the *khānaqāh* both in the city and across Kashmir which it had lacked before.

Regarding the construction of the *khānaqāh*, Khuihāmī ascribed it to Sayyid Buzurgh and gives the date of construction as 1220 AH/1805 CE[31]. Yet, the chronogram written on a stone in the *khānaqāh* gives the date as 1182 AH/1768 CE and the builder's name as Azad, father of Sayyid Buzurgh. The confusion has risen from the fact that Khuihāmī has mistaken the single-story *khānaqāh* with the adjoining double-story hammam mosque, which is also sometimes referred to as the *khānaqāh*. In addition to the mosque, the *khānaqāh* precinct also included two burial chambers including that of Sayyid Fażil and a number of ancillary buildings that had been constructed in the twentieth century CE. This historical precinct of *khanqah* was gutted down during a fire incident in 2012[32].

Spatially, the *khānaqāh* precinct revolves around the burial chamber of Sayyid Fażil. The various buildings in the precinct are organic additions to the burial chamber which remains the spiritual and physical nucleus of the surrounding building and spaces.

The various buildings in the complex are broadly located along a north-south axis with the main entry from the western side, which historically, till early part of the last century, comprised of a water body – Brar-i Nambal. Today, much of the land on the western side has been reclaimed from the Nambal and a road adjoins the precinct on its western edge. On the northern and southern sides, the precinct is surrounded by residential areas: *moḥala* which came up because of the presence of the *khānaqāh*. The residential compound of the descendant of Sayyid Fażil is contagious to the precinct on its eastern boundary.

In terms of the organization of spaces, the two-story hammam-mosque is located on the northern end of the complex, and the *khānaqāh* on the southern end. The burial chamber of Sayyid Fażil, the *ḥujra khāṣ*, is located in between these two buildings. A small narrow chamber which serves as the room for housing the holy relics is located in between the *ḥujra khāṣ* and the hammam-mosque. Of the various buildings in the complex, the *ḥujra khāṣ* is the oldest, though we do not have the year of Sayyid Fażil's death. The chamber housing the relics and the *khānaqāh* dates from 1768 CE, the hamman-mosque as mentioned before from 1805 CE. The *ḥujra khāṣ* was repaired in 1877 CE by a prominent Kashmiri trader, Khawājā Sana-ul Lah Shawl (d.1879 CE), who also constructed a passage along the eastern edge of the complex to serve as a connecting corridor between the various buildings. In the post-Independence period, the *khānaqāh* was expanded on the northern side, and the entire walls of the *khānaqāh* and the corridor leading up to the *khānaqāh* were decorated with *khatamband* work and *naqāshī*.

The *khānaqāh* constructed by Azad comprises a linear 5*taq* building which was extended on the northern side to accommodate two more window bays, making the entire structure a 7*taq* building measuring 24.3m × 12.1m [Figure 5.1]. The building is raised on a high plinth (1.8m) of dressed ashlar masonry. The original height of the plinth was almost that of a full floor and boats used to be moored alongside the plinth, before the entire area was filled in for construction of a road. Internally the *khānaqāh* comprises a double height hall measuring 22.5.m × 10.06.m. The ceiling of the *khānaqāh* is supported on four wooden columns, centrally located on the original eighteenth century CE plan. During the extension on the northern side, the wall on that side was opened and wooden columns inserted in between. Similarly, the entrance doorways to the *khānaqāh* on the south-western side were also removed during the extension that was carried on that side. Consequently, the *khānaqāh* does not have a separate entrance, but can be accessed from both the hammam-mosque (north-east corner) as well as the ante-chamber leading to the eastern corridor. The main *ḥujra khāṣ* (7.0m × 5.5m), constructed entirely in wood, is also accessed from the *khānaqāh* on its eastern side. The hammam-mosque has a small separate entrance located on the north-eastern corner. The doorway in turn leads to the *ṣufa* of the hammam with bathing cubicles on its northern side and the main mosque hall measuring 9.75m × 9.75m on the

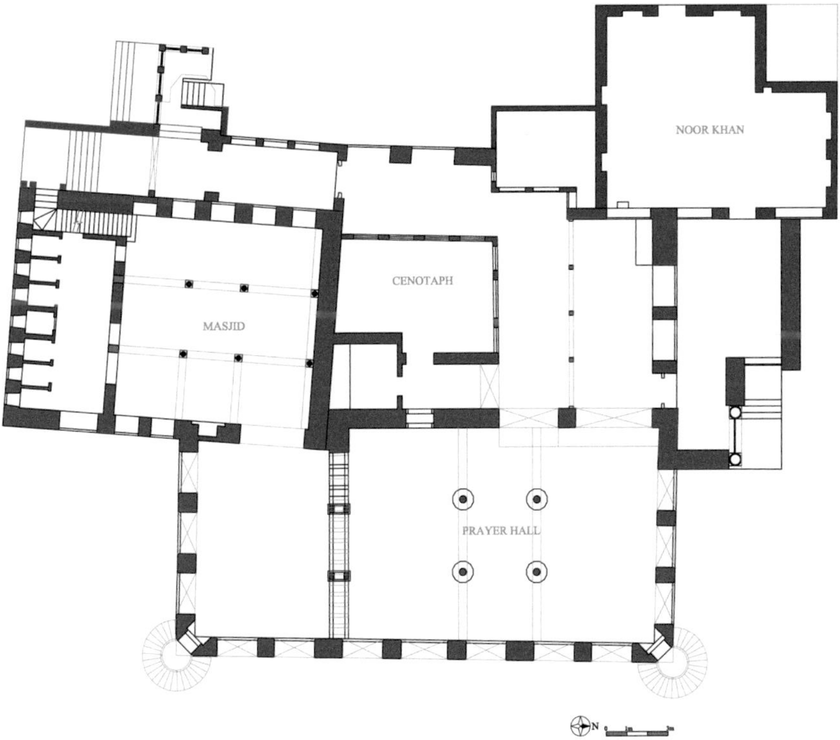

Figure 5.1 Khānaqāh-i Ghusīyah, ground floor plan, © INTACH, Kashmir.

other side. As with many hammam-mosques that were constructed in the eighteenth-nineteenth century CE, the *ṣufa* of the hammam opens directly into the prayer hall of the mosque. The low-height ceiling of the mosque is in turn supported on two rows of wooden columns. Traditionally, the upper floor of the hammam-mosque could be approached from a steep staircase that was located on along the north-eastern corner of the mosque, but this was closed during the twentieth century CE, and a separate staircase constructed along the corridor. The upper floor of the hammam-mosque comprise a lofty hall measuring 14.32m × 9.75m with a height ceiling (4m), supported on two rows of columns parallel to the *qiblā* wall. This hall was used on the occasion of *ʿurs* and during summers only, while the low-ceiling smaller prayer hall on the ground floor was used during winters.

Architecturally, the complex draws inspirations from the two highly revered Muslim shrines of Srinagar city: the old *Asār-i Sharīf* at Hazratbal and the *Khānaqāh-i Mʿaulā*. Like the Hazratbal shrine, the *Khānaqāh-i Ghusīyah* was constructed as a double-height hall, with big arched window openings surmounted by rectangular clearstory ventilators. The use of molded lime plaster work can be seen in both the buildings. Similarly, both the buildings are raised on a high stone plinth of ashlar masonry and a traditional Kashmiri *char-bām* roof. Internally, the redesigning of the *khānaqāh* interiors was modeled heavily on the interiors of the *Khānaqāh-i M'aulā* [Plate 11]. The designs, patterns and motifs and even the colors bear a remarkable degree of similarity, both in the decoration of the walls with *khatamband, naqāshī* and calligraphy. Similarly, the design motifs in the ceiling as well as the decoration of the wooden columns, with wooden beading in herring bone patterns, the lotus-shaped pseudo-wooden base and capital of the columns draw their inspiration from the interiors of the *Khānaqāh-i M'aulā.*

The *Khānaqāh-i Ghusīyah* apparently was without a spire, and this would also be in keeping with the design of the Hazratbal shrine. The small rectangular pavilion with a wooden open pseudo-dome was constructed after the shrine was extended in the 1950s. The hammam-mosque on the other hand was surmounted by a multi-tiered pyramidal roof with a square pavilion at top. The pavilion was covered with the quintessential Kashmiri spire with brass finial and gables at the base. The reconstruction work on the *khānaqāh* complex has recently been completed based on architectural and photo documentation [Plate 11]

Khānaqāh-i Nazkī (Qadri), Qadi Kadal, Srinagar

Another building dating to the eighteenth century CE is the *Khānaqāh-i Nazkī* at Qādi Kadal, Srinagar. The building stands in the same compound as the shrine of the sixteenth century CE, Qadrī shaykh, Mīr Nazuk Nazkī-Qadri. The *Kashur Encyclopedia* dates the construction of the *khānaqāh* to Jahāngīr's reign[33], but this is based neither on any epigraphical, stylistic nor textual evidence. Though we cannot discount the possibility that a lesser institution such as a madrasa might have existed at the site from where members of the Nazkī[34] family would have continued their preaching, yet the present structure based on its architecture alone can be safely posited as an eighteenth-century CE building.

The *khānaqāh* itself comprises of four-story high cuboidal building, measuring 8.53m × 10.66m, comprising two lofty prayer halls located on different levels [Figure 5.2]. The building has been constructed on top of the stone retaining wall that served as the embankment wall for the Nallah Mār canal. The canal which was dug in the sixteenth century CE by Zain-al Ābidīn to serve as a secondary spine of water-borne transportation in the city, continued to function till the 1970s when it was filled in and converted into a road. The main entrance to the *khānaqāh* is from the western side facing the small compound that also houses the shrine of Mīr Nazuk on its north-west. A small low-height door located on the south-western corner of the building provides access to a narrow 1.2m wide passage running along the length of the wall on the southern side. This passage also has small space for ablution as well as a narrow wooden staircase that leads to the upper floor.

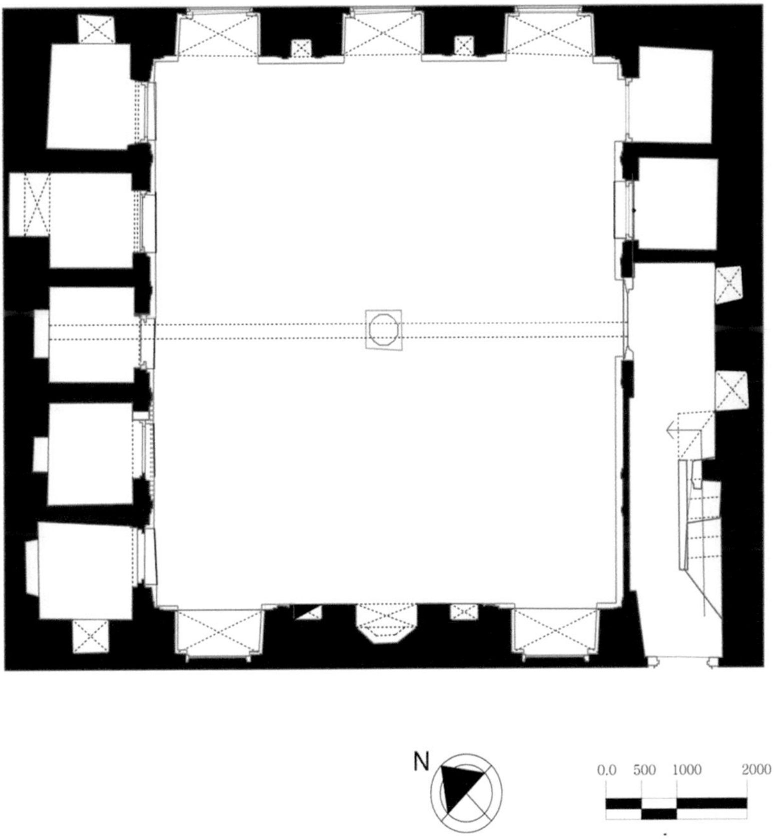

Figure 5.2 Khānaqāh-i Nazkī, ground floor plan, © INTACH, Kashmir.

The prayer hall of the *khānaqāh* is located on the other side of the passage and comprises a double-height hall measuring 7.0m × 6.0m with a series of cells (*ḥujras*) located on the northern side of the hall. In terms of spatial arrangement, the positioning of the *ḥujras* on the side of the main prayer space can be seen both in bigger monuments such as *Khānaqāh-i Mʿaulā* and smaller buildings such as Zakir masjid, and emerged as a preferred plan form for designing of *khānaqāhs* in Kashmir. Nevertheless, given the organic development of some of the *khānaqāhs* in Kashmir, we also see an entirely different arrangement of spaces in some of the *khānaqāhs* that are more or less coeval with the *khānaqāh* of Mīr Nazuk. These include the *Khānaqāh-i Ghusīyah* as well as the *Khānaqāh-i Naqshbandiya*, though the present building of the *Khānaqāh -i Naqshbandiya* dates from the reconstruction that was undertaken in the twentieth century CE. The ceiling of the *khānaqāh* itself is supported on a wooden column, with wooden beams running in opposite direction in a plus-shaped (+) arrangement, again a typical example of wooden trabeated construction system adopted in Kashmir.

The wooden staircase opens out onto a narrow passage on what is essentially the first floor, but here also functions as a *dalān*. An openable wooden lattice work screen in the passage (*varusī*) provides a clear view down into the prayer hall of the *khānaqāh*. Unlike the *Khānaqāh-i M'aulā*, where an internally located staircase connects the various building levels, the staircase in the Mir *khānaqāh* are screened from the main hall. Additionally, the side *dalāns* looking down in the main hall at *Khānaqāh-i M'aulā* are spatially more elaborate and well decorated as compared to that found in *Khānaqāh-i Nazkī*. From this narrow *dalān,* another wooden staircase provides access to the upper floor of the *khānaqāh* which comprises a single large hall measuring 7.0m × 9.4m running all across the building. This part of the *khānaqāh* was traditionally used in summer, and with a high ceiling (3m) and window openings on all sides, it gives a feel of spaciousness and light. Again, this is a feature we find at *Khānaqāh-i Ghusīyah*.

The pivotal decorative feature of the hall is a single wooden column which supports a wooden beam running parallel to the *qiblā* wall. The wooden column rests on a stone base with a bold floral motif running along it. The column itself is shaped as *sarv-i tham* (baluster column) with the capital fashioned as a half-finished *muqarna*. The baluster columns owe their origin in the Mughal architecture to Shāh Jahān and were introduced in Kashmir during his reign. The design found great favor in the wooden architecture of the region after its widespread use in the reconstruction of the *Khānaqāh-i M'aulā* in eighteenth century CE. This again advances our hypothesis that the *Khānaqāh-i Nazkī* is not a construction from the Jahāngīrī era, but from a later date. The *vas tālāv* ceiling of the *khānaqāh* is a feature that is widely used in both religious and domestic architecture of the region from eighteenth century CE onwards.

Externally, the building façade comprises arcade in exposed brick masonry. The brick used in the walls helps in establishing the date of the building construction which is commonly dated to Jahāngir's period. However, the size of the brick, 20cm × 10cm × 3.8cm, resembles brick sizes that were used during late seventeenth-eighteenth century CE. Given that the production of bricks during Mughal period was fairly standardized, it seems highly improbable that the *khānaqāh* was constructed during Jahāngir's reign.

The outer character of the building and the articulation of the building façade also shows influence from the Mughal architecture of the region. These influences can be observed in the designing of arched window openings in the façade, set within slightly recessed rectangular panels. The earliest trace of such a detailing in the Islamic religious architecture of Kashmir, where the window panel is set within a rectangular frame of the masonry pier, can be found in Mughal buildings of Kashmir, of which the oldest is *Masjid-i Naū*[35].

To relieve the monotony of a regular arrangement of window openings, the builders made a slight change in both the height of the windows as well as the profile, with the lower arches being more pronounced and those at the top being rendered as segmental arch. Combined with the rectangular shape of the window openings on the ground floor, we find an arrangement of opening that not only makes the building façade interesting, but also, given the solid cuboidal form of the *khānaqāh,* take away from some of the massiveness of the exposed brick masonry planes. The play on the building façade through an arrangement of varying window shapes combined with the basic clean cuboidal massing gives the *khānaqāh* an architectural affect that would find resonance in modern architecture. Still, the building which would have been the tallest structure along the Nallah Mār canal does not lose any of its robustness and exudes the same sense of permanence that we find associated with Mughal buildings in Kashmir. Unlike the masonry dome of a Mughal building, the *khānaqāh* is covered with a traditional Kashmiri *char-bām* roof with elaborate ornamental wooden eave boarding[36].

The architecture of the *Khānaqāh-i Nazkī* represents an emerging trend during which Mughal architectural traditions were transmitted into native practices during eighteenth century CE. It is possible that such a practice had started at an earlier date, especially in the field of vernacular architecture, with city elite modeling their houses on the *ḥavelīs* of the Mughal emperors and their *ṣubedars,* but of this we have no evidence[37]. It is only in the religious architecture of the region in the *Khānaqāh-i Mʿaulā* and *Khānaqāh-i Nazkī* that we see early examples of this transmission, though in case of the *Khānaqāh-i Nazkī,* this happened after the end of Mughal rule in Kashmir.

Khānaqāh-i Khawājā Masʿud at Pampore

Of the various surviving Muslim religious monuments of Kashmir, the *Khānaqāh-i Khawājā Masʿud*, Pampore is of an uncertain date [Figure 5.3]. No date has been recorded or is offered for the construction of the *khānaqāh*. Khawājā Masʿud was wealthy merchant who adopted the path of Sufism, becoming a disciple of Bābā Dāwūd Khākī. Initiated into the *Suharwardī silsila*, Khawājā Masʿud spent his time in religious preaching and community welfare before passing away in 1047 AH/1637 CE[38]. On his death, he was buried at Pampore. According to local traditions, the *khānaqāh* was constructed by Bābā Muhammad Ṣādiq, a disciple of Khawājā Masʿud, and forms part of a larger precinct that includes a mosque and the shrine of Masʿud. Dedhmārī in his work on political and social history of Kashmir makes a detailed mention of the life of Masʿud, but is silent on the existence of a *khānaqāh* at Pampore. Similarly, Khuihāmī in his nineteenth century CE account of Muslim religious places and saints make no mention of the shrine, though he too records the life of Khawājā Masʿud in detail[39].

Figure 5.3 Khānaqāh-i Khawājā Masʿud, north-eastern façade of the building, Pampore, 2007, © Hakim Sameer Hamdani.

The *khānaqāh* is mentioned in the Gazetteer of 1873 as well in Kak's selection of monuments of Kashmir. Kak also has an image of the *khānaqāh* in his book which would tentatively indicate a later-day origin for the building instead of seventeenth century CE. While the building has been heavily restored in the twentieth century CE, also involving major changes to the building fabric, yet the basic structure of the *khānaqāh* comprising wood structural system has remained unchanged from what can be observed in the archival images of 1930s. An examination of the exposed wooden members of the structure with its freshness of grains does not support dating the building to the seventeenth century CE.

The *khānaqāh* of Khawājā Masʿud follows the principles that were established in the reconstruction of the *Khānaqāh-i Mʿaulā* at Srinagar during early eighteenth century CE. Like the *khānaqāh* at Srinagar, the *khānaqāh* at Pampore is based on a square plan measuring 17.3m × 17.3m. The main entrance to the building is from the eastern façade from a low-height entrance doorway flanked by a rectangular window on either side. Archival images of the building from the early part of the twentieth century CE indicate that the eastern façade of the building was preceded by a double-story rectangular *dalān* supported on plain rectangular wooden columns.

The ground floor of the *khānaqāh* comprises a single hall 15.2m × 15.2m, with the ceiling of the double-height hall (6m) supported on four wooden columns. A narrow U-shaped gallery (3.6m-2.7m wide) extends on the first-floor level on three sides looking down into the main hall. This feature finds a parallel in the *Khānaqāh-i Naqshbandī* in Srinagar. Similarly, given their small size, both the *khānaqāh* at Naqshabandh Ṣāhab and at Pampore are devoid of solitary cells (*chillā kuth*) that can be found at the *Khānaqāh-i M*ʿ*aulā*. Following the pattern of the *Khānaqāh-i M*ʿ*aulā*, the *khānaqāh* at Pampore also includes a second prayer hall on the second-floor level which is rarely used.

The height of the building from the ground till the top of the spire stands at 27.0m which, given the small size of the building, is comparable to that of the *Khānaqāh-i M*ʿ*aulā*. The square pavilion, spire and brass finial of the *khānaqāh* are again modeled on the *Khānaqāh-i M*ʿ*aulā* which served as the design prototype for the builders at Pampore. The resemblance between the two shrines finds another parallel in the designing of the cantilevered eaves.

Structurally also, the *khānaqāh* at Pampore follows the wooden construction system of alternative layering of wooden logs that defines the *Khānaqāh-i M*ʿ*aulā*. The only difference lies in the choice of filler material. While at *Khānaqāh-i M*ʿ*aulā,* thin burnt bricks were used as filler in between the wooden logs, at Pampore, compacted clay was used for the same purpose. Unfortunately, like with much of the buildings which has undergone major renovations, the clay filling has been replaced with metric bricks during repairs undertaken in the twentieth century CE.

The building interiors have also been changed considerably due to refurbishment carried out by the caretakers in the last decade which have totally obscured original details and appearance of the building.

Terracotta spire of the *rūżā* of Sayyid Qasim

In central Kashmir, on the road to the picturesque meadow of Dudh Pathri, are located two small shrines dedicated to the memory of two brothers, Sayyid Qāsim and Sayyid Yʿaqub. Not much is known about the two, whether they were native Kashmiris or arrived in Kashmir as a part of a religious mission. According to the shrine custodian (*mutwalī*),[40] the two were associates of Mīr Sayyid ʿAli Hamdanī, a claim which could not be substantiated based on any textual or historical references.

The site itself comprises two small shrine buildings located adjacent to each other, located on a slightly elevated plateau (*wudar*). While the lower shrine is oriented along the east-west direction, the other shrine is located further up and oriented along the north-south axis. Both the shrines have been reconstructed recently in 2015. Before their reconstruction, the shrines represented an older vernacular architecture, entirely based on wood that was widely prevalent in rural Kashmir. Based on a sole surviving image of the shrine and local observations, we can summarize the architecture of the old buildings as comprising a square plan form of approximately 3.8m × 3.8m [Figure 5.4]. The size corresponds to the present building plan for both the shrines. The square wooden plan comprising the shrine

Figure 5.4 Shrine of Sayyid Qasim, Budgam: 2010, © Mukhtar Ahmad.

proper was surrounded by a narrow colonnade supported on plain wooden columns, serving as an outer circumambulatory. The entire structure was covered with a low-pitched pyramidal roof that according to the *mutwalī* was originally covered with the birch bark roof. The original plan form of both the shrines correspond to that of Sultan Shams-al Dīn, the founder of the *Shahmīrī* dynasty, with an outer circumambulatory (*pradikshana pat'h*) surrounding the main structure.

Significantly, both the shrines had a terracotta finial, unlike the usual umbrella-shaped brass finial that is common with major *khānaqāhs* and shrines of Kashmir. Today, only a few examples of such finial survive in the region, though the feature seems to have been widespread till mid-twentieth century CE[41]. Fragments of the terracotta finial are located at the site, providing enough information for their reconstruction.

The 1.5m high finial comprises four parts, with the lower part based on a circular plan of 1.75m diameter. Interestingly, the Buddhist *chorten* also comprises four parts: *bumpa*, *harmika*, *yasti* and the *chatravali*[42]. The lower part of the finial is clearly modeled on the *bumpa* with its oblong shape and arched gateways, much like in the *chorten* with openings along the cardinal directions. The upper receding parts of the finial evoke the outer profile of the *chorten* without the arrangements of rings that are ubiquitous to a *chorten*. Below, what can be interpreted as the umbrella or *chatravali*, the spire assumes the shape of cone with projecting curvilinear stems at the base. Whether these stems represent the horns of an animal or a neck of a bird or are based on any other symbolic iconography is a matter of conjecture. And like a *chorten*, which culminates in a closed lotus, the last part of the spire is fashioned into conical shape almost resembling the jewel that forms the pinnacle of a traditional *chorten*. The two-tiered conical finial is also reminiscent of the shape of the two-tiered pyramidal roof that surmounts the stone temples of medieval Kashmir. It is quite possible that the shape and the form of the spire was derived from Buddhist *chortens* before being incorporated into vernacular form of Hindu temples from where it was inherited by the Muslims builders.

Unfortunately, the reconstruction of the shrine has resulted in the loss of this architectural detail that was once widespread in rural Kashmir. The art of crafting the spire is also no longer available with what can be seen as an increasingly dying tradition of pottery in the valley. Though there are reports of similar surviving structures, but the only one I could actually locate was at Neva, Pulwama. There, a small square shrine (3.9m × 3.9m approx.) is also surmounted by a terracotta spire, though given the small size of the shrine, it is of smaller size.

Conclusion

The eighteenth and nineteenth century CE represent a period of sustained political instability in Kashmir, following the demise of Mughal rule. Contemporaneous sources from the period are replete with instances of oppression, calamities and indifference of the Afghan and Sikh rulers towards the welfare of the people. The period also marks a hiatus in new building activity and a general dilapidation of existing buildings, structures and sites. In these tiring times, it was the patronage of local community that sustained any rebuilding, repair or construction activity of communal nature. This period also marks the transition of patronage from the state to community elders for protection and preservation of places of worship. Communal funding, especially drawing upon the lucrative shawl industry, formed the backbone of Muslim religious architecture in the eighteenth and nineteenth century CE, which with the fall of the Mughal Empire had reverted to its native idiom. This period also marks the end of both the extended medieval period of Kashmir as well as the Muslim rule which had lasted for more than five centuries.

Notes

1 Thus, we witness repeated Hindu-Muslim as well as Shi'a-Sunni riots under the Afghan rule, for details see Khuihāmī, *Tārīkh-i Hasan* and Hamdani, *Shiyan-i Kashmir.*

2 In addition to Abdālī, the Afghan kings who ruled over Kashmir are Taimur Shāh (r. 1772–93 CE), Ẕaman Shāh (r. 1793–1800 CE), Shāh Shujā (1795 CE) and Muhammad Shāh (1795–1819 CE).

3 The annual collection of revenues from Kashmir at the Afghan court mounted to an amount of 40 lakh rupees, B Hopkins, *The Making of Modern Afghanistan* (New York: Palgrave Macmillan, 2012), 132.

4 Emperor Alamgir II, Sufi, *Kashir*, 309.

5 Sūkh Jiwan rebellion against Aḥmad Shāh is said to have been partly due to the exorbitant financial demand made on him.

6 Khuihāmī, *Tārīkh-i Hasan*, 741–49.

7 George Forster, *A Journey from Bengal to England through the northern part of India, Kashmir, Afghanistan and Persia, and into Russia by the Caspian Sea* (London: R. Faulder, 1798), 36.

8 Khuihāmī, *Tārīkh-i Hasan,* 785.

9 Sufi, *Kashir*, 323.

10 Sufi, *Kashir,* 726.

11 Ibid.

12 'At Hasanabad, which is next reached, is a ruined mosque, once a handsome building, as the carved limestone remains amply testify [...] when Mean Singh was Governor of Kashmir. He ordered its destruction, and carried away some of the limestone blocks to form the ghat, at Basant Bagh, opposite the Maharajah's palace', J Collett, *A Guide for Visitors to Kashmir* (Calcutta: W. Newman & Co., 1898), 107–08.

13 In all, twelve *ṣubedars* ruled Kashmir during the Sikh rule, with Colonel Miyan Singh (1834-41 CE) being the longest serving *ṣubedar,* who tried to bring relief to the people.

14 The population of Kashmir is said to have reduced from 8 lakhs to 2 lakhs during the famine, which took place during the *ṣubedari* of Sher Singh the son of Maharaja Ranjit Singh, Sufi, *Kashir*, 738.

15 Shaykh Muhyi-al Dīn was a disciple of a prominent Sufi, Shaykh Aḥmad Tarbalī, Khuihāmī, *Tārīkh-i Hasan*, 873.

16 Sufi, *Kashir*, 745.

17 The same can be deduced from Forster's remark on seeing the ruins of Amīrabad in Dal lake, which had been built only eight years before his arrival in Kashmir by the Afghan *ṣubedar*, Amīr Khān. For Afghan additions at Shalimar bāgh, see Baron C. Hugel, *Kashmir and the Punjab* (Jammu: Light & Life Publishers, 1972), 111.

18 Forster seems to have been left unimpressed by local architecture including the Jamia Masjid, Forster, *A Journey from Bengal,* 10.

19 The dating of the shrine is based on inscription that was carved on the wooden door frame, Mohammed Yosuf Teng, ed., *Kashir Encylopedia*, 3 vols. (Srinagar: Jammu & Kashmir Academy of Art, Culture and Languages, 1986), 251.

20 Though Forster (travelling as he was with a Muslim noble, Zulfikar Khān) does not mention it, this facility would be available only to travelling Muslims. In the city, the same facility was provided by bankers within their residences, Forster, *A Journey from Bengal,* 304.

21 The nature of this maintenance works was centered around repairs to the birch bark roof of the mosque, though the work was left incomplete.

22 *Nūr Khāna*, literally 'the house of light' is used for chamber reserved for women at *khānaqāhs*. The main hall of the *khānaqāh* used for prayers is invariably reserved for men. In some of the *khānaqāhs*, such as *Khānaqāh-i M'aulā*, this main congregational hall is referred to as *Buqa aali,* 'revered house'.

23 INTACH J&K (2007:127).

24 The Sikh court had extensively patronized the use of wall murals on religious sites under their territory and *naqāshī* or *moḥarqashī* as it was known in Punjab became an important tool of façade decoration, see Kanwarjit Singh Kang, *Wall Paintings of Punjab and Haryana* (Delhi: Atma Ram and Sons, 1985) and Susan Stronge, *The Arts of the Sikh Kingdoms* (London: V & A, 1999).

25 For a general discussion on Sikh Art, see Stronge, *The Arts of the Sikh Kingdoms.*

26 Hugel, *Kashmir and the Punjab*, 159.

27 Maḥmud Ghāmī achieved acclaim through his *Khamsa* which reads as a translation of the Persian poet Niẓāmī Ganjavī's (d. 1209 CE) *Khamsa.*

28 Aside from his *Gulraiz*, Maqbool Shah also composed *Pīr nāma*, *Grist nāma* etc., works which provide a glimpse into the social life of nineteenth century CE Kashmir.

29 Parmanad is best remembered for his *mathnawi* Akanandu which was adopted by the twentieth century CE Sufi poet Samad Mīr's in one of his major work.

30 1096AH/1684CE.

31 Khuihāmī, *Tārīkh-i Hasan*, 434.

32 The *khānaqāh* complex was reconstructed by INTACH based on its extensive architectural documentation of the site.

33 Majid Aasmi, ed., 'Srinagar Number, vol. 1' in *Saun Adab* (Srinagar: J&K Academy of Arts, Culture & Languages, 2007), 331–32.

34 We find references to members of the Nazkī family serving as *sajada nishīn* indicating their role as custodians of the shrine, not that they presided over an established *khānaqāh*. Additionally, a reading of Dedhmārīs, *Waqāt-i Kashmir* does not indicate that a *khānaqāh* stood near the shrine of Mīr Nāzuk even as late as 1159 AH/1746 CE, the date of compilation of this general history of Kashmir, Dedhmārīs, *Waqāt-i Kashmir,* 281, 365. Also see, M Ahmad Andrabi, ed., 'Awliya Number', in *Hamara Adab* (Srinagar: J&K Academy of Arts, Culture & Languages, 1997), 195–96.

35 Similar can be seen in other Mughal era religious buildings like the Dara's mosque, Thag Bābā's shrine as well as secular edifices constructed by the Mughals such as the hammam at Shalimar bāgh as well as the Mughal era retaining wall and *burj* in Nishat bāgh. In the pre-Mughal era, Islamic religious buildings of the region the same affect is achieved by projecting of a narrow band from the main masonry panel, examples can be seen at Dumath, mosque at Zaina Lank and the *Khānaqāh -i Naū* which have been studied earlier.

36 A series of wooden brackets support the roof eaves.

37 The oldest residential building in Srinagar city dates back to the latter part of the nineteenth century CE, see INTACH (2010).

38 Dedhmārī, *Waqāt-i Kashmir*, 279.

39 In addition to the *khānaqāhs* described in this chapter, other buildings belonging in this typology that find mention in the nineteenth century CE history of Khuihāmī include, *Khānaqāh-i Walā, Khānaqāh-i Aala, Khānaqāh-i Kubarwī, Khānaqāh-i Faiż Panāh, Khānaqāh-i Sayyid Barkhudār, Khānaqāh-i Bābā Ismāīl, Khānaqāh-i Malīk Jalāl, Khānaqāh-i Shamsī, Khānaqāh-i Drugjan, Khānaqāh-i Chistī, Khānaqāh-i Sopur, Khānaqāh-i Makhdūmī, Khānaqāh-i Bijbehara, Khānaqāh-i Shaykh-al Alam, Khānaqāh-i Jelānī, Khānaqāh-i Khawja Shāh and Khānaqāh-i Dangerpora,* see, Khuihāmī, *Tārīkh-i Hasan,* 402–438. Of these *khānaqāhs,* many were no longer extant at the time Khuihāmī wrote his account, which he recorded only for preserving their historical memory.

40 Abdul Ghani Mir, *Mutwalī*, author interview, Budgam, 21st May, 2018.

41 M Saleem Beg, Convener INTACH J&K Chapter, authors interview, Srinagar, 1st July, 2017.

42 W S Wong, 'Stupa, Pagoda and Chorten-Origin and Meaning of Buddhist Architecture', *Athens: ATINER's Conference paper Series*, No: ARC 2014–1094, 2014.

6

CONCLUSION: TRANSITION TO A PAN-ISLAMIC IMAGE IN POST-INDEPENDENCE PERIOD

Man kunam az sar birūn Saib hawa-i khuld rā,
bakht agar az sākinān-i shahr-i Kashmīram kunad
I would take my head out in the air of paradise,
If fate would destine me a resident of Kashmir
Ṣaʿib Tabrizī (d. 1676 CE) (Translation mine)

The religious architecture associated with Muslim faith in Kashmir epitomizes the continuity of an architectural tradition that precedes the establishment of Muslim rule in the region in the early fourteenth century CE. While unraveling the threads of this architectural phenomenon, we perceive its root in a culture of syncretism, yet we also see periods of tension with organized attempts at changing the dynamics of the society as well at is architectural manifestation. These are traditions that Kashmiri society has inherited from its past traditions that continue to dictate the narrative of contemporary life in the region.

In the early medieval period, before the commencement of the *Shahmīrī* Sultanate, Kashmir had enabled itself as a productive cultural center, providing cultural cues and artistic inspirations for the surrounding hill principalities and kingdoms. Though by the eleventh century CE, Kashmir could perceive changes in the political situation on its western borders with incursion of 'the chief of *mlecchas*'[1], yet in the isolation of its frontiers, it continued to maintain its unique cultural experience albeit with limited resources that the kingdom had now at its hand.

The establishment of Muslim rule in Kashmir was preceded by the emergence of the nascent Muslim community of migrants at Srinagar dating to late twelfth-early thirteenth century CE. Was this a community of mercenaries searching for opportunities in the political chaos that was hallmark of Kashmir at this time? Or a community of traders travelling along the Silk route that had settled down in Kashmir? Although this research does offer an understanding of this period based on available historical and archeological records, yet it hopes that future studies examining the roots of this nascent Muslim community are undertaken. The nature of this early Muslim community needs to be revisited so as to get a clear understanding of this crucial yet obscured part of Kashmir's history. Nevertheless, as shown in this study, this small community and its progression in the socio-political life of the region establishes the antecedents of future Muslim society in Kashmir.

The early *Shahmīrī* Sultans ruled over a kingdom whose population was of non-Muslim belief, the Muslim community both at the court and in the region being miniscule. During the early Muslim rule in Kashmir, Islam as a religion did not serve as a source of legitimacy for the rule of the Sultans. The power that these sultans exerted was through bonds of patronage and marriage which formed the linkages joining them to their subjects, and the land. Changes affected in the society were intermittent and limited[2], we see no striking sudden transformations. The establishment of Muslim rule in Kashmir marks neither the end of an epoch nor the beginning of a new era. Such an interpretation was envisioned at a much later date in the seventeenth century CE, which sees the establishment of the Sultanate as origin of Islam in Kashmir. This retrospective reworking of past that has emerged as standard narrative in recent times needs to be revisited, especially based on architectural evidences that this study has surveyed.

In the initial years of the Sultanate rule, there was no attempt by the state at proselytizing of the local community or even the courtiers. We find no mention of non-native Muslim missionaries arriving in the land for propagating of the faith. It was in these years of Muslim rule in Kashmir that the germ of a future Muslim community was laid – a community that was molded in the native cultural ethos. And it was from these traditions rooted in the memory of land that the architectural traditions related to Islam in Kashmir were born. The context of the foundational Islamic religious architecture lies in this socio-political cultural milieu in which the footprints of a new belief system were gradually adopted. Representative both of a process to ingrain themselves within the larger non-Muslim native community as well as to limit any divulgation of cultural idiosyncrasy that would set them apart, the early Muslim community of Kashmir aimed at cultural integration rather than segregation. Thus, the requirements of the faith were realized in a localized architecture on a scale nearer to the vernacular rather than the monumental buildings of medieval Kashmir.

This study was started with an aim at understanding the representation and meaning of the Islamic religious architecture of Kashmir and see if such a meaning establishes a tradition of transcendent cultural uniqueness in Kashmir. This study aims at filling the evolutionary context of Islamic religious architecture of Kashmir that has been stymied by the absence of a widespread field of survey of existing buildings representing this architectural tradition. Or a discussion on how these buildings relate to the political, cultural and artistic outpourings of the period of their construction. This limitation has been further magnified by the absence of historical textual evidence on the subject of construction of these buildings which could relate to our understanding of this architectural genre. What we have mostly inherited in terms of research on the subject is a standard colonial interpretation based on a generalization derived from the study of few isolated buildings. This argument gets repeated ad hominem in contemporary writings on the subject some of which continue to see this architectural tradition as being rooted in all lands and culture but Kashmir. Such a view argues that the unique resemblance between a Muslim mosques and shrines of Kashmir to pre-Muslim architecture of region as a simple case of appropriation and conversion, albeit through the use of force. In doing so, the boundaries of difference between arrival, reception and development of Islam in Kashmir and in areas to the south of Pir Panjal are obscured – the uniqueness of Kashmiri experience is relegated to the standard generalization of wider Indian experience, especially that of Northern India. The continuity of architectural traditions of Kashmir as we traverse from Hindu to Muslim rule shows not only the strength and uniqueness of this cultural uniqueness, but also provides us with a theoretical model to identify this historic phenomenon.

Historically, the period of Kashmiri Sultans (1322–1558 CE), spanning more than two centuries, forms the formative as well as the period of consolidation Kashmir's religious architecture linked to Muslim faith. It was a style which sought to maintain a sense of continuity with Kashmir's pre-Islamic past. The heart of this architectural experience was rooted in native architecture and it was for this very reason the architecture as an expression of a community did not evoke any incongruous tone.

These architectural traditions as well as the entire cultural milieu which had given birth to it, continued to operate even in the face of challenges orchestrated by Muslim missionaries who arrived in Kashmir from the Persia and areas dominated by Persianate culture. In the name of Islamization of the society, attempts were made to introduce ideas and customs linked to the wider Persian culture, some of which did, over the time, achieve a certain degree of success with the court. The arrival of these missionaries, their association with the royal court and their interference in the life and customs of the people evoked both a political and a religious opposition of which the native *Reshī* order of mendicants is the most obvious manifestation. It is in this period of consolidation and challenges that the image of Muslim religious architecture of Kashmir was firmly established, even in instances wherein the initial concept was of non-native derivation[3].

We also see that an experimentation of form and imagery was taken up, drawing upon during the reign of Zain-al Ābidīn, whose rule is representative of a process of trans-cultural engagement, of attempts at forging new ideas while continuing with older established principles. Thus, while the Sultan's continued patronage of what was by this time the standard repertoire of Kashmir's Islamic religious architecture, he also patronized architectural projects based on the principles of Timurid aesthetics. The rule of Zain-al Ābidīn's successors proves that his ecumenical state policy was not an exceptional interlude but a normative trend in the functioning of the state which had nevertheless assumed a deeper Muslim hue. The establishment of the Chak rule in the wake of the collapse of the *Shahmīrī's* was laid on sound Shi'a foundation and its initial years mark a renewed process of targeted conversion and desecration of non-Muslim religious sites, with the active participation of the *Nurbakshī* order. The *Nurbakshiya's* represent the same disdain for native cultural practices and architectural achievements as was witnessed in the *Kubrawī* order earlier, both being linked in their Persian roots. Yet, gradually as the initial fervor and missionary zeal of the order waned, we find that under later Chaks the same acceptance of the non-Muslim community as before. The Chaks also patronized *khānaqāhs* that were essentially a part of the Sunni belief system as representative of inter-sectarian piety, of which the most famous was the rebuilding of Char shrine. The rebuilding at Char of the shrine complex linked with Shaykh Nūr-al Dīn, who had by this time acquired the status of patron saint of Kashmir, took place at a time when the region was under threat of annexation from the Mughal Empire. The reconstruction undertaken in a highly disturbed political atmosphere can also be seen as building of symbols linked to Kashmiri identity in face of external aggression.

Though after the fall of the Kashmiri Sultanate to Mughals, these local building traditions no longer formed part of the projects executed under royal supervision, yet local patronage and preference insured their survival. The building traditions of the region were revived following the end of Mughal rule in the mid-eighteenth century CE. During their six-decade governance of Kashmir, the Afghans rulers offered little in terms of state patronage or artistic inspiration in the vast field of Islamic religious architecture in Kashmir. Most of the constructions that took part in this period were part of independent and localized projects funded by the community under the supervision of elite of the society. In some cases, prominent traders financed the construction or repair work. Given the exploitative nature of Afghan rule in Kashmir, the period of previous Mughal rule in Kashmir was recast as an idealized, romanticized past of abundance and good life. As a result, many architectural elements and symbols linked with Mughal architecture were incorporated in both the residential vernacular architecture of Kashmir as well as Islamic religious architecture.

The political events of the nineteenth century CE marked the end of Muslim rule in Kashmir. In these changed, and what was perceived by the Muslim community of Kashmir as testing times, we again see importance of the role of local community and community elders in patronizing the construction and repair of Muslim religious places. This was a relationship that would form the dominating theme of patronage of building activity in Kashmir for the rest of the nineteenth century CE. Yet, the scope and extent of this patronage was limited both by financial resources as well as spiritual and social importance of these sacred sites[4]. To a large extent, the architectural outpourings as well as artistic embellishments were limited to designing and repairs of major *khānaqāhs* and *rūżās*. The genre of mosques was mostly ignored and the building belonging to this typology were at least in rural setting seen as 'no better than the meanest cultivator's cottage'[5].

Prominent Muslim religious building that got constructed in Kashmir during the nineteenth century CE include the shrine and *khānaqāh* at Rehbāb Ṣāhab, *Khānaqāh-i Makhdūm* (c. 1871 CE, Srinagar), *Thung-i Masjid* (1854 CE, Srinagar), shrine of Jānbāz Saheb (Baramulla), *imāmbāda* at Zadibal and Hasanabad (Srinagar), *Khānaqāh-i Naqshbandī* (c. 1886 CE, Srinagar), *Masjid-i Qaẓi Jamāl-al Dīn* (Srinagar), *Masjid-i Zain-al Ābidīn* (Srinagar), *Masjid-i Hājjī Eidāh* (Srinagar), shrine at Dadasar and *Asār-i Sharīf* Danagerpora (c. 1871 CE, Srinagar).

While most of the buildings followed the traditional Kashmiri architectural style, the mosque of Hājji ʿEidāh[6] was strikingly different in its architectural vocabulary. The mosque was built at Zadibal in Srinagar city by a member of Kashmiri Diaspora community who had immigrated to Peshawar. The mosque with its façade of an open arched arcade[7], twin minaret and domed hall follows a plan form comprising a single aisle divided into three bays by masonry piers evokes the architectural preferences of its patrons rather than of the local community. Unlike traditional Kashmiri mosques in Srinagar, the mosque of Hājjī ʿEidāh was set within a larger compound comprising a separate hammam as well as other ancillary buildings. Other members of Kashmiri Diaspora in the Indian plains were also responsible for funding major additions or repairs to major religious buildings in Kashmir. Nawab Iḥsan-ul Lah of Decca, who traced his ancestry to Kashmir, was responsible for building a major hammam at *Asār-i Sharīf* Hazratbal, the principal shrine of Kashmir.

One of the leading Kashmiri traders of late nineteenth century CE, who funded building construction and renovation of major Sunni shrines and mosques of Srinagar was Khawājā Sona-ul Lah Shāwl of Khanyar. Mīrzā Muhammed ʿAli, another prominent trader, was responsible for construction of an *imāmbāda* at Hassanabad while also contributing with other Shi'a traders in repairing the historic *Mʿārak* at Zadibal.

The transfer of Kashmir to the Raja Gulāb Singh in 1847 CE by the British colonial administration of India resulted in the establishment of the princely state of Jammu and Kashmir. Under Maharaja Gulāb Singh (r. 1847–57 CE) and his successors, we find gradual increase in the influence exerted by the British colonial administration in the affairs of the state. Though this process was started during the reign of Gulāb Singh's successor, Maharaja *Ranbīr* Singh (r.1857–85 CE), it was only under Maharaja Pratap Singh (r. 1885–1925 CE) that a British Residency was established in the state. It was also during the 40-year rule of Pratap Singh that a number of modern civic and infrastructural facilities were created in the state with British technical help, and under their supervision. These include construction of school, colleges, power plants, establishment of Srinagar Municipality and most importantly the construction of the Jhelum Valley Cart road in 1889–1890 CE. In 1897 CE, the road was extended to Srinagar, the summer capital of the state, and provided an alternative mode of travel within the valley from the traditional water-borne route. In the field of architecture, European colonial influences were introduced to the region with the reconstruction of the Shergahri palace (1885 CE)[8] in Srinagar during the reign of Ranbir Singh, after it was gutted down in a fire incident. This style was continued in the construction of buildings such as Amar Singh College, SP College, Silk factory, Power house (Solina) and other similar structures in the region constructed by the state. The construction of the Residency building in the latter part of the nineteenth century in the British country manor style further popularized the architecture amongst the *darbāris* of the Dogra court. Gradually, elements form this architectural style were also adopted in the local vernacular – as well as the Muslim religious architecture.

Significantly, it was in the temple architecture of Kashmir that the Dogra rulers made a significant contribution, when they commissioned the construction of two significant temples in the valley, the Gadadhar temple and the Vijeshwara temple at Bijbehara. Though patronized and popularized by the Dogra court, the first recorded temple in Kashmir designed in this new style is the Anandeshwar Bhaironath mandir constructed by the Sikh governor of Kashmir, Dīvān Moti Ram (1819 CE). The origin of this style lie in the architectural contours and predilection of the Lahore *durbār,* of which both Moti Ram and Gulāb Singh were important functionaries and adherents.

Gadadhar temple was constructed within the palace complex of Shergahri at Srinagar and though small in size, as royal temple it set the precedent for future temples to be constructed in Kashmir. This involved an entirely new architectural vocabulary, drawing inspirations mainly from the Indian plains with cubical masonry structure covered with shallow domed ceilings and hemispherical *shikhara*. Similarly, when Maharaja Ranbīr Singh decided to rebuild the Vijeshwara temple at Bijbehara, the building, though constructed in local *devrī* stone, was again constructed in the style of traditional North Indian temples, especially the variant that was flourishing in Jammu. This style was followed in the designing of the royal Dogra *samadhis*, built in Srinagar in memory of Maharaja Gulāb Singh and his successor Ranbīr Singh. Within the heart of the city, this new architectural style assumed an iconic status with the construction of Raghunath mandir[9] at Fateh Kadal by Ranbir Singh in 1875 CE. Initially, it was the Dogra kings who served as patrons of this new language of constructing temples, but soon it was copied by Kashmiri Pandits courtiers[10] at the Dogra court as well as the Pandit community at large. Setting a point of departure from the architectural vocabulary of the medieval stone temples of Kashmir, this new Dogra-style of temple construction found favor with the local Kashmiri Pandit community. The continued popularity of this new genre with both the Dogra court and the Kashmiri Hindu community can be assessed by the fact, that in 1912, Maharaja Pratap Singh designed a new miniature temple in this style at Kheer Bhawani at

Figure 6.1 Kheer Bhawani, the main miniature marble temple at Kheer Bhawani, constructed in 1912, Ganderbal: 2018, © Hakim Sameer Hamdani.

Tulmula, a shrine which serves as one of the foremost *tiratha* (pilgrimage center) for Kashmiri Pandits [Figure 6.1].

After centuries of living under Muslim rule, the Kashmiri Pandit community associated itself both politically and architecturally with the power of the Dogra state as well as its cultural manifestation in the field of architecture. It is worthwhile to note that a century earlier, Kashmiri Muslim community had not been able to form a similar cultural link with the architectural enterprise of the Mughal Empire. Why then did the Kashmiri Pandit community behave in a different manner to a non-native architectural idiom being introduced is a question that future research may take upon. The dialectic nature of the event can be understood once we reflect and analyze on how Kashmiri Pandit community has been traditionally seen as preserver and promoter of Kashmiri culture. Nevertheless, as an architectural tradition, the style outlived its patrons and remained the preferred architectural vocabulary even in the post-Independence period for Kashmiri Pandit community in their construction of temples.

It was also during the Dogra rule when the government took some albeit small steps to help the Muslim community of Srinagar in persevering prominent Muslim religious sites. This though did not remove friction between the Hindu rulers and the Muslim community as has been demonstrated by Mridu Rai, yet the period also marks the first effort by the government at conserving Kashmir's built heritage – heritage linked with Muslim places of worship. This includes both the repair to the Jamia Masjid and ʿĀālī masjid in Srinagar under technical help from Archaeological Survey of India. The repairs were carried out with substantial financial contribution from the local Muslim community. An earlier attempt at arresting the decay at Jamia Masjid had been carried out by Mīr Husayn Qadrī in 1297 AH/1879 CE with a financial contribution of 60,000 rupees from Maharaja Ranbīr Singh (r. 1830–1885 CE) while a similar attempt was made during the reign of Maharaja Pratap Singh in 1912 CE. Still, some of the Muslim religious sites which had been closed during the Sikh rule continued to remain out of bound to the local Muslim community and contributed to the feeling of rising discontent and friction between the community and the government[11].

The repairs to both the mosques were completed in the 1920s and were almost immediately followed by a period of political agitation that became a part of the wider freedom struggle sweeping through colonial South Asia. In the aftermath of Independence, we find that many of the older mosques and shrines were rebuilt both in the city of Srinagar and in the surrounding towns and villages. A major project undertaken in the post-Independence period was the reconstruction of the Jamia Masjid at Shupian in South Kashmir. The mosque construction was again financed by prominent trader of the area, and the design was based on the pattern of the Jamia Masjid at Srinagar. Built on a smaller scale, the mosque follows the same courtyard plan of the Srinagar Jamia with four main *iwans* surmounted by the traditional pyramidal spire[12]. While traditional architectural features and elements continued to be used in designing or redesigning of Muslim religious places in the post-1947 period, yet some subtle changes were also affected. The more monumental wooden construction system, such as employed in the construction of *Khānaqāh-i Naqshbandī*, was increasingly proving unsuitable given the vast amount of wood required in its construction. The wooden trabeate system had in the initial years of community found favor with Muslim builders because of the ease of its construction. The same was now replaced by a more effective and economical load-bearing masonry construction involving the use of standard metric brick that had been introduced in the region by the British in the twentieth century CE. Many of the European colonial influence that had made their way into the local vernacular in the late nineteenth and early twentieth century CE, were also transmitted into the building of mosques and shrines. An especially fine example of this transfer of ideas can be seen in two important mosques of Srinagar, that near the shrine of Alam Ṣāhab at Narwara and the Kanil Masjid at Maharaj Gunj.

Also, in the post-Independence period, we see that within the wide field of Muslim religious architecture in Kashmir, a great focus revolved around the construction of mosques. While some of this was understandable as part of urbanization of the city and towns of Kashmir, yet given the resources spent on the construction and embellishment of the buildings, it can also be seen as reworking of the outpouring of Muslim religiosity. The heart of Kashmiri Muslim culture had revolved around shrines and *khānaqāhs*, not mosques. This in earlier times had earned the Kashmiri Muslims the unsympathetic sobriquet of being *pīr parast*[13].

Given that many of the older surviving mosques at this period were either in a dilapidated condition or hardly differentiable from the surrounding residences, an age of experimentation set in the designing of mosques, in certain cases involving the services of qualified engineers. This involved treatment of building façade in a new eclectic style with juxtaposition of local as well as imported elements. The main mosque at Habba Kadal chowk and Saraf Kadal, both of which were located on prominent junctions of the city, were designed in this style, involved a combination of Dutch gable, arched windows and in case of Habba Kadal mosque dome-shaped pavilion and minarets. Nevertheless, the architectural landscape of the region comprising its mosques, *khānaqāhs*, shrines and *imāmbādas* remained mostly unchanged. Till the reconstruction of the *Asār-i Sharīf* at Hazratbal, we see that in the area of Muslim religious architecture of Kashmir, a creeping spirit of innovation could be seen but as of yet no distinct dichotomy between the past and the prevailing architectural traditions had taken place.

It was the reconstruction of the Hazratbal shrine in the 1970s that marks a paradigm shift in the Islamic religious architecture of Kashmir. The project was undertaken in the 1970s by Shakyh Muhammad ʿAbdullah (d. 1984 CE)[14] after his return from a tour of West Asian countries and performing of the Hajj pilgrimage. Aside from the political implications behind the shrine's reconstruction and its ramifications on Shaykh ʿAbdullah's personal standing within the Kashmiri Muslim community, is the question of architectural imagery involved in the construction of this highly revered shrine[15]. Shaykh ʿAbdullah had emerged in the 1930s as the spokesman for Kashmiri Muslim community in their struggle against the Dogra regime. During the course of the freedom struggle, he aligned with the Indian National Congress and was instrumental in Kashmir's accession with India in the 1947. In between the 1930s and 1940s, he transformed from being a leader of the Muslim community to the spokesman of Kashmir, which was reflected in his party's vision for Kashmir enshrined in a document, *Nayā Kashmir* (New Kashmir)[16]. As a pan-Kashmiri leader, Shaykh ʿAbdullah and his party were representatives of a sense of Kashmiri identity – Kashmiri nationhood[17]. Yet, in designing the Hazratbal shrine, a process that he was deeply involved with, no respect was shown for native-local architectural sensibilities. Projected as *Madina-i Sani* (The Second Madina), the building design is based a contemporary reworking of elements of Mughal architecture in a canvas which would appeal to modern architectural sensibilities given the building's clear and distinct lines. The new building at Hazratbal with its bulbous white marble dome, marble *chatrī's* and a slender single minaret also showcased the appeal of a more widely recognizable Islamic building, an appeal which became more and more widespread with every passing decade [Plate 12].

Unfortunately, though the Hazratbal project was completed through public donations, no public discourse ever took place on its architectural language. What has been written about the project relates to its political importance. The architecture of the shrine itself has largely remained untouched. The redesign of the Hazratbal shrine was based on a universalist pan-Islamic inspiration that ignored centuries of what can be understood as particularist realities rooted in the experience of Islam in Kashmir.

The decision on the shrine's new design was undertaken by the architect in consultation with the spirit behind the project – Shaykh ʿAbdullah. Should the design be seen as an attempt by its patrons to evoke an image that they believed was more Islamic than what was being replaced? Or did it represent a notion of novelty, simply of doing something new then what was there before? Or was the symbolic association between the shrine and the Prophet's shrine at Madina the guiding factor which weighed on the design process?

The reconstruction of the Hazratbal shrine in the 1970s in a modern and a non-Kashmiri architectural idiom did not start a public debate on what should be the 'physical' form of future Muslim religious buildings of Kashmir. But it offered the Kashmiri Muslim community with a new visual image – a new design pattern to employ in the construction of its religious places. The new shrine building emerged as a prototype that would, in coming years, increasingly influence the shape of *masjids* and *rūżā* in Kashmir.

The pre-eminence of the Hazratbal shrine as the principal Muslim shrine of Kashmir drawing devotees from all across the region added to wider propagation and dissimilation of this new architectural style. It's worthwhile to note that in the post-1970 period, as ever-increasing number of Kashmiri pilgrims started visiting the Arabian Peninsula for performing *hajj*, they became acquainted with a totally different image of what an Islamic building constitutes. These new images must have certainly made a deep impression on the minds of these pilgrims, images that carried back to the various ends of their native land. While not all of these *hājjīs* would have been actively engaged in the building activity centered on mosques and shrines of their localities, yet an appreciation for what was witnessed in the sacred land of Islam did make itself manifest over a period of time. And as the required technology and building material became readily available, this trend also became more widespread. Interestingly, even before the usage of reinforced cement or concrete became prevalent in the region, wooden domes with iron sheet cladding had made their presence felt. This has to a large degree resulted in the eclipse of the indigenous building traditions of the region especially in the design or redesigning of major Muslim shrines in the area. Though largely ignored for most of its historic past in Kashmir, domes and minarets are increasingly becoming an important part of contemporary Islamic architecture of Kashmir. The form has been adopted not only by architects and engineers but also by local masons and carpenters who, for most part of the preceding century, remained the actual designers on site. The work of these masons and carpenters has resulted in the creation of an eclectic architectural style many a times at variance with the historical architectural traditions of the region.

The burning of the shrine of the Shaykh Nūr-al Dīn, the patron saint of Kashmir, at Char in 1998 brought this debate to the forefront. The architect was asked to revisit his initial design for the gutted shrine so as to incorporate features such as the dome and minaret. This was certainly at variance with the life and teaching of the saint, who is generally seen as the face of Kashmiri order of Sufism, the *Reshīs*. The saint is also said to have resisted attempts by missionaries of Persian origin to 'Persianize' the lifestyle of native Kashmiri Muslims in the name of Islam. The building was later on modified to a more Kashmiri style, though the end image is more of an architectural kitsch.

The ongoing reconstruction of the historic *imāmbāda* at Zadibal can also be seen as a distinct echo of what happened almost half a century back at Hazratbal. The original building, with its wooden columns, *papier-mâché* ceiling and lattice work was demolished in 1999 to make way for a modern cement concrete building of dome and minarets. The building design with its *Safavid* dome also makes a clear and manifest reference to its Shii'te origin, stressing the Iranian connection.

An interesting phenomenon related to both the Hazratbal as well as Zadibal reconstruction is the association amongst the local community, of the new design with holy Islamic building – an association belied by the actual building design. The generally held belief at the time of reconstruction of the Hazratbal shrine which still lingers on was that the building was based on the design of *Masjid-i Nabvi* at Medina. Similarly, widespread credence was given to the idea that the new *imāmbāda* at Zadibal was based on the design of *al-Aqsa* mosque at Jerusalem.

The second half of the twentieth century CE also witnessed renewed public interest within the Muslim community on repair and reconstruction of various religious sites. Unfortunately, this well-intentioned philanthropic process was marred by a severe lack of understanding of the historic character of the associated built fabric of these sites. Coupled with a functional need to accommodate an increasing number of worshippers, introduction of new building material, loss of traditional building knowledge was the emergence of a new middle-class spirit, the nouveau-riche which looked down upon anything old as being representative of an image that is in essence 'poor and backward'. Consequently, a number of old buildings were demolished and new modern structures constructed in their place, a majority of which lack any contextual connection with their surroundings as well as the required esthetes. Far more than any natural or manmade threat, it is this spirit which essentially verges on ignorance and lack of respect for the past that has emerged as the greatest threat to historic built fabric of the area, both religious as well of a more secular nature.

When the revered Dastgir Ṣāhab shrine of Srinagar was gutted down in a mysterious fire incident in 2012[18], the nature of the reconstruction featured in public debates both online and in print media. After much deliberation within government circles as well as in the larger civil society, it was finally decided to rebuild the shrine in its original form, based on the extensive documentation INTACH had carried out in 2010. The Chief Minister of the state at that time, ʿUmarʿAbdullah, remained the main force behind the decision to recreate the old shrine. Historically, this choice marks a reversal of what his grandfather, Shaykh ʿAbdullah, had undertaken at Hazratbal in the 1970s, and offers hope for future conservation works in the region.

Today, the mountain frontiers of Kashmir are no longer a physical barrier; Kashmir is no longer an isolated cultural outpost. Still, weaving its image of an earthly paradise, the land has much changed. To a large extent, with the mass exodus of Kashmiri Pandits from the valley in the early 1990s, the nature and character of Kashmiri society has changed, it no longer represents a multi-confessional, cosmopolitan social fabric. And in an increasingly Muslim-alone valley, the contours of Muslim society of Kashmir are being reorganized; historical realities associated with Islamic experience of Kashmir are being questioned, reinterpreted and reworked. The quintessential Kashmir spires of the mosques, shrines and *khānaqāhs* are being increasingly replaced with domes and minarets. Rituals and customs associated with these shrines and *khānaqāhs* are being questioned as being un-Islamic, as an unacceptable innovation – *bid'a*. And as Kashmir finds itself increasingly drawn into the sectarian and communal discourses originating from lands located geographically to its west in the traditional heartland of Islamic world undergoing through cataclysmic changes of its own, we may pause and wonder what of Kashmir's native identity, will it survive? The search for pure Islamic culture, an authentic experience of Islam, is slowly and steadily effacing out traces of Kashmir's own Islamic past which was built on a tradition of assimilation and syncretism. Today, it seems that this represents the future, but then it is in no way certain that is 'the only future' of Kashmir. In a global world of heightened interconnectivity, with waves of new ideas and challenges emanating from outside, a return to roots may still offer the land the path forwards towards carving new ideas, new symbols and a new language for its architecture.

Notes

1 Kalhānā, *Rajatarangini,* 217.
2 An example of this change can be seen in the adoption of a new calendar coeval with the establishment of the Muslim rule as well change in the epigraphy relating to minting of coins.
3 Jamia Masjid, Srinagar.
4 '[...] I have often seen a mosque without a thatch and a beautiful old shrine tumbling to pieces for want of some simple repairs ', W R Lawrence, *The Valley of Kashmir* (Jammu: Kashmir Kitab Ghar, 1996), 285. Some prominent shrines mentioned by Lawrence include those of various *Reshī* saints at Watlab, Aishmuqam, Bamzu, Tangmarg, Dedsar as well as the shrines at Kulgam, Keeri, Lolab and Pampore, ibid, 258,288 and 289.
5 Ibid, 285.
6 Haji 'Eidah was a leading trader of Peshawar, whose family traced their roots back to Kashmir, Hamdani, *Shiyan-i Kashmir*, 287.
7 Given the local climatic needs, the open arcade has been screened with wooden window and door frames.
8 This happened in the wake of a devastating earthquake that took place in 1885 CE and badly damaged the palace.
9 The temple was named after a similar temple complex at Jammu: Ragunath mandir (c. 1835 C) that served as the family temple of Dogra kings.
10 An example would be the Ram Mandir constructed by the influential Dhar family at Safa Kadal.
11 As late as 1911 CE, the Maharaja came with a proposal to convert Pather Masjid into a orphanage to be named after the Hindu deity Hanuman, but the proposal was not realized, Rai, *Hindu Rulers, Muslim Subjects*, 211–13.
12 The name of the carpenter who oversaw the construction of mosque in the 1930s is preserved in local memories as Habib-ul Lah of Srinagar.
13 A rough translation would be saint worshippers. See, Lawrence, *The Valley of Kashmir, 286.*
14 Shaykh Muhamad 'Abdullah (d. 1982) was the leading twentieth century CE political figure of Kashmir, who is also referred to as *Shīr-ī Kashmir* (Lion of Kashmir).
15 The building was designed by a renowned architect form Hyderabad: Fayaz-al Dīn Beyhzad, Shuja Husayn, Engineer, authors interview, 1st May, 2018, Srinagar.
16 The document was formulated in the aftermath of the Second World War, somewhere in and around 1944.
17 This Kashmiri distinctiveness can be seen as an expression of regional identity, sub-national or national identity based on the observers personal standing on the subject.
18 The fire incident occurred on 25th July 2012.

APPENDIX

The origin of Major Sufi orders in Kashmir

S. No.	*Sufi Shaykh*	*Area of Arrival*	*Order*	*Date*
01.	Sayyid Sharif- al-Dīn (Būlbūl Shāh)	Ardebil, Iran or Turkistan (not established).	*Suharwardī* or Shi'a (not established)	Early 14th century (d.1327CE)
02.	Mīr Sayyid ʿAli Hamdanī	Hamadan, Iran	*Kubrawī*	Late 14th century Arrival: 1379CE
03.	Sayyid Muhammad Hisarī	Saman, Balkh (modern Afghanistan)	*Qadrī*	Late 14th-early 15th century During Sultan Sikandar's regin
04	Sayyid Muhammad Madnī	Mawara-an Nahar (Trans-Oxiana)	Possibly Shi'a	Late 14th-early 15th century During Sultan Sikandar's regin
05.	Qazi Jamāl	Hindustan (Indian mainland)	Hanafī scholar, Serves as *Qazi-al Quzat* (Chief Judge)	Mid 15th century During Sultan Zain-al Ābidīn 's reign
06.	Shaykh Nūr-al Dīn	Native Kashmiri	Founder of *Reshī* order	Late 14th-mid 15th century
07.	Sayyid Bilāl**	Not mentioned but Iran or Central Asia	*Naqshbandī*	Mid 15th century
08.	Sayyid Muhammad Isfahanī	Isfahan, Iran	*Suharwardī*	Mid 15th century
09.	Sayyid Hājjī Murad	Forefathers were from Bukhara.	*Shattārī**	Mid-15th century
10.	Sayyid Barkhudar Bukharī	Bukhara	*Suharwardī*	15th century
11.	Mīr Shams-al Dīn ʿIraki	Irak, Iran	*Nurbakshiyā*	15th century
12.	Shāh Nʿimat-al Lah Qadrī	Khwarazm, Iran	*Qadrī*	Late 16th century
13.	Sayyid Ismāʿīl Shāmī	Syria	*Qadrī*	Late 16th century

14.	Shaykh Yʿaqūb Sarfī*** Or Shaykh Ismāʿīl	Native Kashmir	*Chisti*	Late 16th century 17th century

Notes:

* The order did not gain much hold in Kashmir, where it seems Sayyid Murad adhered to the older established *Kubrawī* order.

** Also referred to as Sayyid Hilāl.

*** Shaykh Yʿaqūb along with Bābā Dāwūd Khākī was a leading disciple of *Suharwardi* saint, Shaykh Hamza Makhdum and was also linked with Emperor Akbar's court. Limited *Chistiī* presence in the city of Srinagar could be seen in the 17th century. The arrival of *Chistīs* is coeval with Mughal rule in Kashmir.

GLOSSARY

āastān shrine
Asār-i Sharīf shrine housing holy relic belonging to the Prophet
bāgh garden
bārādarī pavilion
brangh spire
chār bām pyramidal slopping roof
chillā forty-day retreat for Sufis
dalān wooden columned portico
darshan dīr ceremonial window for viewing
devrī limestone (also, for fine dressed ashlar stone masonry)
dub projecting wooden balcony
dūr earring, used for pendants at roof corner
durbār court/assembly of ruler or noble
garbhagriha innermost sanctum of temple
ghāt steps for disembarking along a riverfront
ghulām gardish circumambulatory
ḥauz pool
ḥavelī mansion
ḥujra cell or chamber (also, burial chamber of a saint: *ḥujr-i sharīf*)
ʿīdgāh open field for offering *ʿīd* prayers
imāmbādā house of Imam, Shi'a place of mourning (also, *imāmbārā*)
jālī pierced screen of stone, brick or wood
khānaqāh Sufi hospices, a place where Sufis meet, pray and hold solitary penances (also, *ribāt*)
līwān vaulted, arched hall opening into a courtyard
madrasa school or college
Mʿārak imāmbādā (at Zadibal)
masjid mosque
miḥrāb prayer niche facing Kaaba
moḥala residential area or ward
mūi-i pāk Holy Hair
naqāshī art of painting, used for both mural and fresco
pinjrakārī latticework (wooden)

pīshtāq high portal gate
pūkhīr raised central platform in an *imāmbādā*
qiblā direction of Kabba
rūżā shrine
ṣaḥn courtyard
sarā'ī caravanserai
ṣubedar provincial administrators
ṣufa raised masonry platform
ṭaraḥ design/style
'urs death anniversary of a saint, commemorated as day of union with God.
varusī wooden partition screen
vihāra monastery
ziyārat shrine

BIBLIOGRAPHY

Manuscripts

Munshi Hasan Ali, *Tārīkh-i Kashmir*. (Srinagar: Private collection of Munshi Ghulam Hasan, Nowpora Srinagar, 19th century).

Pandit Birbal Kāchru, *Majmat-al Tārīkh*. (Srinagar: Research Library, Acc. no: 130, 1846 CE).

Bābā Khalil-al Lah, *Rūżā-al Riyaz*. (Srinagar: Sheikh-ul Alam Chair, Kashmir University, Acc. no. 123, 1894 CE).

Mulla Muhammad Khalil Mirjānpurī, *Tārīkh-i Kashmir*. (Srinagar: Research Library, Acc. no: 1074, 19th century).

Mulla Abdul Nabī, *Wajiz-ut Tārīkh*. (Srinagar: Research Library, Acc. no: 1048, 1857 CE).

Mirza Saif-al Din, *Akhbarat-i Mirza Saif-al Din*, 12 vols. (Srinagar: Research Library, Acc. no:1420–27, 1429,1430,1433,1434,1435,1436, 1846–53CE).

Mir Sad-all Lah Shahabadī, *Bāgh-i Sulieman*. (Srinagar: Research Library, Acc. no: 51, 1780 CE).

Unpublished thesis

Abdul Majid Mir, *Al Qasaid-al Arabia: A critical study* (PhD. Thesis: Centre of Central Asian Studies, University of Kashmir, 1995).

Kashi Gomez, *Beyond Sacred Landscapes: Poetic Illuminations of Local Experience in Maṅkha's Śrīkaṇṭhacarita* (M.A. Thesis: University of California, Berkeley, 2016).

Books and journals

A Ahmad, W Mujani and R Othman, 'Architecture According to the Perspective of the Quran: An Evaluation', *International Journal of Academic Research in Business and Social Sciences*, Vol. 7, no. 8, 2017.

A A Maudoodi, *Political Thought in Early Islam*, in *A History of Muslim Philosophy*, 2 Vol., ed. M M Sharif. (Delhi: Adam Publishers & Distributors, 2001).

A Guillaume, *Islam*. (England: Penguin Books Ltd, 1982).

A J Arberry, *An Introduction to the History of Sufism*. ((UK: Orient Longman Ltd., 1992).

A Lambah and A Patel, *The Architecture of Indian Sultanates*. (Mumbai: Marg Publications, 2006).

A N D Haksar, *Subhāshitāvali: An Anthology of Comic, Erotic and Other Verse*. (Delhi: Penguin, 2007).

A Rippin, *Muslims: Their Religious Beliefs and Practices*. (New York: Routledge, 2012). (First published: 1990).

Abbas Amanat, *Iran: A Modern History*. (New Haven: Yale university Press, 2017).

Abbas Khansarwani, transl. B.P. Ambashthya, *Tārīkh-i Ser Sahi*. (Patna: K.P. Jayaswal Research Institute, 1974).

Abū' Naeem Ghulam Qadir, *Munkathab Kalam-i Shaykh ul Alam*. ((Srinagar: Best booksellers, 2015).

Abū'l Fażl, transl. H Blochmann, *Ain-i Akbari*. (New Delhi: Sangh-e Meel Publications, 2003).

Abū'l Fażl, transl. H. Beveridge, *Akbar Nama*, 3 vols., (New Delhi: Low Price Publications, 2011)

Abū'l Rahim al Berunī, transl., W C Sachan, *Alberuni'S India*, 2 Vols. (Delhi: S Chand & Co., 1964).

Akbar S Ahmed, *Postmodernism and Islam: Predicament and Promise*. (New Delhi: Penguin Books India, 1993).

Akhtar Mohi-ud Din, 'Social Ideals and Patriotism in Kashmiri Literature (1900–1930)', *Indian Literature*, vol. 20, May–June 1977.

Andrew Petersen, *Dictionary of Islamic Architecture*. (New York: Routledge, 1999).

Annemarie Schimmel, *Islam Literature of India in A History of Indian Literature, Vol. VII*, ed. Gonda, J. (Wiesbaden: Otto Harrassowitz, 1973).

Annemarie Schimmel, *Islam in the Indian Subcontinent*. (Leiden: EJ Brills, 1987).

Annemarie Schimmel, S.C. Welch, M. L. Swietochowski and W.M. Thakston, *The Emperors' Album: Images of Mughal India*. (New York: Metropolitan Museum of Art, 1987).

Annemarie Schimmel, *A Two-Colored Brocade, The Imagery of Persian Poetry*. (The University of North Carolina Press, 1992).

Anthony Kennedy Warder, *Indian Kāvya Literature: The Art of Storytelling*, vol. 6 (Delhi: Motilal Banarsidass Publishers, 1992).

Anthony Welch. 'The Emperors Grief, Two Mughal Tombs in Frontiers of Islamic Art and Architecture', in Essays in Celebration of Oleg Gebbar, ed. Gülru Necīpoğlu and Julia Bailey, *Muqarnas* (Boston: Brill, 2008).

Antonio Gramsci, Q. Hoare and G. Nowell-Smith, *Selections from the Prison Notebooks of Antonio Gramsci*. (*New York*: Lawrence & Wishart, 1971).

Asad-al Lah Aafaqi, *Hayat Shaykh-ul Alam*. (Char: Life Foundation, 2014).

Avinoam Shalem, 'What Do We Mean When We Say "Islamic Art?' A Plea for a Critical Rewriting of the History of the Arts of Islam', *Journal of Art Historiography*, no. 6, 2012, 1.

Azfar Moin, *The Millennial Sovereign – Sacred Kingship and Sainthood in Islam*. (NewYork: Columbia University Press, 2012).

B Gascoigne, *The Great Moghuls*. (London: Jonathan Cape Ltd, 1976).

B Hopkins, *The Making of Modern Afghanistan*. (New York: Palgrave Macmillan, 2012).

B K K Deambi, *Corpus of Sarada Inscriptions of Kashmir*. (Delhi: Agam Kala Prakashan, 1982).

B Sahu, *Proceedings of the Indian History Congress*. (Delhi: Indian History Congress), vol. 74, 2007.

Bābā Dawud Khākī, transl. Qari Saif-al Din, *Dastur-al Sīlikin* (Srinagar: Ashraf Book Center, 1971).

Bābā Dawud Khākī, transl. S M Habib, *Vird-al Muridīn*. (Srinagar: Sultaniya Book Depot, 2012).

Bābā Nasīb al-Dīn Ghāzī, transl. Marghub Banhali, *Nūr Nāmā* (Srinagar: Markaz-i-Nur, 2013).

Bahāristān-i Shāhī, transl. K N Pandit, (Srinagar: Gulshan books, 2013).

Banarsi Prasad Saxeena, transl. R A Hashmi, *Tarikh-i Jahāngīr*. (Delhi: National Council for Promotion of Urdu Language, 1979)

Banarsi Prasad Saxeena, *Tārīkh-i Shah Jahān*. (Delhi: National Council for Promotion of Urdu Language, 2000).

Baron C Hugel, *Kashmir and the Punjab*. (Jammu: Light & Life Publishers, 1972).

Erich Baron and Schonberg, *Travels in India and Kashmir*. (London: Hurst & Blackett, 1853).

Beatrice Forbes Manz, *Power, Politics and Religion in Timurid Iran*. (Cambridge: Cambridge University Press, 2007).

Bernard Lewis, ed. *The World of Islam*. (London: Thames & Hudson, 1976).

C Geertz, *The Interpretation of Cultures*. (New York: Basic Books, Inc., 1973).

C M V Stuart, *Gardens of the Great Mughals*. (London: A. and C. Black, 1913).

C W Ernst and G M Smith, ed., *An Indo-Persian Guide to Sufi Shrine Pilgrimage in Manifestations of Sainthood in Islam*. (Istanbul: The Isis Press, 1999).

Catherine B Asher, 'Sub-Imperial Palaces: Power and Authority in Mughal India', *Ars Orientalis*, vol. 23.

Catherine B Asher, *Architecture of Mughal India*. (Cambridge: Cambridge University Press, 1992).

Catherine B Asher, *Delhi's Qutb Complex: The Minar, Mosque and Mehrauli*. ((Mumbai: The Marg Foundation, 2017).

Charles Ellison Bates, *A Gazetteer of Kashmir*. (Srinagar: Gulshan Books, 2005).

Chitralekha Zutshi, *Languages of Belonging*. ((Delhi: Permanent Black, 2003).

Christopher Tadgell, *Architecture in Context*. (London: Routledge, 2008).

Diana L Eck, *India: A Sacred Geography*. (New York: Three Rivers Press, 2012).

Dr. N Tsering, *Alchi*. (Leh-Ladakh: Central Institute of Buddhist Studies, 2009).

E B Havell, *Indian Architecture, Its Psychology, Structure & History from the First Mohammedian Invasion to Present Day*. (London: John Murray, 1913).

E F Neve, *Beyond The Pir Panjal*. (Srinagar: Gulshan Books, 2011).

Ebba Koch, *Mughal Art and Imperial Ideology*, collected essays. (New Delhi: Oxford University Press, 2001).

Ebba Koch, *Mughal Architecture*. (New Delhi: Oxford University Press, 2002).

Ebba Koch and Ali Anooshahr, ed., *The Mughal Empire Between Jahangir and Shah Jahan*. (Mumbai: Marg, 2019).

Edward H Madden, 'Some Characteristics of Islamic Art', *Journal of Aesthetics and Art Criticism*, Vol. 33, no. 4, 1975.

Edward W Said, *Orientalism*. (London: Penguin Books, 1995).

Edward W Troll, ed., *Muslim Shrines in India*. (New Delhi: Oxford University Press, 2004).

Ernst J Grube, in *Architecture of the Islamic World, Its History and Social Meaning*, ed. George Michell, (London, Thames & Hudson, 1978).

F Bernier, *Travels in Mughal Empire*. (New Delhi: Chand, 1972).
Finbarr Barry Flood and Gülru Necipoğlu, ed., *A Companion to Islamic Art and Architecture*. (John Wiley & Sons, 2017).
Finbarr Barry Flood, Before the Mughals: Material Culture of Sultanate of North India', *Muqarnas* (Leiden: Brill, 2019).
Francesca Orsini and S Sheikh, ed., *After Timur Left: Culture and Circulation in Fifteenth- Century North India*. (Delhi: Oxford University Press, 2014).
Fredrick W Bunce, *The Mosques of the Indian Subcontinent*. (New Delhi: DK Printworld, 2008).
G M D Sufi, *Kashīr, Being a History of Kashmir from the Earliest Times to Our Own*, 2 vols (Srinagar: Gulshan books, 2008).
G N Gauhar, *Kashmir Mystic Thought*. (Srinagar: Gulshan Books, 2009).
G S Khawja, *Islamic Architecture of Delhi*(Delhi: Bharatiya Kala Prakashan, 2012).
G T Vigne, *Travels in Kashmir, Ladak Iskardo, 2 vols*. (Srinagar: Gulshan Books, 2008).
George Forster, *A Journey from Bengal to England Through the Northern Part of India, Kashmire, Afghanistan, and Persia, and into Russia by the Caspian Sea*. (London: R Faulder, 1798).
Ghulam Qadir Bedar, *Mukhtasar Tārīkh -i Kashmir*. (Srinagar: Sultaniya Book Depot, undated).
Gregory S Hutcheson, 'Contesting the Mezqita Del Cristo De La Luz', *La Corónica*, Vol. 43, no. 1, 2014.
Gustave E Von Grunebaum, *Medieval Islam: A Study in Cultural Orientation*. (Chicago: University of Chicago Press, 1969).
H Gotez, 'Two Illustrated Persian Manuscripts from Kashmir', *Asia Asiatiques*, Vol. 9, no. 1/2, 1962-63.
H Goetz, *Studies in the History and Art of Kashmir and the Indian Himalayas*. (Wiesbradan: Otto Harrasswitz, 1969).
H H Cole, *Illustrations of Ancient Buildings in Kashmir*. (London: WH Allen & Co, 1869).
H Le, *Buddhist Architecture*. (Lakeville: Grafikol, 2010).
H Beveridge, *The Rashahat-i-'Ainal-Hayat (Tricklings from the Fountain of Life*. (Cambridge University Press, 1916).
Haidar Malīk, transl. Razia Bano, *Tārīkh-i Kashmir: History of Kashmir*, (Delhi: Bhavna Prakashan, 1991).
Hakim G Safdar Hamdani, *Shiyan-i Kashmir*. (Srinagar: Ali Muhammed & Sons, 1974).
Hamid Naseem, *Muslim Philosophy: Science and Mysticism*. (Delhi: Sarup Publishers, 2001).
Hayat Aamir Husseni, *The Religious Thought of Mir Saiyid Ali Hamdani*. (Srinagar: Jay Kay Bookshop, 1998).
Ibn Battuta, transl. H A R Gibb, *Travels in Asia and Africa, 1325–1354* (Delhi: Low Priced Edition, 1999).
Inayat Khan, transl. by A R Fuller, rev. and ed. by W E Begley and Z A Desai, *The Shah Jahan Nama of `Inayat Khan* (New Delhi: Oxford University Press, 1990).
INTACH, *Shehar-i-Kashmir, Cultural Resource Mapping of Srinagar City*. (Srinagar: INTACH J&K Chapter, 2010).
Irfan Habib, 'Baranī's Theory of the History of the Delhi Sultanate', *The Indian Historical Review*, Vol. VII, no. 1–2, (Delhi: Motilal Banarsidass) 1980.

Irfan Habib, *Akbar and His India*. (New Delhi: Oxford University Press, 2010).
J Collett, *A Guide for Visitors to Kashmir*. (Calcutta: W. Newman & Co, 1898).
J L Bhan, *Kashmir Sculptures*. (New Delhi: Readworthy Press Corporation, 2018).
J R Dupuche, *Abhinavagupta: The Kula Ritual, as Elaborated in Chapter 29 of the Tantrāloka*. (Delhi: Motilal Banarsidass, 2003).
Jadunath Sarkar, *Fall of Mughal Empire (1771–1778)*, Vol. III. (Calcutta: MC Sarkar & sons, 1938).
James Arbuthnot, *A Trip to Kashmir*. (Calcutta: Thacker, Spink & Co, 1900).
James Fergusson, *History of Indian and Eastern Architecture, Vol. I & II*. (New Delhi: Low Price Publications, 2006).
James L Wescoat and J Wolshke-Bulmahn, *Mughal Gardens: Sources, Places, Representations, and Prospects*. (Dumbarton Oaks, 1996).
Janet Rizvi and Monisha Ahmed, *Pashmina, The Kashmir Shawl and Beyond*. (Mumbai: Marg Publications, 2009).
Jaun Cole, *The Roots of North Indian Shi'ism in Iran and Iraq: Religion and State of Awadh*. (University of California Press, 1989).
John Bray, Trader, Middleman or Spy? The Dilemas of a Kashmiri Muslim in Early 19th century Tibet in *Islam and Tibet*, in *Interactions Along the Musk Routes*, eds. A. Akasoy, C. Burnettand and R. Yoeli-Tlalim, . (Routledge, 2011).
John Burton-Page, ed. George Michel, *Indian Islamic Architecture: Forms and Typologies, Sites and Monuments*. (Leiden: Brill, 2008).
John J Curry and Erik S Ohlander, *ed., Sufism and Society*. (New York: Routledge, 2012).
John Siudmack, *The Hindu-Buddhist Sculpture of Ancient Kashmir and Its Influences*. (Lieden: Brill, 2013).
Jonarāja Shrivara, Shuka et.al, transl. J C Dutt, *Rajatarangini:Kings of Kashmira, a Translation of Sanskrit Work*, 3 vols. (Srinagar: Gulshan Books, 2009).
K Ayyappa Paniker, ed., *Medieval Indian Literature, 4 vols*. (New Delhi: Sahitya Academy, 1997).
K Brown, *Sikh Art and Literature*. (Hoboken: Taylor and Francis, 2012).
K Salma Jayyusi, ed., *The City in the Islamic World*, vol. ii. (Boston: Brill, 2008).
Kalhānā, transl. M A Stein, *Rajatarangini*, 2 vols. (Srinagar: Gulshan Books, 2007)
Kanwarjit Singh Kang, *Wall Paintings of Punjab and Haryana*. (Delhi: Atma Ram and Sons, 1985).
Keith Critchlow, *Islamic Patterns: An Analytic and Cosmological Approach*. (New York: books, 1976).
Kenneth Cragg, *The Event of Quran: Islam in Its Scripture*. (Oxford: Oneworld Publications, 2006).
Khawājā Nizam-al Dīn Aḥamd, transl. B De, *Tabaqāt-i Akbarī* (Calcutta: Asiatic Society of India, 1927).
Khawājā ʿAzam Dedhmārī, transl. Z S Azhar, *Waqāt-i Kashmir* (Srinagar: Gulshan Publishers, 2003)
L C Brown, *Religion and State, The Muslim Approach to Politics*. (New York: Columbia University Press, 2000).
Laleh Bakhtiar, *Sufi: Expressions of the Mystic Quest*. (London: Thames and Hudson, 1976).
Lisa Balabanlilar, *Imperial Identity in the Mughal Empire: Memory and Dynastic Politics in Early Modern South and Central Asia*. (New York: I. B. Tauris, 2012).

Luther Obrock, 'Landscape in Its Place: The Imagination of Kashmir in Sanskrit and Beyond', *History and Theory*, Vol. 59, no. 1, 2020.
Luther Obrock, 'History at the End of History: Śrīvara's Jainataraginī', *The Indian Economic and Social History Review*, Vol. 50, no. 2, 2013.
M A Ali, *Mughal India*. (New Delhi: Oxford University Press, 2010).
M A Sells, *Early Islamic Mysticism*. (Srinagar: Gulshan Books, 2009).
M A Shah and M M Khan, *Medieval Kashmir*. (Delhi: Dominant Publishers, 2013).
M A Stein, *Ancient Geography of Kashmir*. (Srinagar: Gulshan books, 2005).
M Ahmad Andrabi, ed., 'Awliya Number' in *Hamara Adab* (Srinagar: J&K Academy of Arts, Culture & Languages, 1997).
M Alam, *The Languages of Political Islam: India 1200–1800*. (Chicago: Chicago University Press, 2004).
M Alam, *The Crisis of Empire in Mughal North India*. (New Delhi: Oxford University Press, 2013).
M Allen, *Ornament in Indian Architecture*. (Newark: University of Delaware Press, 1991).
M H Zaffar, 'Lal-Ded: The Mystic of Kashmir', *Sutra Journal*, March, 2016.
M Hattstein and P Delius, ed. *Islamic Art and Architecture*. (Königswinter: Konemann, 2004).
M I Khan, *History of Srinagar*. (Srinagar: Cosmos Publications, 1999).
M I Khan, *Kashmir's Transition to Islam*. (Srinagar: Gulshan Books, 2005).
M M Sharif, *A History of Muslim Philosophy, Vol. I & II*. (Delhi: Adam Publishers & Distributions, 2001).
M Maqbool Muqbil, *Abu'l Fuqra*. (Jammu: Qasmi Kutub Khana, undated).
Majid Aasmi, ed., 'Srinagar Number, vol. 1' in *Saun Adab* (Srinagar: J&K Academy of Arts, Culture & Languages, 2007).
Manohar Kaul, *Kashmir: Hindu, Buddhist and Muslim Architecture*. (New Delhi: Sagar Publications, 1971).
Marg, Vol. 57, No. 1, September 2005. (Mumbai: Marg Publishers).
Marshall G S Hodgson, 'Islam and Image', *History of Religions*, Vol. 3, no. 1, 1964.
Marshall G S Hodgson, *The Venture of Islam, 3 Vols*. (Chicago, IL: University of Chicago Press, 1974).
Martin Frishman and Hasan-ud din Khan, ed., *The Mosque, History, Architectural Development & Regional Diversity*. (London: Thames & Hudson, 1994).
Maulana M H Azad, *Darbar-i Akbarī*. (Delhi: National Council for Promotion of Urdu Languague, 2000).
Mīrzā Haidar Dughlat, transl. E D Ross, *Tārīkh-i Rashidī: A History of the Moghuls of Central Asia*, (Srinagar: Gulshan Books, 2012).
Mirza Muhammad Aslah, ed., S H Rashdi, *Tazkira-i Shura-i Kashmir*. (Lahore: Iqbal Academy, 1983).
Mohammed Yosuf Teng, ed., *Shireen Kalam*. (Srinagar: Jammu & Kashmir Academy of Art, Culture and Languages, 1978).
Mohammed Yosuf Teng, ed., *Kashir Encylopedia*, 3 vols. (Srinagar: Jammu & Kashmir Academy of Art, Culture and Languages, 1986).
Mohibbul Hasan, *Kashmir Under The Sultans*. (Srinagar: Ali Mohammad and Sons, 1974).
Monica Juneja, ed. *Architecture in Medieval India: Forms, Contexts, Histories*. (New Delhi: Permanent Black, 2001).

Moulvi Ahtiram-ud Deen, *Sahifey Khushnavisan*. (Delhi: National Council for Promotion of Urdu Language, 1987).

Mridu Rai, *Hindu Rulers, Muslim Subjects*. (Ranikhet: Permanent Black, 2004).

Mrs J C Murray Ansley, *Our Visit to Hindustan, Kashmir and Ladakh*. (London: W. H. Allen, 1879).

Mrs Hervey, *The Adventures of a Lady in Tartary, Thibet, China, & Kashmir Through Portions of Territory Never before Visited by European*. (London: Hope & Co, 1853).

Muhammad Qasim Shāh Farishtā, *Tārīkh –i Farishtā*. (Lucknow: Munshi Nawal Kishore, 1823).

Mulla Mohammad ʿAliʿA, transl. Ghulam Rasul Jan, *Tuḥfatūl Aḥbāb*. (Srinagar: Jan Publications, 2006).

Mulla Muhammad Tahir Ghani, *Dewan-i Ghani*. (Srinagar: J&K Academy of Arts, Culture & Languages, 1984).

Muzaffar Khan, *Kashmiri Muslims*, 2 Vols. (Srinagar: Humanizer Publications, 2012)

N Isaeva, *From Early Vedanta to Kashmir Shaivism: Gaudapada, Bhartrhari, and Abhinavagupta*. (New York: State University of New York Press, 1995).

Nader Ardlan and Laleh Bakhtiar, *The Sense of Unity: The Sufi Tradition in Persian Architecture*. (Chicago: University of Chicago Press, 1971).

Nasser Rabbat, 'What Is Islamic Architecture Anyway?', *Journal of Art Historiography*, no. 6, 2012.

Nawab Samsam-ud Dawla Shah Nawaz Khan and Hayy Abdul, transl. H Beveridge, *The Maathir-Ul Amra*. (Patna: JankiPrakashan, 1979).

Neil Leach, ed., *Rethinking Architecture, A Reader in Cultural Theory*. (New York: Routledge, 1997).

Nile Green, *Making Space: Sufis and Settlers in Early Modern India*. (New Delhi: Oxford University Press, 2012).

Nile Green, ed., *Afghanistan's Islam*. (University of California Press, 2017).

Nūr-al Dīn Jahāngīr, transl. A Rogers, *The Tuzuk-i Jahangiri* (Delhi: Low Price Publications, 1999).

O Handa, *Temple Architecture of the Western Himalaya: Wooden Temples*. (Delhi: Indus Publishing Company, 2002).

Oleg Grabar, *The Formation of Islamic Art*. (New Haven: Yale University Press, 1987).

P A Khaliq Tahirī, *Awliyā-i Kashmir*. (Srinagar: Gulshan Publication, 2003).

P N K Bamazai, *Cultural and Political History of Kashmir*. (New Delhi: MD Publications, 1994).

Pandit Anand Koul, *Archaeological Remains of Kashmir*. (Srinagar: The Kashmir Bookshop, 1935).

Pandit Hargopal Kaul Khastā, *Guldasta-i Kashmir*. (Srinagar: Shaheen Book Stall, 1987).

Patricia Crone, *From Arabian Tribes to Islamic Empire: Army, State and Society in the Near East*, c.600–850. (New York: Routledge, 2008).

Patricia Crone, *Slaves on Horses: The Evolution of the Islamic Polity*. (Cambridge: Cambridge University Press, 2008).

Percy Brown, *Indian Architecture, Islamic Period*. (Bombay: D.B. Taraporevala Sons & Co, 1942).

Philip Davies, *The Penguin Guide to the Monuments of India*, vol. II. (London: Viking, 1989).

Pīr Hasan Shāh Khuihāmī, transl. Shams-ud Din Ahmad, *Tārīkh-i Hasan*, vol. I (Srinagar:1999).

Pīr Hasan Shāh Khuihāmī, transl. Shams-ud Din Ahmad, *Tārīkh-i Hasan*, vol. II (Srinagar:2002).

Pratapaditya Pal and Frank Ames, *The Arts of Kashmir*. (Cincinnati Art Museum: Asia society, 2007).

R K Parimu, *A History of Sikh Rule in Kashmir, 1819–1846*. (Srinagar: Jammu and Kashmir Government: Department of Education, 1977).

R A Jairazbhoy, 'The Taj Mahal in the Context of East and West: A Study in the Comparative Method', *Journal of the Warburg and Courtauld Institutes*, Vol. 24, no. 1/2, 1961.

R Aquil, *Sufism, Culture and Politics*. (New Delhi: Oxford University Press, 2015).

R Bernier and D Lama, *Himalayan Architecture*. (London: Associated University Presses, 1997).

R C Agrawal, *Kashmir and Its Monumental Glory*. (*Delhi*: Aryan Publications, 1998).

R C Kak, *Ancient Monuments of Kashmir*. (Delhi: Sagar Publications, 1971).

R Ettinghausen, Oleg Grabar and Marilyn Jenkins-Madina, *The Art and Architecture of Islam, 650–1250*. (New Haven, CT: Yale University Press, 2001).

R M Eaton, *Essays of Islam and Indian History*. (New Delhi: Oxford University Press, 2010).

Ranjit Hoskote, *I Lalla, The Poems of Lal Ded*. (Gurgoan: Penguin Random House India, 2013).

Robert Hillenbrand, 'Turco-Iranian Elements in the Medieval Architecture of Pakistan: The case of the Tomb of Rukn-i ʿAlam at Multan', *Muqarnas*, (Leiden: Brill, 1991).

Robert Hillenbrand, *Islamic Art and Architecture*. (London: Thames & Hudson Ltd, 2004).

Roland Barthes, trans. du Seull, *Elements of Semiology & Writing Degree Zero*. (Boston: Beacon Press, 1976).

Romila Thapar, *The Past Before Us – Historical Traditions of Early North India*. (Harvard University Press, 2013).

S Jayyusi, R Holod, A Petruccioli and A Raymond, *The City in the Islamic World*. (Leiden: Brill, 2008).

S M H Tabatabai, transl. William C. Chittick, *A Shi'ite Anthology*(Tehran Ansariyan Publications, 1980)

S Srivastava, *Jahangir, A Connoisseur of Mughal Art*. (New Delhi: Abhinav Publications, 2001).

S Verma, *Mughal Painters and Their Work. A Biographical Survey and Comprehensive Catalogue* (Delhi: Oxford University Press, 1994).

Saima Bhat, 'Islam's First Kashmir Address', *Kashmir Life*, May 23, 2018.

Samer Akkach, *Cosmology and Architecture in Pre Modern Islam: An Architectural Reading of Mystical Ideas*. (Albany: State University of New York Press, 2005).

Satish Chandra, *Parties and Politics at the Mughal Court, 1707–1740*. (Delhi: Oxford University Press, 2002).

Sayyid ʿAli, transl. G R Bhat, *Tārīkh-i Kashmir* (Srinagar: Center of Central Asian Studies, 1994).

Seyyed Hossein Nasr, *Islamic Art and Spirituality*. (Albany: State University of New York Press, 1987).

Seyyed Hossein Nasr, *The Garden of Truth*, transl. (New York: Harper Collins, 2008), 82.

Shahzad Bashir, *Messianic Hopes and Mystical Visions: The Nūrbakhshīya between Medieval and Modern Islam*. (Columbia: University of South Carolina Press, 2003).

Shaykh Muhammad Murad Teng, ed., S Ruqiya, *Tuhfat-ul Fuqra*. (Srinagar: Shalimar Art Press, 1997).

Sheila S Blair and Jonathan M Bloom, *The Art and Architecture of Islam, 1250–1800*. (Ahmedabad: Mapin, 1995).

Sheila S Blair and Jonathan M. Bloom, 'The Mirage of Islamic Art: Reflections on the Study of an Unwieldy Field', *The Art Bulletin*, Vol. 85, no. 1, 2003.

Sheila S Blair and Jonathan M Bloom, *The Grove Encyclopedia of Islamic Art and Architecture*. (New York: Oxford University Press, 2009).

Shelton Waldrep, *The Dissolution of Place: Architecture, Identity and the Body*. (Farnham: Ashgate Pub Co, 2012).

Suvir Kaul, ed., *The Partitions of Memory, The Afterlife of the Division of India*, (Delhi: Permanent Black, 2001).

Sunil Sharma, *Mughal Arcadia – Persian Literature in an Indian Court*. (Cambridge: Harvard University Press, 2018).

Surgeon Major Henry Walter Bellew, *Kasmir and Kashgar: A Narrative of the Journey of the Embassy to Kashgar in 1873–74*. (London: Trubner & Co, 1875).

Susan Gole, *Indian Maps and Plans*. (New Delhi: Manohar Publications, 1989).

Stronge Susan, *The Arts of the Sikh Kingdoms*. (London: V & A, 1999).

Sylvia Crowe, Sheila Haywood, Susan Jellicoe and Gordon Patterson, *The Gardens of Mughul India*. (Srinagar: Jay Kay Bookshop, 2006).

T N Madan, *Family and Kinship, A Study of the Pandits of Rural Kashmir*. (New Delhi: Oxford University Press, 2007).

Timothy Insoll, *The Archeology of Islam*. (Oxford: Blackwell publishers, 1999).

Titus Burckhardt, *The Art of Islam: Language and Meaning*. (London: World of Islam Festival Publ. Co, 1976).

Travis Zadeh, *Mapping Frontiers Across Medieval Islam*. (London: I.B. Tauris & Co, 2011).

Tuḥfatūl Aḥbāb: A Muslim Missionary in Medieval Kashmir: Being English of Tuḥfatūl Aḥbāb K N Pandita *Tuḥfatūltranslation*. (New Delhi: Eurasian Human Rights Forum, 2009), 118–119.

Victor Jacquemont, *Letters from India 1829–1832*. (London: Macmillan & Co, 1936).

Vincent A Smith, *The Oxford History of India*. (Oxford University Press, 2002).

W H Nicholls, 'Muhammadan Architecture in Kashmir' in *ASI Annual Report* (New Delhi: ASI, 1906–07).

W Moorcroft and G Trebeck, *Travels in the Himalayan Provinces of Hindustan and the Punjab; in Ladakh and Kashmir, in Peshawar, Kabul, Kunduz, and Bokhara, 2 vols*. (Srinagar: Gulshan books, 2000), 118–123.

W R Lawrence, *The Valley of Kashmir*. (Jammu: Kashmir Kitab Ghar, 1996).

W S Wong, 'Stupa, Pagoda and Chorten-Origin and Meaning of Buddhist Architecture', *Athens: ATINER'S Conference paper Series*, No: ARC2014–1094, 2014.

W Wakefield, *The Happy Valley: Sketches of Kashmir and the Kashmiri*. (London: Sampson Low, Marston, Searle & Rivington, 1879).

Walter D Mar, *The Romantic East, Burma, Assam & Kashmir*. (London: Adam and Charles Black, 1906).

Yassir Tabbaa, *The Transformation of Islamic Art During the Sunni Revival*. (London: University of Washington Press, 2001).

Yves Porter and Richard Castinel, 'Jahanpanah's Jamiʿ Masjid (circa 1343): A Reassessment', *Muqarnas*, vol. 35 (Leiden: Brill), 2018.

Zia-al Haq Nazimī, *Kashmir mein moi-hai-i mubarak*. (Bijbehara: IdaraAuqaf Islamia Hazratbal Khiram, 1997).

INDEX

ʿAālī Masjid 96–99,170, 194
Akbar 61, 62, 91, 128–131, 162, 170, 171, 201
Alā'-al Dīn Khalji 91
Alā'-al Dīnpūrā 66, 67
Alā'-al Dīn 26, 27, 45, 54
Alā-i Darwaza 91
Alam Ṣahāb mosque 194
Alchi (temple) 38, 42, 80
Anderkote 21, 26; for shrine *see* Shams-al Dīn
Asār-i Sharīf Hazratbal 149, 150, 191, 195; at Kalashpora and Narwara 150; at Lal Bazar 150, 151, 165; originally *Bāgh-i Ṣadiq Abād* 150, 152, 153; rival shrine at Soura 151
Ashoka 3, 22, 30, 31, 52
Aurangzeb 83, 131, 140, 147, 149–151, 162, 165
Avantiswami temple 39

Babā Bam-al Dīn 111; Bamzu cave 108, 125
Bābā Dāwūd Khākī 105, 119, 162, 179, 201
Bābā Nasīb-al Dīn Ghazī 118, 119; *khānaqāh* 153–156
Babā Zain-al Dīn 109; shrine at Aishmuqam 112; shrine at Shree Gupwara 111–112
Bābur 60, 62
Bāgh-i Farāh Baksh 152
Baihaqī Sayyids 59, 60
baluster column 116, 155, 159, 172, 178
Bamiyan 7
bārādarī 70, 140, 141, 150, 152, 164, 202
Barar-i Nambal 99
Begampuri mosque 66, 84
Bīlhanā 3
brangh 43, 85, 86, 118, 155, 202
Būlbūl Shāh 25, 29; *khānaqāh* of 71; 200

chādhar 141
chār bām 37, 43, 153, 155, 158, 202
Chār-i Sharīf 170
Chillā 69; *chillā khanā* 74; *chillā kuth* 158, 181

dalān 97, 98, 105, 115, 116, 149, 153, 155, 156, 158, 159, 178, 181, 202; derived from *tālār* 98
Dārā Shīkoh 137, 138, 147, 163
Diddā 26, 30, 50, 122
Dīvān Moti Ram 192

Gandhara (influences) 26, 50
ghulām gardish 115, 202
Ghurids 9
Gulāb Singh 169, 191, 192
Gupta 29, 38

Hājji ʿEidāh mosque 191, 199
Hājjī Piyāda mosque (Balkh) 79
Hasan Shāh 54, 59, 76, 103; *ṣufa* 67
Hasanabad (mosque) 159–161, 168, 184; vandalized for Basant bāgh *ghāt* 161, 168, 184
ḥauz 141
Hindu Shahiya 22, 50
ḥujrā 94
Husayn Bayqara 70
Husayn Shāh Chak madrasa 71

ʿīdgāh 96, 97, 99, 202; for mosque *see* ʿAālī Masjid
Imāmbāda (Mʿārak) 114–117, 191, 195, 197; Hassanabad 159, 160

I'timād-al Daula tomb 148
iwān 83–85, 122, 137, 145, 194, 202

Jahān Ārā 137, 138, 140, 163
Jahāngīr 87, 94, 95, 122, 128, 130, 131, 133, 135, 147, 148, 162, 164, 171, 176, 178
jālī 81, 202
Jamāli-Kamālī shrine (glazed tiles) 66
Jamia Khiva 85
Jamia Masjid Srinagar 66, 73, 83–86, 96, 97, 99, 101, 103, 114, 116, 117, 153, 156; at Bijbehara 125, 128; ASI repairs 194; Aurangzeb's reconstruction 131; closed 167, 168; reopening 169; Shahābpur 28; Shupian 194
Jhelum (Vitastā) 3, 25, 36, 71, 76, 104, 108, 132, 146, 156, 191
Jonarāja 28, 45, 50, 119

Kabba 48, 70, 79, 139, 202
Kalhānā 22, 30, 31, 65
Kanil Masjid 194
Kanīshkā 3, 22, 66
Kathi Darwaza 129, 130; Sangin Darwaza 129
Khānaqāh-i Ghusīyah 173–178
Khānaqāh-i Khawājā Mas'ud 179–181
Khānaqāh-i M'aulā 16, 68, 69, 71, 80, 108, 131, 132, 156–159; *Buqa Aali* 185; closure 167, 168, 175–181; interiors 170; *Nūr Khāna* 171
Khānaqāh-i Naū 71–74
Khānaqāh-i Nazkī 176–179
Khān-i Jahān mausoleum (Delhi) 64
khatamband 80, 156, 158, 159, 174, 176
Kheer Bhwani 192,193
Khurasan 14, 35, 59, 118
Kotā Rani 24–26, 45
Kubrawī 37, 55–57, 60, 62, 85, 99, 123, 190, 200

Lachma Khātūn 101, 124
Ladakh 3, 22, 23, 27, 38, 61, 70, 112, 161
L'alā Ded 26, 27, 51
Lalitāditya Muktāpīda 18, 23, 24, 27, 30, 32, 37, 38, 49, 65
Loduv temple 32, 57, 108, 110, 111

Mahasen temple 69
Mahmud Ghazni 22
Malīk Abdul Rahim (shrine) 105–107
Malīk Ahmad mosque 76, 77; *khānaqāh* 68
Malīk Jalāl-al Dīn 73; *mazar* 101–103
Malīk Ṣaif-ul Lah Dar *(mazar)* 103–105
Maṅkha 3
Masjid-i Naū (also Shāhī Masjid, Pather Masjid) 132–135, 139, 162, 178
Mauryan rule 3, 22, 30, 31; influences 42
Mazar-i Salātīn 64, 90, 102, 105
Mīr Masjid 21, 37–45
Mīr Sayyid 'Ali Hamdanī 37, 55, 65, 66, 68, 118, 121, 158, 181, 200
Mīr Sayyid Muhammad Hamdanī 37, 55, 56, 85
Mīr Shams-al Dīn 'Iraki 59, 60, 67, 69, 114, 121, 200
Mirkula Devi (temple) 38
Mīrzā Haidar Dughlat 61, 71, 114, 123; on Kashmir 62; crafts 120; criticism of *Reshīs* 109
mlecchas 31, 187
Mughal architecture 13, 16, 127–161, 166, 170, 171, 178, 190, 196
mūi-i pāk 202; at Hazratbal 149,150; at Soura 151; at *Khānaqāh* Dangerpora 151
Mullā Shāh: mosque at Ganderbal 140–144, 163, 173; mosque at Nāgar Nagar 81, 137–140
Mullā Tāhir Ghanī 162
muqarna: in arch 149; in capital 178; in dome 94

naqāshī 66, 148, 149, 158, 159, 171, 174, 176, 202; *moḥarqāshī* 185
Naqshbandī 57, 200; *Khānaqāh-i Naqshbandī* 177, 181, 191, 194
naskh 139, 147, 160
Naushera (Srinagar) 74, 76, 78, 144
Nilmāt Puranā 2, 17
Nūr Jahān 133, 135, 160
Nūrbakshī 57, 60, 68, 114, 190; *Khānaqāh-i Nūrbakshiya* 69–71, 74

Padmaswami temple 39
Padshāhī kul 141
Pandrethan temple 39, 53, 85
Parvarpura 32
Payar temple 38, 53
pinjrakārī 46, 48, 115–117, 154–156, 159, 202

pīshtāq 73, 134, 135, 138, 139, 144, 161, 203
plan: at Balkh 79, 80; centralized octagonal plan 63, 64, 66; four-*iwan* plan 84; Mughal, based on *hasht bihisht* 141; nine bay at Toledo 164
Pratap Singh 191, 192, 194

Qādrī 57, 163, 170, 171, 173, 176, 200
qiblā 37, 39, 41, 72–74, 88, 92, 97, 116, 134, 139, 141, 143, 175, 178, 203
Quṭub Minar 34, 52
Quṭub-al Dīn 12, 117; mausoleum 62–66
Quwat-al Islam mosque 9, 34, 49, 52

Raghunath mandir 192
Raja Pratap Singh (Udaipur) 38
Ranbīr Singh 191, 192, 194
Ranjit Singh 168, 172, 184
Reshī 15, 54, 56–58, 60, 69, 92, 117, 118, 153, 155, 189, 197, 199, 200; cave shrines 106–113, 125
Rīnchanā 23, 24, 26, 27, 29, 50, 56; Jamia Masjid 52; *khānaqāh* at Rīnchanāpūrā 28; mosque of 21, 25, 35–37, 39, 45, 48; palace 50
Rukn-i ʿAlam shrine (Multan) 64

sabaq-i hindī 128, 162, 172
Safavid art influences 126, 145, 197
Samarra (glazed tiles) 66
Sarnath 42
Sayyid Husayn Khurazmī shrine 99–100
Sayyid Muhammed Madnī 200; mosque of 11, 40, 41, 43, 78–81, 105, 107; shrine of 12, 81–82; Mughal gateway 144–146, 164; mosque in vicinity of 74–76
Sayyid Qasim (shrine) 181–183
Sayyid Yʿaqūb (shrine) 181–183
Shāh Jahān 129, 131, 140, 144, 148, 149, 161, 162, 172, 178; shāhjahāni arch 139
Shahāb al-Dīn 18, 26, 27, 28, 54, 55, 59; Shahāb al-Dīn porā 28
Shams-al Dīn 26, 45, 46, 48, 49, 54, 183; ziyārat of 45–49
Shaykh ʿAbdullah 195, 196, 198, 199
Shaykh Abū'l Fażl 128
Shaykh Ahmad Yasavi *khānaqāh* 70
Shaykh Amin Mantāqī (shrine) 149
Shaykh Ghūlām Muhyi-al Dīn 147, 149, 169, 171; son (Imām-al Dīn) 169
Shaykh Hamza Makhdum 92; Akbar constructs shrine 105, 130, 165, 201; mosque at Aham 92; shrine complex at Koh-i Maran 93–95
Shaykh Nūr-al Dīn 56, 71, 108, 109, 119, 168, 190, 197, 200; cave 111; Koimuh cave 125; Loduv cave 108, 111; Tapil cave 108–111
Shaykh Yʿaqūb Sarfi 201
Sher Shāh Suri 87
Shi'a-Sunni riot 122,169, 184
Shi'a 9, 144, 145, 164, 161, 197`
Sikander 56–60, 62, 99, 104, 124, 153; architecture 66, 67, 96; construction of Jamia Masjid 83–86, 103
ṣufa 66, 67
Suharwardī 57, 92, 105, 107, 153, 165, 179, 200
Sunni 9, 60, 92, 130, 167, 170, 190, 191

Tambulan Begam's tomb 94
Thag Bābā (Shaykh Ibrāhīm) shrine 146–149
thuluth 70, 76, 77, 100, 160
Timurid architecture 55, 62, 65, 66; 70, 101, 127, 129, 164, 189; court 69
Tughlaqs 9, 20; architecture 66, 84, 90, 97; Fīrāz Shāh 27; Sultan Ghiyās-al Dīn 23, 87, 90
tughra 160
Turuskā 22

varusī 116, 155, 178, 203
vernacular architecture 29, 30, 69, 80, 87, 122, 171, 179, 182, 183, 188, 190, 192, 195

Zafar Khān 144, 161
Zaina Lank 11, 73, 74, 86–91, 105, 186
Zain-al Ābidīn 54, 57–59, 62; construction of Dumath 64–65, 67, 73, 74, 80, 101, 103, 105, 111, 118, 123, 124, 164; construction of Nallah Mār 176, 189, 191
Zakir Masjid 93–95
Zulchu's invasion 24, 35, 50, 59